Praise for *The Secret South*

The more insights we can gain into this important expedition, the better. Ivan Mackenzie Lamb's account of Operation Tabarin is both fascinating and absolutely unique. Its publication will be welcomed by all who seek a better understanding of the trials, tribulations (and occasional comedy) of life in the far south.

SIR RANULPH FIENNES, OBE, FRGS,
VICE-PATRON, UK ANTARCTIC HERITAGE TRUST

The Secret South gives new understanding and perspective to Operation Tabarin ... Bringing Ivan Mackenzie Lamb's remarkable experiences and observations to light is a most valuable contribution to polar literature.

BEAU RIFFENBURGH, AUTHOR OF *NIMROD:
THE STORY OF SHACKLETON'S FIRST EXPEDITION*

Antarctica is the most enigmatic of places, the least discovered and understood continent on earth. The work of the early scientists of the Falkland Islands Dependencies Survey was key to unlocking its secrets. This book reveals an important part of that extraordinary story.

CAPTAIN TIM STOCKINGS, OPERATIONS DIRECTOR,
BRITISH ANTARCTIC SURVEY

Ivan Mackenzie Lamb's *The Secret South*, now published for the first time, is an exceptionally interesting account of British wartime activities in Antarctica.

DR ISOBEL WILLIAMS, MD, FRCP, FRGS,
AUTHOR OF *WITH SCOTT IN THE ANTARCTIC*

Ivan Mackenzie Lamb's work laid the foundations of Antarctic botanical science. In the year of the 75th anniversary of Operation Tabarin ... Lamb's account of his experiences will be a welcome addition to our understanding of this most important of British Antarctic endeavours.

CAMILLA NICHOL, CHIEF EXECUTIVE,
UK ANTARCTIC HERITAGE TRUST

Ivan Mackenzie Lamb, October 1944.

THE
SECRET
SOUTH

A Tale of
Operation Tabarin,
1943–46

Ivan Mackenzie Lamb

Edited by
Stephen Haddelsey & Ronald Lewis-Smith

Greenhill Books

The Secret South
This edition published in 2018 by
Greenhill Books,
c/o Pen & Sword Books Ltd,
47 Church Street, Barnsley,
S. Yorkshire, s70 2as

www.greenhillbooks.com
contact@greenhillbooks.com

ISBN (hardback): 978–1–78438–325–1
ISBN (paperback): 978–1–78438–420–3

CIP data records for this title are available from the British Library

Designed and typeset by Donald Sommerville

Printed and bound in the UK by TJ International Ltd, Padstow

Typeset in 12.5/16.5 pt Arno Pro Regular

Dedicated, as we believe
Ivan Mackenzie Lamb would have wished,
to his children,
Eric, Frank and Nina,
and to his grandchildren,
Antonio, Catherine and Elizabeth

O Lord . . .

Whither shall I go from thy spirit? or whither shall I flee
from thy presence?

If I ascend up into heaven, thou art there: if I make my
bed in hell, behold, thou art there.

If I take the wings of the morning, and dwell in the
uttermost parts of the sea;

Even there shall thy hand lead me, and thy right hand
shall hold me.

Psalm 139: 7–10 (King James Version)

tale/terl/ n. 1 a narrative or story, esp. fictitious and
imaginatively treated.

The Concise Oxford Dictionary

Contents

Acknowledgements

FOR THEIR ASSISTANCE AND SUPPORT for this, the first publication of Ivan Mackenzie Lamb's account of Operation Tabarin, the editors would like to thank his children, Eric, Frank and Nina, for permission to publish their father's work and for supplying so many of the photographs that he took with his Leica camera during the expedition; Ieaun Hopkins and Joanna Rae of the British Antarctic Survey's Archives Department for facilitating access to relevant manuscripts, maps and photographs; Dr Irwin Brodo, the late Dr George A. Llano, and the late Dr Andrew Taylor for sharing their recollections of Lamb; the late Alan Carroll for imparting his knowledge of Operation Tabarin's Base 'A' at Port Lockroy; I-Ting Weicht, who undertook the transcription of the manuscript while working in Vienna, Austria and Hualien City, Taiwan; Dr Steve Colwell, Dr John King and Professor John Turner of the British Antarctic Survey for providing an excellent summary of modern theories on Antarctic wind generation; and Michael Leventhal of Greenhill Books for seeing the potential of the manuscript and for agreeing to publish it.

Finally, we would like to express our gratitude to our wives, Caroline Haddelsey and Elinor Lewis-Smith, for their love and support during the completion of our editorial labours.

Stephen Haddelsey
Ronald Lewis-Smith

Plates and Illustrations

Unless otherwise stated, all photographs, maps and other illustrations are courtesy of the British Antarctic Survey Archives, copyright the Natural Environment Research Council. Photograph references listed all have the prefix AD6/19/1.

Plates

Lamb in his laboratory at Base 'A', Port Lockroy, 1944. (A8/2)

Unloading stores on Goudier Island, February 1944. (A1/29)

Bransfield House under construction, 12 February 1944. (A1/31)

Base 'A' from the east, showing the Nissen hut. (A119)

Base 'A' with the Sierra du Fief in the background. (A121)

The completed Bransfield House. (B67/5)

Andrew Taylor (A50), James Marr (A55), 'Chippy' Ashton (A56), 'Taff' Davies (A57), Tom Berry (A58), 'Fram' Farrington (A60), Eric 'Doc' Back (A61), John Blyth. (A62)

Midwinter's Day celebrations, 21 June 1944. (A8/20)

Lamb, with a lichen-covered rock. (*Lamb family album*)

Returning from a seal hunt. (A8/28)

Setting a fish trap at Port Lockroy. (A8/3)

Lamb emerging from his igloo. (A11/21)

Marr unloads a sledge, caught in a crevasse. (A40/24)

Surveying at the foot of the Wall Range, Wiencke Island. (A42/7)

Lamb at Camp 'A' during the Wiencke Island survey. (A40/35)

Lamb and his tent during the Wiencke Island survey. (*Lamb family album*)

Maps and Illustrations in Text

Editors' Introduction

ON 8 FEBRUARY 1942, A SMALL PARTY of uniformed sailors stepped from their ship's dinghy onto the black sand of Deception Island in the South Shetlands. Having pulled their boat up onto the beach, they could then stand for a moment to admire their unusual surroundings.

Formed from the sea-filled caldera of an active volcano, Deception Island consists of a ring of snow-capped mountains which rise to nearly 2,000 feet to enclose a deep lagoon accessible only via a narrow and dangerous passage, variously called Neptunes Bellows[1] or Challenger Pass. Periodically the island demonstrates its latent power, with violent tremors sending rocks and boulders skittering and bouncing down the mountainsides to land with a thud or a splash on the beach or in the waters of Port Foster. Even in dormant periods sulphur fumes pervade the atmosphere and clouds of steam rise continually from the beaches; indeed, so hot is the volcanic ash of the island that one later resident found that he 'could cook a penguin egg quite well by burying it'.[2]

A decade or so earlier the now deserted harbour would have been full of noisy life – and death. In 1912 the Norwegian Hektor Whaling Company had built a shore-based whaling station here; thereafter, throughout the three-month hunting season of every year, the narrow passage that gives access to Bransfield Strait would have been clogged with traffic: grimy, slow-moving factory ships seeking safe anchorage away from the turbulent waters of the Southern Ocean, and their squadrons of fast, steam-driven catchers towing in their collections of balloon-like whale carcasses for dismemberment on the wide wooden 'plan' of the whaling station before hurrying out again to continue the profitable work of slaughter. In the grey but near-continuous daylight of the Antarctic summer in these latitudes the flensers worked around the clock, and their victims were so numerous that they could afford to concentrate solely on the process of tearing the great slabs of blubber from the bodies, allowing the less easily harvested remains, or *scrott*, to float away and litter the beaches. At the height of the season, the waters of Port Foster were actually dyed red with blood, and the nightmarish quality of the scene was heightened still further by the appalling stench: the naturally sulphurous air of the island being overlaid with the distinctive aromas of industrialized blubber reduction, memorably described by one naturalist as 'being like a mixture of the smell of a tanning factory and that of fish meal and manure works together with a sickly and almost overpowering odour of meat extract'.[3]

By 1942 the butchery and the vast profits it generated were things of the past, but still the facilities, equipment and by-products of the industry lay all around: the flensing platform on which the giant carcasses were stripped; the gaunt ruins of the factory building with its mechanical winches and vast cauldrons for boiling down the blubber; the giant rusty oil storage tanks, each capable of holding the essence of thousands of whales; the low wooden and corrugated-iron dormitories, offices and hospital that had once served the small community of whalers; and, on the beach, piles of ships' chandlery, ready to service the needs of the whale-catchers. Whale bones, too, were everywhere: enormous ribs, collapsed in on themselves like the walls of abandoned houses, skulls and colossal vertebrae, all picked clean by the seabirds which flocked to this charnel house from far and wide, and sheets of the once highly prized baleen, turned green by algae so that they had come to resemble a peculiar form of tussock grass, incongruous in a world almost devoid of vegetation and dominated by black and white.

Undeterred by these eerie surroundings, or by the unexpected crash and bang of loosened sheets of corrugated iron flapping in the wind, the sailors made their way up the black beach and, under the watchful eyes of their officers, began their work. First, with tins of paint specially brought for the purpose, they adorned the giant rusty oil storage tanks with large, if somewhat crude, representations of their national flag; with all due ceremony, they unfurled the flag itself on a pole erected beside the derelict factory buildings; at the foot of the flagstaff they buried a sealed bronze cylinder; finally, and perhaps most tellingly, a sailor drove a number of long nails through the flagstaff – a simple expedient designed to deter any subsequent visitors from interfering with the flag that they had just raised.

Deception Island, along with the rest of the South Shetlands, the South Orkneys, the South Sandwich Islands, and the great arc of the Antarctic Peninsula had long been claimed by Britain by right of their discovery by British mariners between the last quarter of the eighteenth century and the middle of the nineteenth. But the flag now daubed on the oil tanks and fluttering at the top of its pole was not the Union Flag and the sailors were not Royal Navy officers and ratings. They belonged to the Argentinian Navy's transport ship *Primero de Mayo,* and the cylinder buried in the volcanic ash contained a message asserting that, with immediate effect, all lands lying between longitudes 25°W and 68°34'W, and below latitude 60°S, fell under the sovereignty of the Argentine Republic. With these simple actions, Argentina added to its dominions an area of roughly 564,000 square miles and increased its population by countless millions of penguins and seals but by not a single human being. In terms of international diplomacy, Argentina had just crossed the Rubicon.

*

Argentina had protested British control of the Falkland Islands ever since 1834 but it was not until the beginning of the second quarter of the twentieth century that it formally asserted its rights over any territory farther south. This claim dated to 1927, when officials in Buenos Aires advised the International Bureau of the Universal Postal Union that, in addition to the Falkland Islands – or Islas Malvinas – Argentina now counted both the South Orkneys and South Georgia among its possessions. Most aggravating of all to the British government was that these claims were based in no small part on the fact that, since the beginning of 1904, Argentina had continuously occupied and operated a small meteorological station, Orcadas, at Scotia Bay on Laurie Island in the South Orkneys: a station established by William Speirs Bruce during his Scottish National Antarctic Expedition, but which – with the belated sanction of the British government – he had handed to Argentina in January of that year. Crucially, in the absence of any documented agreement signed by the representatives of both nations at the time of this transaction, it was in vain for the British to aver later that they had intended to transfer Bruce's facility but not Laurie Island or the South Orkneys as a whole.[4]

This embarrassing ambiguity was entirely of Britain's making. Civil servants in Whitehall had recognized almost immediately that the transfer of Bruce's meteorological station had been poorly managed and that a lack of clarity could lead to a dispute at some point in the future – but a combination of apathy, indifference and a wonderfully English reluctance to 'rock the boat' had resulted in no action being taken to address the matter in a timely fashion. Besides, with the exception of the Falklands, whose strategic location enabled them to dominate the mouth of the River Plate and the shipping lanes around Cape Horn, the South Atlantic island groups appeared almost worthless. With their wave-whipped shores and barren ice-clad interiors they offered no opportunities for trade or agriculture, and if they possessed any mineral wealth their location in such high latitudes rendered exploitation virtually impossible. At the time, an accidental weakening of British claims in the region had seemed a matter of very little significance.

It was only at the end of 1904, when Carl Anton Larsen, an entrepreneurial Norwegian sea captain, proved the viability of Southern Ocean whaling that the colossal economic potential of the islands began to be fully appreciated. In the decades preceding the introduction of pelagic whaling, all flensing operations had, perforce, to be conducted at shore stations – meaning that the nation, or nations, claiming those lands and their surrounding territorial waters could charge for whaling licences. British officials recognized that, almost overnight, the barren lumps of rock that they had previously dismissed as valueless had developed the potential to generate vast revenues. Although this realization prompted them to clarify the extent of British claims in the region through the issue of Letters Patent in 1908, to many observers this act bore all the hallmarks of an attempt to slam the stable door after the horse had bolted.

Over the ensuing decades the attitude of successive Argentinian administrations hardened, with the unauthorized establishment of a wireless telegraph station on Laurie Island in 1925,[5] a refusal to apply for a telegraph licence from the Falkland Islands Government in order to operate it, and the claims made at the International Bureau of the Universal Postal Union all constituting major escalations. In response to these challenges, the British government struggled to identify a clear and coherent policy: on the one hand, the existence of a large British population in Argentina and significant levels of British investment in the country made it reluctant to antagonize Buenos Aires without very good cause; on the other, it needed to maintain its claim to territories which were now far from being profitless. More broadly, any failure to defend its rights in the South Atlantic could be interpreted as weakness and have profound implications for other parts of the Empire.

Throughout this period the only truly meaningful British initiative was the launch of the *Discovery* Investigations. As early as 1917, it had been recognized that if southern whales were not to be driven to extinction by prodigal hunting practices it was essential to introduce regulations that were themselves based upon a detailed understanding of the whale's lifecycle: of its patterns of migration, feeding and breeding. Such knowledge could be obtained only by a properly instituted programme of oceanographic research, undertaken by scientists and provided with the latest equipment and with ships suited to work in some of the most tempestuous waters on the face of the planet. Crucially, the resulting series of annual research voyages, which began with the National Oceanographic Expedition of 1925–7, was not only highly profitable in scientific terms, it also provided the British government with a means by which to assert its interests in the region without directly addressing the issue of Argentina's territorial claims.

With the outbreak of war in 1939, subtlety gave way to direct action – on both sides. To Argentinian observers, Britain's attitude towards its far-flung outposts of empire had long seemed confused and noncommittal – but, throughout this period, the undisputed power and reach of the Royal Navy had made anything more than diplomatic posturing appear altogether too dangerous a proposition. Any overt attempt to capitalize on the apathy so far displayed by Foreign Office mandarins in Whitehall and by their political masters in Westminster might result in a swift and decisive return to the kind of gunboat diplomacy so favoured by Lord Palmerston in the previous century. By 1942 the situation had changed radically. A string of defeats in France, Norway, Greece, North Africa and the Far East, had left Britain fighting for its life. More locally, while Winston Churchill had ordered that the Falkland Islands garrison be reinforced in order to counter a perceived threat from the Japanese in the aftermath of Pearl Harbor, the placing of an embargo on the scientific work of the *Discovery* Committee and the commandeering of its two research ships by the Admiralty clearly signalled a relaxation of British control in the region.

Watching these developments, the government of President Roberto María Ortiz concluded that if ever a time was to arrive when Argentina might be able to fulfil its territorial ambitions in the South Atlantic, then surely that time was now. After all, whatever resentment Britain might feel at Argentina's actions, with its forces fully engaged in other far distant theatres of war, what chance was there that it would have either the resources or the will to retaliate? There was, it seemed, only one way to find out. The *Comisión Nacional del Antártico* and the Argentinian Navy were instructed to prepare for a voyage of exploratory activity in the Argentinian sector of Antarctica – the voyage to include visits to various sites in what Britain called the Falkland Islands Dependencies – and very soon the plans that would ultimately result in the raising of the Argentinian flag on Deception Island began to take definite shape.

*

Given its previous dilatoriness and the mass of more pressing issues that it must deal with relating to the conduct of the war, the response of the British government to what it perceived as Argentinian encroachments proved surprisingly determined. After a number of preliminary interdepartmental meetings, during which Foreign Office representatives pleaded for restraint and their Colonial Office counterparts called for decisive action, a War Cabinet of 28 January 1943 agreed not only that a Royal Navy warship should proceed immediately to the Falkland Islands Dependencies but also that 'permanent occupation should be established next year on all Islands except probably Laurie Island'.[6]

Shortly after the cabinet meeting, the armed merchant cruiser, HMS *Carnarvon Castle*, dropped anchor in Port Foster and its crew immediately began the process of obliterating all marks of foreign sovereignty by lowering the Argentinian flag and daubing its painted representations on the oil tanks with red oxide paint. They also hoisted the Union Flag, erected four 'British Crown Land' signs at conspicuous points, and recovered the bronze cylinder and message left by the Argentinian sailors a year earlier. The ship then steamed to Signy Island in the South Orkneys, where the same protocols were followed, before finally making a cordial visit to the Argentinian meteorological station on Laurie Island.

Throughout this voyage – and in accordance with the instructions with which he had been issued – *Carnarvon Castle*'s captain, Lieutenant-Commander E. W. Kitson, advised all interested parties, particularly the Argentinian meteorologists on Laurie Island, that he was engaged in a search for German surface raiders and submarines. Like all good cover stories, this fiction – which had been created in response to Foreign Office fears that a more overt statement of British motives might provoke Argentina into interrupting exports of beef to Britain, or otherwise interfering with British interests in the region – did possess a kernel of truth. In the early years of the war German *Hilfskreuzer* such as *Pinguin* and *Atlantis* had posed a real threat to Allied shipping in the South Atlantic, but by 1943 the vast majority of these raiders had been sunk and the residual threat was deemed negligible. Of course, the Argentinian government knew this as well as anyone and the following month *Primero de Mayo* again visited Deception Island, where its crew repeated the tasks completed by Kitson's men in January, removing the symbols of British sovereignty and re-erecting their own.

These actions made two things very clear to the British cabinet: first, that, Argentina had no intention of backing down and gracefully accepting the restoration of British hegemony in the region; second, that the current rather ridiculous game of tit-for-tat might go on for years, with expensive warships being diverted from other duties in order to redecorate not only Deception Island but also other relatively accessible locations in the Dependencies. This being the case, a policy of occasional visits must be replaced by one of physical occupation. An interdepartmental meeting discussed the matter again on 27 May 1943, and planning for the expedition that would soon be given the codename 'Operation Tabarin' began at last.

Although the expedition's organising committee included officials from various government departments, ranging from the Colonial Office to the Ministry of War Transport, from the very outset a trio of highly experienced polar veterans took the lead in defining the objectives of Operation Tabarin: James Wordie of Shackleton's *Endurance* Expedition, Neil Mackintosh of the *Discovery* Investigations, and Brian Roberts of the British Graham Land Expedition (BGLE). Crucially, while all three recognized and wholeheartedly supported the primary geopolitical goals of the operation, they also shared the conviction that bases established for political and economic reasons could provide useful platforms for valuable scientific and survey work. They also hoped that an expedition intended to meet immediate short-term objectives might ultimately evolve into a long-term programme of scientific research in the Antarctic.

According to the plans developed by these 'benign paladins',[7] the newly appointed leader of Operation Tabarin, Lieutenant-Commander James William Slessor Marr of the Royal Naval Volunteer Reserve, would be expected to establish two bases during 1944: one on the oft-visited Deception Island and another at Hope Bay on the northern tip of the Antarctic Peninsula. Marr himself would be stationed at Hope Bay, a location that offered the greatest opportunities for scientific work and sledging. As a professional zoologist with many years of service with the *Discovery* Investigations, he would be ideally qualified to oversee an ambitious programme of research and he would be supported by civilian experts in the fields of geology, meteorology, glaciology and botany. Survey work would also be undertaken – most notably a journey down the east coast of Graham Land intended to complement the sledging expeditions completed by the BGLE along the west coast during 1934–7 – and to assist in the achievement of this objective, surveyors from the Royal Engineers and Royal Navy would be detached from their military duties. Depending on the course of the war – and upon the availability of funding – additional bases might be established and the scientific programme expanded still further at a later date.

Despite the expedition's complex programme of science and survey, Marr soon came to realize that his greatest challenge would be to meet his geopolitical objectives – a challenge made even more difficult when circumstances forced him to establish his main base not at Hope Bay, but on the tiny Goudier Island in Port Lockroy off the western edge of the Peninsula. Prior to sailing he was issued with a lengthy set of 'Political Instructions' which would have left even the most experienced of military attachés scratching his head in bewilderment. This document made it clear that a confrontation with Argentinian personnel must be anticipated, but that 'violence should at all costs be avoided'.[8] Having made this unambiguous opening statement, the author of the instructions then sought to predict every possible scenario and to provide detailed orders as to how each should be handled:

> … it may not always be possible or desirable to avoid the purely technical use of force in such instance as, for example, pushing past a man standing with outstretched arm or vice versa … If the expedition finds Argentines and/or Chileans already installed at a place where it is proposed to land, you should nevertheless make it your object to land also, to establish yourselves, preferably at a suitable distance from the other party, and to maintain towards the latter an attitude of politeness and even cordiality, while making it unmistakably clear that it is your duty to assert and to maintain British Sovereignty over the territory concerned …
>
> If an Argentine and/or Chilean party already established on an island show an unmistakable intention of resorting to violent force in order to prevent the expedition from landing on the territory concerned, an attempt should be made to dissuade

them tactfully from this intention. Should this fail, however, and violent force be directed against your landing, the expedition should return under protest to His Majesty's Ship, remain at the island concerned and seek wireless instructions forthwith.[9]

Basically, an attitude of 'live and let live' should be adopted locally, while the larger issues of sovereign rights were debated by the opposing governments. Unfortunately, this well-meaning attempt to leave nothing to chance left Marr with practically no room for manoeuvre, and one can only smile at the picture of this dour polar veteran standing in front of an Argentinian officer, desperately leafing through his voluminous instructions in an attempt to identify the most appropriate course of action.

*

So far as the selection of personnel was concerned, despite being able to call upon the social and professional networks of Wordie, Mackintosh and Roberts, the expedition committee managed to recruit only two scientists for the first year of Operation Tabarin: William Flett, a lecturer in geology at the University of Glasgow who would lead the five-man party on Deception Island, and the author of *The Secret South*, Ivan Mackenzie Lamb. The latter choice, in particular, would prove to be an inspired one.

According to his own account, published in the expedition's periodical news-sheet, *The Hope Bay Howler*, at the time of his recruitment Lamb was employed as Assistant Keeper in the Department of Botany at the British Museum (Natural History), researching the lichen collections of the early British, Belgian, French and Swedish Antarctic expeditions and preparing reports on the lichen finds of the BGLE and the *Discovery* Investigations:

> This work was well under way when one day in September the Keeper of my department sent up word that he would like to see me at once in his *sanctum sanctorum*. Hastily reviewing in my

mind and preparing a defence for all recent sins of commission and omission which might underlie this request, I presented myself before the Presence, whose first action was to impress upon me, by appropriate words and gestures, a solemn warning that the information which he was about to convey to me was of such profound significance and secrecy that the discussion of its terms, even in lowered voices and behind locked doors, almost bordered on the profane.[10]

Though somewhat bemused by the explanation offered by his superior, Lamb nonetheless agreed to proceed to the Colonial Office building at 2 Park Street, where he met 'Jimmy' Marr for the first time.

At the time of this encounter, the contrast between the two men could hardly have been more marked. Forty years old, stocky of build, balding, bespectacled and distinctly weather-beaten, Marr had spent almost his entire adult life on the windswept decks of polar research ships. He had authored a popular account of his part in Shackleton's *Quest* Expedition[11] and an important treatise on the South Orkneys,[12] and his RNVR uniform, in addition to its two-and-a-half gold stripes on each sleeve, displayed the coveted white ribbon of the Polar Medal, which he had been awarded in 1934 and again in 1941. Though somewhat serious, even grim, of visage, Marr combined a dry sense of humour with an almost childish delight in inventing jingles, playing his harmonica at bar-room singsongs, and performing comic turns to round off an evening's boisterous and well-lubricated frivolity.

For his part, Lamb was thirty-two, a little over six feet tall, slim, blue-eyed, with a long, sensitive face and straight black hair, which he swept back from his brow and retained in place with an application of brilliantine. Although he had been born in London on 11 September 1911, Lamb's family were Scottish and he had spent his formative years in Edinburgh where, in the words of one contemporary, he 'had been well inculcated with many of the more admirable of the

Scottish national characteristics'.[13] He also claimed connection with the aristocracy of exploration – though of Africa rather than the polar regions – in the form of the Scottish missionary David Livingstone, his grandmother's great-uncle. His academic credentials were no less impressive: following graduation from Edinburgh University in 1933 with a BSc with Honours in Botany, he had spent two years undertaking botanical research at the Universities of Munich and Würzburg in Germany, before accepting the post of Assistant Keeper at the British Museum in 1935. This appointment had given him the financial security necessary to marry, in 1936, his Finnish sweetheart, Maila Laabejo of Tampere, and, in 1940, to become a father for the first time. Finally, just a year prior to his meeting with Marr, Lamb had been awarded the degree of Doctor of Science by Edinburgh University, with a dissertation concerning the hypothesis of the movement of the Southern Hemisphere continents based on his studies of the Antarctic lichen flora.

Clearly, this tall, impeccably dressed and somewhat ascetic-looking scientist impressed Marr because, having articulated the purpose of Operation Tabarin more successfully, and more enthusiastically, than the Keeper of Botany had been able to do, he immediately reaffirmed the offer of a place for Lamb among his personnel. In reply, Lamb told Marr that he 'considered it a privilege to be asked to accompany the Expedition in a scientific capacity',[14] and accepted.

Given the breadth and depth of his research into Antarctic flora, there can be little doubt that the chance to undertake fieldwork in the very places where many of his specimens had been collected must have been very appealing to Lamb. However, by his own admission, he also harboured an ulterior motive for accepting the post of expedition botanist. Being both philosophical and religious in nature, he had become deeply disillusioned by the war and by what it had revealed of humanity's extraordinary capacity for destruction. These feelings had crystallized when, on arriving for work one day, he discovered that an enemy bomb had devastated a large part of the British Museum's herbarium and its invaluable plant collections. 'To me,' he wrote,

> the event brought only mistrust in the usefulness of scientific effort, and an obsessive realization that human progress depends, at any rate in our latitudes, entirely on good roofing and protection from the elements, and is therefore something essentially artificial, fugacious and undependable. The sight of the sacred volumes of our scientific lore mouldering in their charred and watery grave seemed a preliminary vision of what must come to all the effort which we lovingly expend during our brief contact with the physical universe.[15]

In accepting a role in Operation Tabarin, Lamb sought either to confirm or to disprove these depressing conclusions; he wanted to recover or completely discard 'faith in science and human progress, by the contemplation of untouched nature and the microcosm of civilization represented by a dozen human beings isolated on a frozen continent'.[16] Over the next two years Antarctica would serve as his laboratory and he and his fellow expeditionaries would be his specimens.

Whatever quixotic objectives motivated him to join the expedition, there can be absolutely no doubt regarding Lamb's contribution to the success of Operation Tabarin. As well as helping to establish its three manned bases – on Deception Island and on Goudier Island early in 1944, and at Hope Bay in February 1945 – he took part in all of the major sledging journeys, manhauling across Wiencke Island in September and October 1944, and covering some 800 miles with dog teams in the area around James Ross Island between August and December 1945. A highly proficient photographer, he also took countless photographs, both at the bases and while sledging, and developed the negatives and printed the images in the base's tiny darkroom.

Surgeon-Lieutenant Eric Back, the expedition's medical officer
and meteorologist (and himself a descendant of the Arctic explorer
Admiral Sir George Back), later said of Lamb that 'although he didn't
look tough, he was',[17] and nowhere was this proved more conclusively
than during the crossing of Erebus and Terror Gulf in the early days
of September 1945, when Lamb found himself pushing his team's
heavily laden sledge almost single-handedly, his dog team being too

exhausted and too hungry to pull. Sub-Lieutenant David James, an assistant surveyor who also took part in this journey, noted in his diary on 4 September that

> Throughout this day my admiration of Lamb, which was always high, grew and grew. No words can adequately depict how exhausting this deep snow is; suffice to say that Victor [Russell] and I, who are twenty-five, of good average physique and very fit, found that half an hour was the absolute longest we could plough through it without having a spell of the comparatively easy task of pulling on skis. Yet he, ten years our senior, was able to continue floundering through it all day, without respite or complaint.
>
> This display of sheer guts, this willingness to drive the body till it drops, fills me with the greatest possible admiration...[18]

At the time, James was not alone in recording his astonishment at the stamina and determination displayed by Lamb during this trial, but only in the pages of *The Secret South*, written a decade later, would Lamb himself reveal just how close the experience came to breaking him both physically and mentally.

When not sledging, he made (unsuccessful) attempts to propagate Falkland Islands flora at Port Lockroy,[19] and conducted a range of environmental experiments. As part of these investigations, he manufactured a five-foot-tall snow gauge to record snow accumulation and used a low-temperature thermometer to observe and record ground surface temperatures beneath the snow layer. On another occasion, he dug into the 'miniature glacier' to the south of 'Bransfield House' on Goudier Island in order to locate bands of ice in the granulated snow, seeking thereby to understand the process by which snow turns to ice without thawing. He also tunnelled into a snowdrift to ascertain the distance light would penetrate through freshly fallen snow. Having crawled into the tunnel, he removed snow from above his head until he could see light and then thrust a ruler upwards in order to measure the depth of the remaining snow. Recording a thickness of twenty-three inches, he surmised that mosses would receive sufficient light to survive despite being buried to a considerable depth, although the light would be at the green and blue end of the visible spectrum – a conjecture that was not experimentally proven in the field until twenty years later. All of these activities revealed the extent of Lamb's inquisitiveness and inventiveness, but they were merely an adjunct to his primary area of interest, the study of lichens. In this arena, Back thought him 'the best botanist to go down since [Joseph Dalton] Hooker, if not even better than him',[20] and Marr would later report: 'I am convinced that, restricted as his field has been, his meticulous and painstaking work here has already gone a long way towards clearing up the somewhat confused taxonomy of the Antarctic lichens'[21] – a conviction fully supported by Lamb's discovery during the expedition of several previously unknown lichens, including *Verrucaria serpuloides*, the only true marine lichen in the world.[22]

Crucially, Lamb also possessed the rare gift of inspiring even his non-scientific colleagues and his enthusiasm for his rather arcane subject proved surprisingly contagious. Again according to Back, 'He encouraged the most uninterested of his companions to an interest in lichens ... He would go around and survey some little growth about half-an-inch long, and this would be described as "luxuriant vegetation" and he really inspired everybody.'[23] Nor would he allow his own meticulousness to dampen the newfound ardour of his apprentice collectors: 'Lamb was so very critical in the selection of his specimens,' wrote Captain Andrew Taylor, senior surveyor and later the expedition's commander in the field,

> that it was seldom that any of us brought him a lichen which
> was of any great interest to him. He would not, of course, create
> this impression when receiving such a botanical gift, but would
> appear most grateful and was always prepared to give a learned

exposition on the species in question. But on more than one occasion, on passing the back of the house shortly afterwards past Lamb's window, particularly at Port Lockroy, I have almost been struck by the specimen in question being tossed through the window.[24]

In some ways, though, perhaps the most important of Lamb's characteristics, at least when judged against the peculiar backdrop of a polar expedition, were his empathy and kindliness. James wrote of him that 'Probably most expeditions have their Dr Edward Wilsons. I have no shadow of doubt who ours is,'[25] and he was not the only member of Operation Tabarin to draw a comparison between Lamb and the man whom many members of Scott's two expeditions called, simply and affectionately, 'Uncle'. In a way that Marr, and certainly Taylor, were unable to do, he appears to have provided the 'glue' that helped to bind the diverse personnel together. Back, who was no mean judge of character, described him as 'completely unflappable, meticulous, a cultured and kindly man . . . a memorable man,' and he seems to have been universally liked and respected by all who came into contact with him. In this context, it is interesting to note that George A. Llano, a post-war colleague, fellow lichenologist, and a close friend of Lamb, described him as being 'a very private man',[26] and none of the other expeditionaries' diaries contain any allusion to Lamb ever having revealed much, if anything, of his inner self. Perhaps, then, Lamb became the character most essential to any small, close-knit community, the 'listener': the man to whom the troubled, the angry, the frustrated and the lonely can talk, without being expected to listen in return.

Taylor became Lamb's closest friend during the two years of Operation Tabarin and they remained in regular contact until Lamb's increasing debility in the last years of his life prevented him from writing. Both men possessed complex personalities, and both were inclined to introspection; perhaps these shared traits enabled

Taylor to assess Lamb's character more completely than any of the other expeditionaries. During the austral winter of 1945, Taylor, who had assumed overall command after Marr's retirement on the grounds of ill-health in February, made a series of notes on the men who now reported to him. Many of these brief sketches are critical, some are scathing. For Lamb, though, he had nothing but the highest praise. The botanist was, he wrote, 'a man and a gentleman, with a philosophic calm that "passeth all understanding"':

> Straight, honest and upright, he is one who appreciates the fairness which I try and inculcate into all my decisions concerning the base here – it is both an honour and a privilege to work with so fine a character. His willingness to accept any task which is given him with the same spirit of unselfishness and willingness which he has always exhibited in all the dealings I have ever had with him makes him stand almost head and shoulders above the rest of us. I feel that in Lamb I have a friend upon whom I may rely utterly in any situation, and I would very much like to feel that even in a small measure, he reciprocates this opinion of me.[27]

Some, like David James, received Taylor's praise in May 1945 but later found themselves excluded from his good graces – but this was certainly not the case with Lamb. Shortly after their return to civilization, Taylor wrote that,

> Events threw me in closer contact with [him], probably, than with any other individual in our party, and I got to know him well. A diligent worker, and a modest and courteous gentleman, he is one of the most unselfish characters I have ever met, a person it is a privilege to have known so well. Having a humour which at times approaches elfishness, he is a most sincere and earnest person who, while he is both logical and imaginative, has a realism about him which would not allow any sense

of histrionics or dramatics to warp the steady judgement he possesses.[28]

*

Lamb and his colleagues had sailed from Avonmouth, Bristol, on 14 December 1943, their wartime expedition and its geopolitical objectives shrouded in secrecy. Following two arduous but productive years in the Antarctic, they returned to England on board the light cruiser, HMS *Ajax*, to find that their very existence had, to all appearances, been entirely forgotten. Although James Wordie made a somewhat belated appearance to greet them at Chatham Dockyard on 9 March 1946, so few preparations had been made for their reception that some of the party actually spent their first night in civilization sleeping on the litter-strewn floor of a now-redundant air raid shelter, accommodation poorer by far than that of the Antarctic base they had left nearly two months earlier. As Taylor remarked bitterly, 'the quietness of our departure was only exceeded by that of our return'.[29]

While men returning from a secret naval operation could hardly expect to be greeted with the kind of euphoria that had marked the reappearance of public heroes like Scott and Shackleton four decades or so earlier, they had every right to feel surprised by the authorities' apparent indifference to the substantial work that they had completed during the expedition. It seems highly improbable that Lamb and his colleagues anticipated the preparation of a full account in the style of Scott's *The Voyage of the Discovery*, or Rymill's *Southern Lights*, but even the scientific and survey reports that they had laboured over so dutifully were quietly received and filed away unobtrusively, with no budget allocated for their publication. Indeed, the only official publication concerning the origins, activities and achievements of Operation Tabarin was a twelve-page summary written by Wordie and published in the *Polar Record* in July 1946.[30] Thereafter, the expedition slipped into an undeserved obscurity.

So far as the explorers themselves were concerned, their overwhelming impression was that they should, in the words of Gwion 'Taff' Davies, the stores officer, 'disappear quietly, and keep our mouths shut'.[31] Whether this injunction was spoken or merely implied, for his part, Lamb followed it without question. After only the briefest of stays in Britain, Uruguay and Sweden, in 1947 he accepted the post of Professor of Cryptogamic Botany[32] at the University of Tucumán where he initiated a series of fieldtrips to collect the lichen flora of several Argentinian provinces, publishing the results of his research in Spanish. He also began work on the Antarctic specimens that he had collected at Port Lockroy, Deception Island, Hope Bay and in the vicinity of James Ross Island.

According to George Llano, Maila Lamb soon found the climate, the insects and the primitive conditions of life in Tucumán intolerable and expressed an urgent wish to move, preferably to the United States. At this point, Andrew Taylor, who had remained with the Canadian Army working on an assortment of cold weather projects, alerted the National Museum of Canada to Lamb's availability, and as a result of this timely intervention he was offered the chance to become the Museum's Curator of Cryptogams, a post he held from 1950 to 1953. This move reduced the strain on the Lambs' marriage, but resettlement in Ottawa proved expensive and Lamb sought to relieve some of the resulting financial burden by selling both his personal library and his private herbarium of some 3,200 European, Patagonian and Antarctic specimens to the museum. Whatever it may have cost him to part with his collection, the benefits to the museum remain incalculable and Irwin Brodo, one of Lamb's colleagues, has stated that, even today,

> His 'spirit' is always present … He was a brilliant lichenologist, far ahead of his time in his considerations of evolutionary and biological aspects of lichens. He was also an extremely good taxonomist, meticulous and thorough in his studies. He prepared

copious notes and drawings on the specimens he examined, all neatly written and enclosed within the specimen packets. His books are annotated with his own observations and comments, and I'm sure there is much to be learned from them.[33]

In 1953 Lamb's growing reputation resulted in his being offered the post of Director of the Farlow Herbarium at Harvard University, a position he held until his retirement two decades later. During this period he concentrated on Antarctic lichen flora, with the intention of publishing a detailed and comprehensively researched ecological, biogeographical and taxonomic *magnum opus*. At the same time he evidenced a growing interest in marine algae and, in 1955, he enrolled on a course dedicated to this subject at Woods Hole, Massachusetts; this was followed, in 1957 and 1958, by visits to marine research centres at the Muséum d'Histoire Naturelle in Paris and at Trinity College, Dublin. Combining this new interest with his abiding passion for Antarctic research, Lamb proposed a study of Antarctic marine algae to be undertaken at bases on the Antarctic Peninsula. As Director of Antarctic Biological Programs at the US National Science Foundation (NSF), George Llano arranged for Lamb to visit McMurdo Sound in 1960, where he was able to familiarize himself with SCUBA techniques in polar conditions. Four years later, with colleagues from the United States, France and Argentina, and with a grant from the NSF, he became a leading participant in what he whimsically referred to as 'Operation Gooseflesh', studying and collecting marine algae at sites along the western Antarctic Peninsula. For this work, Lamb received the US Antarctica Service Medal to add to the British Polar Medal that he had received in 1953 in recognition of his role in Operation Tabarin.

Following the success of this, his last, Antarctic expedition, Lamb suffered professional disappointment of the most profound kind when, in 1973, an American lichenologist, Carroll W. Dodge, published his *Lichen Flora of the Antarctic Continent and Adjacent*

Islands.[34] Dodge, whose work was largely based on the lichen collections made by Admiral Richard Byrd, Sir Douglas Mawson and Dr Paul Siple, had no personal experience of the Antarctic and his work provoked much criticism from several lichenologists, including Lamb, for what they perceived as his inept taxonomic concepts and his 'identification' of innumerable new species based upon minimal evidence. But, whatever its inadequacies, Dodge's study pre-empted the publication of Lamb's work and its effect on Lamb personally was devastating. After thirty-five years of dedicated research, and having published several landmark monographs and many other research papers on both lichens and marine algae, in the final stage of his Antarctic lichen project he admitted defeat in his goal to publish what would have been an extremely authoritative and valuable *Flora*, and he abandoned work. His immaculately prepared notes and descriptions, copiously illustrated by photographs and detailed line drawings of microscopic dissections, remain unpublished.[35]

During the same period, Lamb experienced crises in other areas of his life, financial, familial and personal, all being overlaid by a pattern of deteriorating health. Most significantly, he divorced his wife and, having attempted suicide on at least one occasion,[36] sought psychological help to resolve a torment that left him increasingly uncomfortable with his gender. In order to achieve an identity with which he could feel at ease he underwent gender reassignment treatment in 1971, becoming Elke Mackenzie. But wider attitudes at that time to such issues were, at best, ambivalent, and following the surgery, Mackenzie was 'actively encouraged' to resign her post at the Farlow Herbarium.[37] Perhaps as a result of these traumas, during the later part of the 1970s Mackenzie gave up her interest in cryptogamic botany and turned to translating German botanical text books into English, work which paid for the land and construction of a home in Costa Rica in 1976.

Mackenzie moved back to Cambridge, Massachusetts, in 1980 to live with her daughter, Nina. Around 1983 she was diagnosed with

The Secret South

Lou Gehrig's disease or amyotrophic lateral sclerosis, from which she died on 27 January 1990, at the age of seventy-eight.

*

Like Andrew Taylor, Ivan Mackenzie Lamb was an almost obsessive recorder of his experiences during Operation Tabarin. So far as the former was concerned, in later years Eric Back would state his conviction that Taylor's compulsion to document every detail of the expedition teetered on the brink of monomania, tinged with paranoia:

> He was known as 'Quadruplicate Andy' ... his doctrine was, 'If you put it down in writing and in quadruplicate, nobody can lose it' and, therefore, that if you've done anything, you'll get the credit for it. If you don't write it down, somebody else will get the credit for it.'[38]

Lamb, too, produced multiple copies of his expedition diary, both typed and in his immaculate, almost copperplate, handwriting, but his urge to record events does not seem to have been driven by anything like the doubts and anxieties that motivated his friend. Instead, given his stated wish to contemplate 'untouched nature and the microcosm of civilization',[39] it is perhaps not too much to imagine that his diary came, in some ways, to serve the same purpose as his copious and highly detailed notes on his botanical specimens.

The result of Lamb's observations, *The Secret South*, is the last of four eyewitness accounts of Operation Tabarin to be published. The others, in the order of their publication, are David James's *That Frozen Land* (1949), Harold Squires's *SS Eagle: The Secret Mission* (1992), and Andrew Taylor's *Two Years Below the Horn* (2017). Of these, James's book covers only the second year of the expedition; Squires's is concerned primarily with the trials and tribulations of one of the expedition's supply ships; while Taylor's, which he completed in 1947, might reasonably be described as the 'official' version of events. Lamb's narrative is very different from all of these. In particular, while its author was, by all accounts, a sincere, earnest, logical and imaginative scientist and a kindly and deeply empathetic man, it was what Taylor described as his friend's 'elfish' sense of humour that came to the fore when he sat down to describe the events of 1943–6.

Written in an unusual, occasionally archaic, style, Lamb's story takes the form of an autobiographical adventure, combining personal experiences with relevant historical background, and memories of everyday life on an old-fashioned Antarctic base with the thrills and hazards encountered during long-distance man- and dog-hauled sledging journeys. In his prologue, he not only admits that 'I have endeavoured throughout to see the whole thing from the lighter side, and depict the episodes encountered during my two years' sojourn on that great southern continent in a quasi-humorous vein,' but also acknowledges that his readers 'may maintain all along that I am giving too free a rein to fantasy and imagination'.

Ironically, the prologue in which Lamb makes this admission is itself an example of just this kind of fantasy in that it cites Walter Traprock's *My Northern Exposure* (1922) as an exemplar of polar writing, but fails to mention (as he must have known) that Traprock was a *nom de plume* of George Sheppard Chappell and that his narrative is a comic fiction. Similarly, Lamb's account of a real visit to Deception Island in February 1945 is peppered with (unacknowledged) allusions to another novel, *Le Plan de l'Aiguille* (1927) by the Franco-Swiss novelist Frédéric-Louis Sauser, writing as Blaise Cendrars.[40] As he derived no obvious literary advantage from these eccentric inclusions, we can only assume that they are the product of Lamb's self-confessed constitutional inability 'to resist appreciating a good joke'.

Admittedly such mischievous fabrications are rare, but Lamb uses other literary devices which, from a historical rather than literary perspective, introduce ambiguity to the narrative. For instance, while based at Hope Bay during the period February 1945 – January 1946, he took part in two sledging journeys, 8 August – 11 September and 9 November – 29 December. He recounts events from both journeys in his book but, presumably to prevent repetition, he draws these events into one expedition, covering August–September. From a purely literary point of view, this decision seems logical as the narrative would obtain little benefit from duplicated descriptions of preparations and sledging. But, in other respects, it sows the seeds for confusion and – were the book to be relied upon implicitly – for serious errors. A key example is the sledge party's supposed discovery in mid-August of a Gentoo penguin colony on Vortex Island. If real, this colony would have been both the most southerly of Gentoo rookeries ever discovered on the east coast of the Antarctic Peninsula, and the earliest to nest. In fact, this colony (of Adélie penguins, not Gentoos) was discovered on 20 November, during the second sledge journey. By suggesting that the sledging party discovered a Gentoo rookery so early in the year, Lamb creates a spurious conundrum – a curious, indeed inexplicable, act on the part of a man who dedicated his entire professional life to science. Equally strange in some ways is the fact that, having contorted the facts to create this anomaly, Lamb fails to pass any comment on the uniqueness of the discovery.

As well as compressing events and occasionally embroidering the recorded facts of the expedition, Lamb sometimes introduces personalities who can be difficult to identify accurately. One such is the youthful crewmember of the supply ship, SS *Eagle*, encountered at Deception Island in February 1945. In chapter nine of *The Secret South*, Lamb provides a detailed vignette of this tobacco-chewing adolescent from Twillingate, Newfoundland – but there is no mention of him at all in his diary entries for this period. In the same chapter, he provides a circumstantial account of his meeting with a man whom he identifies only with the official (or invented) acronym of 'CUSCI'. Details found in various expedition diaries make it possible to identify the potbellied, camera-wielding official as Kenneth Bradley, the Colonial Secretary – but not all the facts fit, and the identification can be tentative at best. Perhaps, instead of being reliable descriptions of recognisable individuals, these are literary creations, possibly amalgams of characteristics drawn from a number of sources. Of course, Lamb was neither the first nor the last autobiographical travel writer to adapt the facts to suit his creative purposes, and comparison might be drawn with near-contemporaries like Patrick Leigh Fermor and Norman Lewis, neither of whom believed that the literal truth should be allowed to spoil a good story. And yet it should also be stated that the accuracy of Lamb's descriptions of named members of the expedition – Marr, Taylor, Tom Berry, Gwion Davies and others – can be proved conclusively through comparison with other contemporary sources.

In some respects, Lamb's omissions seem more remarkable than his creative inclusions. By far the most obvious of these is his decision not to tell the story of the near-loss of the *Eagle* following a collision with an iceberg during a gale in Hope Bay in March 1945. Having already lost its anchors, the little ship sustained such serious damage that its captain, Robert Sheppard, was forced to choose between beaching the vessel or attempting to reach the Falkland Islands, a voyage that meant crossing hundreds of miles of some of the stormiest ocean on the face of the planet. The most probable result of either decision would be the loss of both ship and crew. Sheppard chose the latter course and, through a combination of brilliant seamanship and extraordinary luck, succeeded in reaching Port Stanley. Hugely dramatic in its own right, this incident also had profound consequences for the shore party in that Sheppard and his crew had been forced to flee before unloading vital supplies and equipment. As a direct result, the conditions experienced by Lamb and his companions during the second year of Operation Tabarin were significantly more trying than those of their first. In his diary entries for 17 and 18 March, Lamb describes the gale, the enforced departure of the *Eagle* and the enormous relief felt by the whole expedition when they received news of the ship's survival – and yet, inexplicably, he mentions none of these in the narrative he wrote for publication.

*

The Secret South is not, then, a straightforward account of a mid-twentieth-century Antarctic expedition. As a narrative, it is as complex and as multi-layered as its author and, indeed, as Operation Tabarin itself.

Lamb himself remains deeply enigmatic. All the accounts of the expedition, both published and unpublished, make it clear that he was, in many ways, an extraordinary individual – not only as a cryptogamic taxonomist and ecologist of world renown, but also as an erudite intellect, a philosopher, linguist, illustrator, humorist, prolific writer, and most reliable friend. What remains unclear is whether his years in the Antarctic enabled him to meet the challenge he set himself when he accepted his position on the expedition, namely 'that of recovering or completely discarding faith in science and human progress'.

Perhaps, though, if we base our judgement on his pivotal contribution to Operation Tabarin which, like all polar expeditions, relied entirely on mutual cooperation and loyalty, on his dedication to his scientific endeavours both during and after the expedition, on the respect, admiration and affection which he inspired in his colleagues, and on the humour with which he recounted his experiences, we might feel fairly confident that he did indeed leave Antarctica with a renewed faith in both science and humanity.

What follows is his story.

Stephen Haddelsey
Ronald Lewis-Smith

Editors' Note

FOLLOWING SEVERAL UNSUCCESSFUL ATTEMPTS to have his tale published in the United States, in the late 1970s Ivan Mackenzie Lamb asked fellow lichenologist Ronald Lewis-Smith to establish whether a British publisher might be found. Only now, some forty years after this request was made, and twenty-eight after Lamb's death, has publication at last proved possible.

Although it has been necessary to subject Lamb's text to an extensive professional edit, throughout this exercise the primary objective has been to present the manuscript in a form as close as possible to the original. However, as described in the introduction, Lamb's final draft of 1956 contains a number of eccentricities and departures from documented fact; taken *en masse* we believe that these would have distracted the reader and undermined the integrity of the work as an historical narrative. On that basis, many of these portions of the text have been removed. The most significant excisions include a lengthy dream sequence included in Lamb's account of the crossing of Erebus and Terror Gulf in September 1945 and three heavily fictionalized chapters dealing with his experiences in the Falkland Islands on his return from the Antarctic in January 1946. Although these, and some lesser deletions, would probably have disappointed Lamb, and inevitably result in a book slightly different from what he intended, we remain convinced that any publisher approached during his lifetime would have demanded precisely the same alterations. Crucially, their removal in no way interferes with the narrative flow. All major deletions are highlighted in the notes.

Another significant change is to the book's title. Lamb had chosen a phrase from the ninth line of Psalm 139, 'Take the Wings of the Morning', but the publisher and editors agreed that this quotation was, quite simply, too esoteric. Again, we believe that, in all probability, any publisher accepting the manuscript at the time of its completion would have insisted on a title more directly and obviously related to the content. To mark Lamb's original intention, the editors have used the relevant section from the psalm as an epigraph. The second epigraph is the editors' choice and is intended to reflect Lamb's particular – occasionally eccentric – style of writing. The author's American spelling has also been anglicized throughout. In all other respects, the narrative is presented as Lamb left it in 1956 – somewhat shorter as a result of the aforementioned excisions, but otherwise fundamentally unchanged. Finally, when quoting the occasionally profane language of his fellow expeditionaries, Lamb routinely replaces swear words with a form of homonym, leaving its interpretation to his readers. In reality, the homonyms are usually close enough to the original language to require very little imagination in their interpretation. Whether this habit was the result of Lamb's own dislike of bad language or an attempt to appease sensitive readers is unclear. His homonyms have been retained throughout, but they have been *italicized*.

For ease of reading, all adjustments have been incorporated into the text without the addition of square brackets or other markers. The editors have also added extensive explanatory endnotes.

The cartoons on pages 54, 116, 141 and 156 were drawn by Lamb and originally appeared in *The Hope Bay Howler*, the expedition's periodical news-sheet. The hut plans on pages 41 and 145 are by members of the expedition. The maps on pages 70, 109, 173 and 182–3 are the original survey maps completed in the field by Andrew Taylor and other members of the expedition and are reproduced here for the first time.

THE
SECRET
SOUTH

Author's Prologue

IF YOU BELONG TO THAT STRENUOUS, rugged school of polar enthusiasts, whether practical or literary, who regard polar exploration as essentially a high, grim and humourless calling, placing much emphasis on the deadly seriousness of toil and the gruelling struggle against hardships and cold, then shy away from this book right off, for it is not your cup of tea. True, it contains a fair amount of practical and factual information on Antarctica which is, so far as I have been able to make it, essentially correct; it strives in large part to give a day-by-day picture of life in what was perhaps one of the last of the old fashioned pioneering expeditions, carried out with traditional and comparatively rudimentary equipment and means of transportation, without the aid of the extensive mechanization which has now completely revolutionized the technique of polar travel. But my general approach to the subject, I fear, is misguided and all wrong, for I have endeavoured throughout to see the whole thing from the lighter side, and depict the episodes encountered during my two years' sojourn on that great southern continent in a quasi-humorous vein, and that for the simple reason that I seem constitutionally unable to resist appreciating a good joke, even when I myself am the victim of it; and with that damning admission I excommunicate myself forever from the august and straight-faced congregation of the Explorers' Club, and the ranks of those great spirits who contribute such illuminating but deadly serious papers to the *Polar Record*. However, although thus voluntarily excluded from the Pall Mall of the polar elect, where harrowing experiences in Arctic and Antarctic climes are solemnly and shudderingly related in dimly lit and softly carpeted recesses, I have at least one similarly minded and congenial example going before me in that outstandingly unique and gifted polar explorer Dr Walter Traprock, whose exploits in the Arctic, as recounted in his classic book *My Northern Exposure* (1922),[1] were so remarkable as to border on the incredible, and yet are related in such a pleasant and humorous style that we almost forget the unspeakable hardships which he and his intrepid comrades must by all accounts have suffered.

Therefore it seems to me, after due cogitation, that in the annals of polar literature there is a place, however humble, for an unassuming and straightforward account of Antarctic adventure written by one who, without unduly serious pretensions, has felt impelled to illuminate these transactions from the funnier angle, as well as to indicate some of the deeper and more serious layers of their eventual implications. While never aspiring to invite a comparison with either the exploratory or the literary abilities of a writer of the calibre of the inimitable Traprock, I have some hopes that to the general reader who is interested in polar exploration and enjoys a good factual yarn, even though it may not lead to any seriously applicable philosophical conclusions, the rapid skimming through of these pages may serve to provide a few hours' relatively harmless, if hardly inspiring, entertainment.

Because all things, rest assured, do have their funny side, either on the outside or the inside, depending on one's way of looking at them. And it is indeed surprising, when you come to think of it, how few of the chroniclers of polar exploration (with the notable exception, as before, of the abovementioned Traprock) have been able to approach their subject in a spirit of good clean fun and show due understanding of the manifestations of humour which are decidedly not lacking in those white expanses beyond the limits of our familiar inhabited terrain. Here, while wandering in these vast, blank and featureless spaces, the Pole Star and the Southern Cross should be our guides to mirthful, and not woeful, apprehension of our situation as involuntary intruders into polar fastnesses, and of the comical vicissitudes to which we are likely to be exposed therein.

Those who have had the fortune, as I did, to penetrate a good deal farther into them than is possible for the majority of mortals, will surely agree that the unseen guardian of those frozen wastes, when disturbed in his eternal ice-glazed hibernation, does not pull any of those friendly, good natured punches of his to your ribs, jawbone and other parts, both above and below the belt, and may even, in the obvious relish and exuberance of his playful sparring, put you down for the count altogether. In fact, the truth is that on occasion he plays it uncomfortably rough, from which I deduce him to be a rumbustious and primeval old character, well attuned temperamentally to the bleak, raw and inhospitable waste which he inhabits. Of course, you may maintain all along that I am giving too free a rein to fantasy and imagination in this matter, and that nothing of the kind actually exists. I can certainly not contradict you confidently on this head, but would only point out that belief in that sort of thing seems obstinately ingrained in human nature, and if we pay homage to Neptune as ruler of the equatorial seas, and laughably submit ourselves to the indignities of his soap and three-foot razor, why therefore should we be unwilling to concede to the White Expanse its own Abominable Snowman?

1
A Polar Portrait Gallery

ON A BRIGHT ANTARCTIC FEBRUARY DAY in the year 1944, two vessels might have been seen entering Antarctic Sound, which is the strait separating the northernmost tip of the Palmer Peninsula (or Graham Land) from the island of Joinville,[1] lying some eight miles to the north of it. This point is the most northerly extension of the Antarctic continent, the latitude here being sixty-three degrees South. One of the vessels was the SS *Fitzroy*, a cargo–passenger ship belonging to the Falkland Islands Trading Company, and now far off her accustomed route, which lay as a rule between Port Stanley, capital of the Falkland Islands, and Montevideo; the other a small grey craft of indeterminate appearance. Her coat of battleship grey, and the single small cannon at her bows (hardly larger than an elephant gun) announces a warlike character; but the lack of armour-plating, the absence of recognizable uniform among the members of her crew, and the mutton carcasses lashed to her shrouds, indicate rather a mission of exploratory nature. She is, in fact, HMS *William Scoresby*, attached to the *Discovery* Investigations Committee, a branch of the British Colonial Office,[2] and before the outbreak of war saw much service in the southern oceans as a whale-marking vessel for scientific investigations. Now she is entrusted with the mission of piloting the *Fitzroy*, which carries the members of the expedition and their stores, into some suitable Antarctic haven, preferably on the coast of the Palmer Peninsula, where a base will be built and expedition headquarters established.

When I came up on the deck of the *Fitzroy* that morning, we were passing an enormous flat-topped iceberg about four miles in diameter. The weather was calm and sunny, and both sky and sea were blue, blue of a very exceptional purity. For as far as the eye could see, the sea was sparsely littered with lumps of brash ice and a few larger pieces which might almost qualify as icebergs. The crannies and cracks in these were of an indescribably intense cobalt-blue colour, and when the ship passed alongside, one could see the submerged part, somewhat frightening in its cold green underwater gleam, jutting out far below the surface or sloping sheer down until lost in unfathomable darkness in the black depths below. On many of these ice lumps Weddell seals were lying – slug-like and inert, up to two yards in length, of a buffy-brown colour. Small groups of Adélie penguins were travelling swiftly through the water here and there, weaving their way in and out, up and down, like diminutive porpoises. At times a whale would roll to the surface a short distance away, spout up a cone of vapour with a gentle blasting exhalation, and then roll slowly under again, bringing to view the revolving expanse of its tremendous black glistening back.

One by one the members of the expedition now congregated along the rail of the *Fitzroy*, with eyes fixed on the ice-covered mountainous mainland which we intended to make our home for the next two years. I will take the liberty of fixing them immobile in the midst of their gesticulations, and present them as it were in tableau, like the saints of a Baroque sculptor, for your inspection.

Firstly, the leader of the expedition, Lieutenant-Commander James W. S. Marr, a name of some fame in the annals of Antarctic investigation, for he is none other than 'Scout Marr' who accompanied Shackleton on his last Antarctic voyage of exploration.[3] In civil life a professional zoologist, on the staff of the *Discovery* Research Committee in London, he had taken part in several Antarctic voyages, and was obviously well qualified by his experience to take charge of the present expedition.[4] Thickset, long-bodied, dressed in blue seaman's clothing, with a bright red knitted woollen hat (the only item of adornment which I ever knew him to affect), somewhat grim of visage, he little betrays in outward appearance the laboratory scientist; and on ordinary occasions his diction, characteristically nautical, gives equally little indication of his profession. But at intervals, purely for his private satisfaction and without regard for the limited understanding of his hearers, he will suddenly ejaculate an impromptu stanza of great originality and mainly biological content, perhaps not conveying any fathomable scientific information, but nevertheless couched in terms of unmistakable erudition, combined with a sense of rhythm and almost orgiastic climax, Kiplingesque with Gilbertian felicity. Like this:

> And taking the first polyploid
> That chanced to come to hand,
> He rammed it up the lumen
> Of the epithelial gland.

On later occasions, when working on some arduous and long-drawn-out task in cold and uncomfortable conditions, I have caught myself also involuntarily composing similar stanzas, reminiscent of Edward Lear in their inconsequentiality, and always with an earthy biological bias; and I came to realize that it is an escapological exercise of the human brain in solitude, when denied the benefit of communion with others of our kind.

Secondly, we come to Captain Andrew Taylor, of the Royal Canadian Engineers, a surveyor by profession, and chosen to accompany the expedition in this capacity on account of his experience in Arctic overland travel and cartography.[5] Tall and robust, with round face and thinning and greying hair, he would make the impression on strangers of a somewhat silent and taciturn man, although unfailingly amiable and friendly to all around him. Not accustomed to expressing his innermost thoughts to comparative strangers, he was several months in our midst before most of us began to realize the forceful, calm, logical and systematic mind, and the outstanding technical abilities, which informed that bland and apparently acquiescent exterior. It was on account of these characteristics that Taylor, by universal tacit consent, became later the leader of the expedition after the voluntary resignation of Marr for reasons of poor health.

Proceeding further, we come to the form of W. R. Flett, a professional geologist, whom I have inadvertently frozen in the act of scratching his head with both hands, in desperation at our earthly prospects. He holds the position of lecturer in his subject at the University of Glasgow, Scotland. Like many of his countrymen, he finds expression for his sense of humour in ultra-pessimistic utterances concerning our fate, the chances of relief ever reaching us, and the state of the world in general. His dour face, crowned by a head of wiry upright grey hair which no earthly power could ever make lie flat, is enlivened by a pair of twinkling eyes which always betray the jocose intention lying behind the most lugubrious expressions of opinion.

'Doc', as we all affectionately call him (correct title, Surgeon-Lieutenant Eric Back, RNVR), who is standing next to Flett, is twenty-four years of age, and looks even younger. He had just completed his medical studies when World War II broke out, and joined the British Navy, in accordance with a long-standing tradition in his family. Slender, delicately built, with the long sensitive fingers of the surgeon, he inspires confidence by his complete self-assurance and obvious mastery of his profession, which indeed he exercised to good effect on a number of subsequent occasions. His knowledge of the classics is refreshing to meet with in one of his age and generation. By close observation, we detect an initial effort to grow a beard, a laudable intention which was never fully crowned with success during the time I knew him.

Next we come to the figure of Lewis Ashton, commonly known by the name of 'Chippy', a ship's carpenter by profession, and with previous Antarctic experience on the scientific voyages of the Royal

Research Ship *Discovery II*. He is a small man in the late forties, born and bred in the seafaring tradition, a representative of that rare type of individual craftsman to whom the durability and appearance of his work counts above everything else. His manual skill is something to be wondered at, whether it be expressed in the building of a habitation with the odds and ends of unsorted lumber picked up from a derelict whaling station, or in the fitting out in minutest detail of a model sailing ship no larger than his little finger. It is hardly surprising that at times he becomes impatient with the clumsy efforts of those of us who imagine that we are helping him in house building and other technical operations, and particularly so when the landlubbers among our party use certain incorrect terms for nautical objects, such as 'upstairs' and 'downstairs' for 'on deck' and 'down below'. If you utter such a solecism in Chippy's presence, prepare to face his withering scorn, and seek a place wherein to hide your head.

Chippy is an old shipmate of Thomas Berry, quartermaster to the expedition. Tom Berry, who also served on the RRS *Discovery II* prior to the war, is in charge of the satisfaction of our gastronomic needs for two years, a truly herculean task. A jocose and somewhat paunchy individual past the first flush of youth, he is a master of culinary arts, and never failed in any circumstances to bring forth good fare which would do credit to much more civilized surroundings; I have seen him produce a hot meal for thirteen men on an improvised stove out of doors in a heavy snowstorm. Just as Chippy has his professional pride in matters of carpentry, so does Tom Berry in his realm of gastronomy, and he shows an ill-concealed contempt of suggestions to utilize certain indigenous sources of nourishment, such as penguin breasts or Weddell seal steaks. Eventually, however, he overcame to a large extent his aristocratic prejudice against such rank and wild forms of alimentation, and prepared these native foods in a remarkably appetizing manner.

The next two members of our expedition, Jock Matheson and Gwion Davies, both served in the capacity of 'handyman', which is a very far-reaching term, especially in the polar regions. They both fulfilled its implications in its amplest aspects. Matheson hails from the misty Isle of Skye, off the west coast of Scotland, and before the war served on several of the *Discovery* voyages and during the earlier part of the war as a seaman in the Royal Navy. One could never hope to see a truer embodiment of the seaman; everything about him smacks of the sea, and his pale blue eyes have that fixed profundity of gaze which comes to those who spend the greater part of their lives sweeping far horizons, and is never seen in the eyes of the city dweller. His mother tongue is Gaelic, one of the original Celtic idioms of the British Isles, and his English speech, slow and deliberate, retains much of the musical accentuation and poetic imagery of that dying tongue. Similar in this respect is Gwion Davies, known as 'Taff', who was brought up in a Welsh-speaking home and had tried his hand at many trades, although always by some inner instinct drawn back to the seafaring life. Taff is a young man in his twenties, and the most notable feature about him is his intense interest in any and every subject, coupled with a remarkable modesty which tends to hide his real knowledge and accomplishments. It was not until I had known him for some months that I elicited from him by questioning the information that he possessed a degree from Cambridge University in natural sciences. In his simple and forthright language, he used to say that he was not attracted by any 'white-collar job', no matter how well it might be paid, and preferred to work as a simple handyman, whether on land or on sea.

The important function of maintaining radio communication with the outside world was in the hands of two more members of our expedition, J. B. Farrington from Manchester, England, and Norman Layther from Auckland, New Zealand. 'Fram' Farrington, who was formerly radio operator on ships of the *Discovery* Commission, is an Irishman by birth, of a deliberate, humorous and kindly nature, and, if I may here borrow a term from the stage, played the role of 'heavy father' towards his younger colleague Layther, who, to carry on in the same terminology, represented 'light juvenile'. The story connected with Layther's original association with the expedition is somewhat amusing, and perhaps therefore worth a few lines in the telling. It seems that one evening in London, during the hectic weeks of preparation before the expedition left the shores of England, Marr, tired out by a heavy day of interviewing designees for the post of second radio operator who were all for one reason or another unsuitable, swore a great oath that he would take the very next ******* who came into the room, and in that very same moment the face of young Norman, with cocky and self-assured smile, appeared round the door, and accordingly he was enrolled immediately. Had Marr sifted many dozens of further applicants, he probably would not have made a better choice. Layther had been a naval radio operator in the early years of the war, and had seen service off the coasts of North Africa and elsewhere. He completely lacked inhibitions and showed a certain recklessness in his utterances and actions which caused a certain preoccupation from time to time in the minds of the older members of the expedition, but for all that, he adapted himself very soon to Antarctic life and showed surprising stability in the face of trying and monotonous circumstances.

As it was our planned intention to establish two distinct bases in the area, a certain amount of duplication of personnel was necessary. Thus, as we have seen, there were with us two qualified radio technicians, Farrington and Layther. Another and very important field in which duplication of highly competent specialists was vitally necessary was that of gastronomy, and here Tom Berry's faithful satellite was one Charlie Smith, a former naval cook from Gravesend near the mouth of the Thames; he owed his position as a member of the expedition to sheer enthusiasm and tenacity, by which I mean to say that he was not intended at first to form part of the land-based personnel, but to remain on board the ship in his professional capacity, thus spending the greater part of the time in the comparative civilization of the Falkland Islands. But he was so keen to make the acquaintance of Antarctica that he lost no opportunity, in or out of season, of expressing his desire to accompany us. Some of his hints towards this end were, it is true, discreet enough, but most of them were sufficiently broad and pointed to force themselves into the cognizance of even the most obtuse or fully occupied minds. That he succeeded eventually in his endeavour proved to be a piece of good fortune for our expedition, for his initial enthusiasm never waned, and his cheerful Cockney personality did much to keep up morale at the smaller base throughout two Antarctic winters.

At a later date another satellite was to swim into the gastronomer's ken, entering Tom Berry's orbit from the Falkland Islands after our base had been established, and shining faithfully with reflected light for the rest of the time we spent in the Antarctic. His name was Johnny Blyth, and there will be more to tell about him further on; at the present moment he is not in our company.[6]

I count eleven figures, and there should be twelve. Ah yes, myself. A professional botanist then attached to the British Museum (Natural History) in London, I had been asked by the *Discovery* Committee to serve in the capacity of botanist to the expedition, having for some years previously made a special study of lichens, and particularly those of the Antarctic regions. I need hardly say that I accepted gladly this opportunity of studying in the living state the organisms which up till then I had known only as dried herbarium specimens in the dusty archives of the British Museum. At this time I was thirty-three years of age.

I had another purpose also to fulfil on the Antarctic continent, namely that of recovering or completely discarding faith in science and human progress, by the contemplation of untouched nature and the microcosm of civilization represented by a dozen human beings isolated on a frozen continent. In the autumn of 1940, on arriving one morning at the British Museum in South Kensington, I found the botanical section roofless and burnt out, the herbarium cases open and deluged by the firemen's hoses; the specimens, collected with infinite toil over the last 200 years, named and carefully studied by generations of botanists, half burnt and scattered in soggy wads among blackened woodwork and twisted girders. The acrid smell of wood smoke and charred paper assailed the nostrils, and we suffered a psychological trauma in that moment of time. From that day onwards began a hopeless race against time and the growth of the mould fungi, as we peeled apart and dried out the pitiful remnants of what had once been one of the finest plant collections in the world.

Our reactions to this catastrophe at the time were various. One of my older and wiser colleagues expressed the hope that the Royal Air Force would soon return the compliment by blasting and burning the collections of the Berlin Botanic Garden out of existence, and indeed in due course this pious desire was fulfilled. To me the event brought only mistrust in the usefulness of scientific effort, and an obsessive realization that human progress depends, at any rate in our latitudes, entirely on good roofing and protection from the elements, and is therefore something essentially artificial, fugacious and undependable. The sight of the sacred volumes of our scientific lore mouldering in their charred and watery grave seemed a preliminary vision of what must come to all the effort which we lovingly expend during our brief contact with the physical universe.

In the shadowed recesses of the British Museum at Bloomsbury, which had as yet remained untouched by aerial bombardment, the white plaster faces of the Greek philosophers continued to stare with their blank eyeballs into some obscure futurity above the heads of the living, and vouchsafed no encouragement or aid. Perhaps the fibrous, crudely hacked, ochre-bedaubed deities of Africa, upended in a neighbouring gallery, might have a message more relevant to our state and times. During the months to come I hoped to have an opportunity of gaining insight into this fundamental and obsessive problem.

But by now our two ships are barely twelve miles distant from the Antarctic mainland, and I must proceed with my narrative.

Gaining a Foothold on the Seventh Continent

———

UP TILL NOW, AT ANY RATE, Fortune appeared to be smiling upon us in our endeavour to land in Hope Bay, and the *Scoresby* passed almost unhindered through small fields of broken brash ice and large expanses of open water, so that a few hours later we entered the bay itself, and dropped anchor some fifty yards offshore. The boat was lowered, and we rowed to the beach.[1]

Hope Bay, discovered and charted for the first time by the Swedish Antarctic Expedition of 1901–3, consists of a shelf of gently sloping rocky and stony land, three or four square miles in extent, lying at the base of the ice cap, through which project two mountains of moderate size; the larger and nearest, Mount Flora, of somewhat irregular shape and showing distinct stratification in its lower part, and the smaller, situated farther to the south, of strikingly regular tilted pyramidal form. Part of the snow-free land mass runs out in a rocky tongue seawards, and on the western side of this tongue is a deep bay penetrating inland and terminated by the ice cliffs of a small and now rather inactive glacier, the Depot Glacier, thus named by the Swedish expedition. Here appears to be the only landing place for many miles along these coasts, as the rest of the shoreline consists either of sheer ice cliffs thirty to fifty feet high or of precipitous rocks rising abruptly from the water's edge. Almost the whole of the area is taken up by a huge rookery of Adélie penguins, with myriads of birds waddling hither and thither in apparently endless confusion, and from a distance making the impression of mites swarming on a piece of overripe cheese. At this time of year (February) the chicks were already far advanced in growth, almost of the same size as their parents, but distinguishable by their fluffy grey-brown coats which were now being shed in ragged patches to expose the sleek adult plumage beneath.

This landing of ours was merely for the purpose of exploring the terrain and finding a locality suitable for the erection of a base, and our time was short, for the *Fitzroy* was standing out in Antarctic Sound awaiting us. The reconnaissance which we were able to carry out, although a brief one, indicated that there was at least one level place large enough to build a hut on, not too far from the sea, and with a conveniently located snow-melt streamlet which would supply us with abundant fresh water during the summer months.

At two o'clock in the afternoon we rowed back to the *Scoresby* and steamed out of Hope Bay by the same route as we had entered. The weather was still mild and clear, and the vista of the bay, its glacier, and the mountains behind it, stood out in sharp relief against the cloudless azure sky. The *Fitzroy*, in order to avoid any danger of being caught in a field of drift ice which was now tending to accumulate near Hope Bay, had retreated well out into the open waters of Antarctic Sound, and nearly five hours had elapsed before we came up with her. Her motor launch was sent over to transfer us on board, and it was no easy matter to get onto the rope ladder suspended from her side, as the swell was rising and falling a distance of about nine feet.

After some discussion aboard the *Fitzroy*, it was decided to remain in Antarctic Sound for the night, and, provided the fair spell of weather continued, to go ashore from both the ships early the following day in order to commence the establishment of the base. But it was not to be; during the night a sea fog came up, large masses of drift ice began to move into the sound, and it seemed as if our line of retreat might very soon be cut off. And so the two vessels retired hastily westwards right out into the open sea of the Bransfield Strait in order to avoid risking imprisonment in the ice.[2]

For the whole of the following day the fog enveloped us in an impenetrable shroud, and we lay hove to, without exact knowledge of our whereabouts. Twenty-four hours later, however, it was again clear and sunny, with a strong and piercing wind blowing offshore, and the imposing mountainous panorama of the west coast of the Trinity Peninsula running from northern to southern horizons. Close scrutiny through binoculars failed to reveal any possible landing place – sheer rock walls and ice cliffs rose directly from the sea on every flank. Moving slowly southward, we passed Charcot Bay, went in between Trinity Island and the mainland, and passed an island of moderate size which was not marked on any of the charts, and to which at the time we proposed to give the name of Fitzroy Island,[3] after our ship. It was late in the day when we reached Hughes Bay on the Palmer Coast, and once more hove to. From where we lay it seemed as if there might be some possibility of effecting a landing here, and with this end in view a small party, including Marr, Ashton, Back, Davies and myself, embarked in the motor launch and made our way slowly shorewards.

The distance was about two miles, and as we neared the land we ran into much ice, large and small, from brashy lumps, hissing together in the swell, to small icebergs. We had to use the boathook a good deal to fend off the larger pieces from the sides of the boat. An unforgettable sight is a small iceberg at close quarters (small in comparison to others of its kind, but dwarfing to insignificance the puny little craft crossing in front of it) rising and falling in the swell, heaving its mass slowly, inexorably, out of the dark depths below, the sea running off it in cascades as it rises, and the cracks and hollows in its substance of an unbelievably intense blue.

Having passed by several small and precipitous rocky islets inhabited by Adélie penguins, we finally reached the mainland itself, but this again stared us uncompromisingly in the face and forced us to admit defeat. For the rocks, rising so sheer out of the water, and the swell of the sea mounting and falling against their naked slippery sides, showed us that any attempt at a landing was altogether out of the question. And so we made our way, in the shadows of falling night, back to the ship, and resumed our voyage southwards along the coast of the Palmer Peninsula.

By the afternoon of the following day, February 11th, we had passed through the Gerlache Strait and come to the channel between the islands of Antwerp* and Wiencke. Rounding a corner of the latter, we entered a harbour-like bay enclosed and sheltered on three sides by snow slopes, ice cliffs, and a rocky peninsula. This is the anchorage of Port Lockroy, and is a well-known haven hereabouts, having been visited by most of the Antarctic expeditions, many of which have left names and dates painted on the rocks. The *Scoresby* and the *Fitzroy* dropped anchor halfway between the ice cliffs and a rocky islet in the middle of the bay. This islet, named Goudier by one of the French expeditions under Charcot,[4] was to become memorable to us as the site of our first Antarctic base.

Arriving on the rocky promontory nearby in the dinghy and the motor launch, and ascending some way up the slopes, which were occupied by a noisy and odoriferous colony of Gentoo penguins, we were in a position to appreciate the majestic grandeur of the landscape surrounding us. To the west rose the rugged ice-covered bulk of Antwerp Island, separated from us by a narrow arm of Wiencke Island and the Gerlache Strait beyond; its southern extremity forming an irregular mountainous mass, Mount William, with sharply crevassed hanging glaciers depending from its slopes, while out due west, and at a much greater distance, the centre of the island rose evenly to form one of the highest mountains of the Palmer Land region, Mount Français, over 8,600 feet high, a snow-covered cone

---

* Now Anvers Island.

awe-inspiring in its distance and vastness, its virgin snows never trodden by the foot of man.[5]

Behind us and much closer, on Wiencke Island itself, rises a chain of mountains, the Sierra du Fief,* of no great height but nevertheless strikingly imposing by reason of their vertical, unscalable black flanks shooting straight up from a narrow fringing glacier to form a jagged sawtooth skyline of seven peaks intermittently blanketed by the light passing clouds.

Goudier Islet was obviously the most suitable site for the erection of the base, being free from penguins and their concomitant noise and ordure, and having two good level and well-drained places at the summit large enough for the establishment of two huts. Accordingly, we commenced forthwith to bring ashore our stores and building materials. These were hoisted out of the holds of the two ships and lowered into large flat-bottomed scows which had been brought with us, lashed down on deck, for this purpose. The scows, joined in a pair by transverse planks, and loaded down heavily with miscellaneous cargo, were towed ashore behind the motor launch to a part of the islet where the rocks, sloping down steeply into deep water, allowed them to be brought right alongside.

Now a human chain was formed on the natural steps of these rocks, and the stores and building materials were hoisted up from man to man, to be deposited in piles on the summit. The goods came at random, just as they were unloaded out of the ship's hold, so that bundles of lumber would alternate with crates of canned food, boxes of tools and instruments, crates of potatoes, and other wares too varied to enumerate. Occasionally a crate of potatoes would burst open while being manhandled up the slope, and the tubers would go bouncing down the rocks in a cascade and splash into the icy waters below, hastened on their way by suitable comment on the part of those forming the hierarchy of the rocks. The various materials, on

---

* Now the Fief Range.

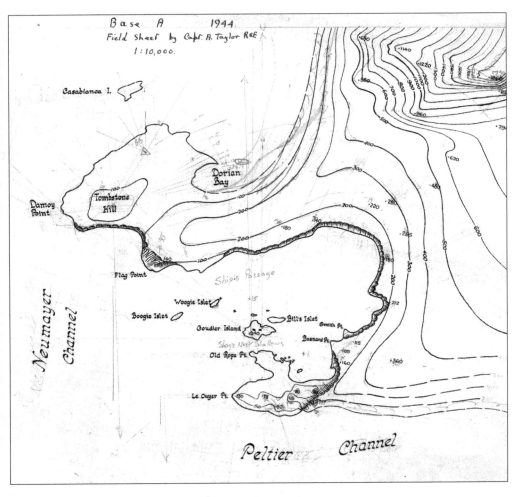

Base A   1944.
Field Sheet by Capt. R. Taylor R&E
1:10,000.

Port Lockroy, 1944.

their arrival at the summit, were sorted into several separate dumps according to their nature, one dump being reserved for building materials, another for victuals, a third for tools, and so forth. A number of mutton carcasses from the Falkland Islands were also brought ashore, and buried in an adjacent snow patch.

This work of offloading continued for several days, but on the second day certain members of the expedition were detailed to assist Chippy Ashton in the erection of the house. At nightfall we all returned to our usual berths on ship-board, and a phantasmagoria of lumber, waves, icebergs, mountain tops, crates of food, rocks, bouncing potatoes, penguins, and sacks of coal would pass before our tired eyes before we slept.

*

Having decided on the site for the house, Chippy Ashton, as mentioned above, had been allotted the services of a number of the other members of the expedition to assist in the labours of its erection, while some of us went back and forth between the site and the lumber pile, looking for, extracting and bringing over baled sections in the order in which they were required. Others of us were busy on the beach with bags of cement, shovels, gravel and sea water, making up concrete for the foundations.

The house, designed under Chippy's supervision before we left London,[6] was a partly prefabricated one, in the sense that all the lumber was cut to size, baled in sections, and each section provided with a number, so that theoretically it was an easy matter to find, unbale, and erect the various sections in their proper sequence. But to those of us who had the task of finding, let us say, bale number DX-4307 (transverse floor joists), the pile of lumber discharged on the rocks appeared of mountainous and dismaying proportions, and we found by repeated experience that DX-4307, or whatever other section we may have been detailed to fetch, would almost invariably be found right down at the bottom of the pile.

'There's no DX-4307, Chippy, but I've got DX-0734, that must be it.'

'No, you silly bugger, DX-0734 is uprights for the wall. Take another look. It's got to be there.'

Half an hour later two individuals return breathing heavily and sweating beneath the burden laid upon them. They deposit it at Chippy's feet somewhat ungently. 'There's your *talking* DX-4307.'

The method of making the concrete foundations was ingenious although hardly labour-saving. Small wooden provision cases, from which the contents had been removed, had the bottoms knocked out so as to make a four-sided frame, which was placed on the bedrock in the required position and rendered immovable by piling rocks all around it. After well wetting the rock at the bottom, the frames were filled up with concrete into which large and small stones were worked, the whole being well pounded down with pieces of lumber from above. One of the most astonishing features of this procedure, from the point of view of those engaged in mixing the concrete on the seashore and staggering up with it in buckets, was the enormous quantity required to fill these moulds, even with the addition of unduly liberal quantities of stones to the porridge-like mass. In some places, where the ground sloped away abruptly, the foundations had to be built up to a height of over four feet, and bucket after heavy bucket of concrete was poured down the mould's ever-hungry maw without seeming to bring up the level to any noticeable extent. Additional supports had also to be poured below that part of the floor beneath the galley which was to bear the weight of the large anthracite-burning all-purpose cooking range, or, according to some humorists, the weight of corpulent Tom Berry himself.

While these things were going on, Farrington had erected the two tubular steel poles for the radio antenna, and with the help of some others, constructed a small shelter of wood and canvas to house the petrol-driven generator. Within a few days of our landing he had the transmitter going in its temporary quarters, and was able to send off a signal to Port Stanley respectfully informing His Excellency, the Governor of the Falkland Islands Dependencies,[7] of the establishment according to plan of Base 'A', as our settlement was to be called.[8]

Within a week things were taking on a very definite shape. By February 14th three walls of the house were standing, complete with windows, and the shell of the roof was extended over them. Between the double wooden layers of walls and roof were extended sheets of shining aluminium foil, which was to serve the purpose (so we were told) of reflecting the heat inwards and the cold outwards.

The stores had by this time been completely segregated into their several categories, and the more perishable of them covered over with large tarpaulins. Tom Berry had supervised the disposition of the foodstuffs, and had erected a small cooking range in a protected niche between two rocks, roofing it over with some spare corrugated iron sheets, and building a third wall with potato boxes. In the cranny he produced for us at regular intervals quantities of boiling hot tea of creosote-like consistency.

Up till now the weather had fortunately remained favourable, and work outdoors was by no means unpleasant; but two days later a change for the worse set in. A bitter wind sprang up, bringing with it driving wet snow which soon thoroughly wetted our clothing and the piles of unprotected stores and materials. At nightfall on the following day, a moderate gale was blowing, and we were indeed glad to return to the ship; this would be for the last time, for on the morrow it would return to Port Stanley and leave us on our island to our own resources.

It was at 3 a.m. on the morning of February 17th when we roused ourselves out of our berths for the last time, got the remainder of our personal gear together, took leave of the officers and crews of the *Scoresby* and the *Fitzroy*, and went ashore in the motor launch in a flurry of driving sleet and snow. Everybody turned to the work in hand with a will, and considerable progress on the building was made by nine o'clock, in spite of the inclement weather. Three walls, the roof, and the floor having been completed, we all crowded together into the shelter afforded by them, and did justice to a copious breakfast of ham, eggs, bread, jam and tea prepared by Tom Berry, after which, overcome by drowsiness, we spread out our blankets on the floorboards, and turned in, wet clothes and all, to enjoy three hours of refreshing slumber. We had been so occupied on our tasks that we had had no time to observe the departure of the two ships until they were just about to round the tongue of land separating us from the Gerlache Strait, when they aroused our attention by giving a farewell blast on their sirens. Within the next two minutes they slid quietly round the point, watched intently by the group of small figures standing on the rocks of their tiny island, now the most southerly inhabited outpost in the world.

By the end of the same afternoon most of the more urgent work had been accomplished, and various minor items could be attended to, such as the assembling and filling of the kerosene pressure lamps, erection of the double-tier iron cots, etc. A large bogey stove was also moved into the hut, and as the outlet for the chimney had not yet been cut in the roof, the smoke stack was taken out through one of the window frames.

During the following days further progress was made, and the house, although still lacking the interior furnishings and finishing touches on the outside, became quite weatherproof and habitable. Much time had been spent by Berry and Taylor on the assembly of the large anthracite-burning cooking range, which had arrived in a multitude of sections, large and small. They found it a Chinese puzzle in its intricacy, but finally got it together, with, if I remember rightly, even a few pieces left over. To kindle a first fire in it was no easy matter; first paper, then sticks, then coal, and finally anthracite chips were introduced tactfully until the firebox was at last in a solid red glow and could be fed thereafter on a diet of undiluted anthracite. On account of its insulated construction, its fuel requirements were very low, only a few pounds of anthracite morning and evening, and it was kept burning constantly, day and night. Its two built-in ovens allowed an ample supply of bread to be baked for the whole party. If you ever want to have a stove like that, be sure to ask for it by name, the 'Esse', and refuse all inferior substitutes.

As we broke newly baked bread for the first time in our new home, we felt ourselves at last soundly established in our vast and frozen realm.

3

A Visit to Cape Renard

WHILE HOUSEBUILDING OPERATIONS were still in progress, the *Scoresby*, contrary to expectations, paid us yet one more visit, on March 19th. She had been favoured with good weather and ice-free waters on this last dash southwards from Port Stanley, and brought us some further supplies and a small additional amount of mail. The weather remained calm and favourable, and the ship lay at anchor during the next three days in the bay beside our islet. Willing hands among the crew gave us welcome assistance in the final stages of our work of organization and construction, and before they left us for the last time we were able to give them a little farewell and house-warming party ashore in our new quarters.

One of the most necessary additions to our supplies which they brought us was a further consignment of flour from Port Stanley. Why were we so grievously short of this staple commodity, this staff of life, it may be asked? The answer was a simple one: our flour, as originally brought out with the other stores from England, had been supplied in soldered tin boxes crated with spaced wooden slats, and without external indication of the contents; and exactly the same type of container had been used for our supplies of cigarettes. During the long outward voyage, with numerous transhipments, the presence of the cigarettes had been discovered, but the only way to find out whether the crates contained cigarettes or flour was to gash the tin open with a knife or cargo hook, and this had been done in nearly every instance so that every time we moved or handled a case of flour, quantities of the precious white powder would sift out, dusting us liberally from head to foot, and most of them, by the time they were stacked up in the galley, proved to be almost empty. What should be done, therefore, on future expeditions, to alleviate this nuisance? Should cases containing cigarettes be clearly marked as such, and flour be packed in containers of quite different type? Should we not rather resort to smuggling procedures to get them through unpilfered and intact, stuffing them into the hollow legs of theodolite tripods, radio poles, and the tubes of our binoculars? All in all, it poses a most difficult problem, and will continue to do so as long as we humans persist in prizing narcotics more highly than the staff of life, misty vapourings more than solid nourishment.

Another item in the additional stores brought down on the *Scoresby* were several tinplate Union Jacks, about four by three feet in size, beautifully enamelled in splendid colours, and destined to be set up in various places along the neighbouring coastline to remind unauthorized marauders that all this barren ice-caked region belonged to the British Crown, and nobody else.[1] This was a right which, at the time, none of us had either the leisure nor the inclination to seriously dispute or examine, being more pressingly occupied with the (to us) more important task of getting a roof up over our heads before the next blizzard should sweep down upon us. The services of Chippy Ashton were requisitioned to frame these visiting cards, as we called them, with strong planking, with the words 'BRITISH CROWN LAND' tastefully painted underneath, and provided with two uprights by which they could be thrust erect between the rocks in conspicuous locations, there to remain eternally, or at least until the next hurricane, and inspire feelings of reverence and awe in the breasts of all two-legged upright creatures, of whatever nationality, who haply might waddle within sight of them from time to time.

On the 22nd of the month it was decided to plant one or more of these visiting cards at some point on the mainland of the Palmer Peninsula, and Doc Back and I, leaning heavily on our unique qualifications as meteorologist and botanist respectively, were fortunate in being able to persuade Marr to include us, with Chippy, among those chosen for the expedition. Early in the morning, after a hasty snack in the galley, we embarked in the dinghy to row over to the *Scoresby*, taking with us the two bulky framed flags, pickaxes, shovels, and also cameras to photograph the ceremony. Shortly afterwards the anchor chain rattled up, and we nosed round the corner of our bay and started to steam down the Peltier Channel towards the southern end of Wiencke Island and the open waters of Flanders Bay and the Bismarck Strait towards the mainland. The weather was miserable, dull and overcast, with something very like rain falling all the time, but windless and otherwise favourable for our designs.

The Peltier Channel is quite narrow, and runs almost immediately beneath the vertical black saw-toothed range of the notable Sierra du Fief, the upper part of which was always visible to us from our base on Goudier Islet. Now we could study it in its entire grandeur, from top to bottom, as it strove up improbably cloudwards from the narrow sloping piedmont glacier which bordered its foot and separated its sheer walls from the ice cliffs at the edge of the channel. The final peak at its southern end forms a promontory of Wiencke Island known as Cape Errera, and soon we steamed past this, out of the channel and into the open waters of Flanders Bay, a great indentation of Bismarck Strait separating the Palmer Archipelago from the mainland.

Out here in the open, well away from the land, the *Scoresby* began to roll somewhat on a long slow swell; there was very little floating ice around, only small scattered milky fields of disintegrated brash, through which we ploughed unhindered with a hissing sound. Eastwards lay the craggy ice-capped mainland, offering to view, among other precipitous capes and promontories almost equally imposing, one grand conspicuous vertical monolith reminiscent in its configuration of the Corcovado in Rio de Janeiro, on the summit of which, with outstretched arms, stands the huge stone figure of Christ looking endlessly out to the east. This mountainous crag, the height of which has been computed at 2,624 feet, is called Cape Renard; and towards it our prow was now pointed, for our lords spiritual and temporal on the bridge had decided that there, if a landing were possible, our flag, as a claim of sovereignty unabated, should, God willing, be planted.

An hour passed, and our ship, a tiny sliver in the limitless rolling expanse, was now half a mile offshore, and hove to. Cape Renard towered up above us, an awe-inspiring conical erection of sheer black rock, its summit lost to view in the shifting folds of the weeping grey sky. At first sight it seemed to spring directly upwards out of the sea, but on scanning it carefully through field glasses we could make out an insignificant rocky shelf or ledge at its base, on which with luck we might effect a landing.

The dinghy was launched over the side, manned by members of the *Scoresby*'s crew at the oars. Marr, Ashton, Back and I tumbled in down the rope ladder, and we were towed alongside some distance further in, then cast off to our own resources and left to cover the remaining distance to shore by ourselves. The swell, already noticeable on the ship, was now felt by us in its full sweep. We rowed our way up the sides of slowly on-rolling mountains of black water, poised a moment on the plateau-like summits, and then swept down into a sagging trough in which we lost sight of our ship, the land, and everything around us except the wimpling and ever-changing crests rearing their mighty bulk momentarily on all sides.

At last we came within a rope's cast of the land, and wondered whether we could get a footing on that forbidding narrow ledge of precipitously tumbled rocks continuously troubled by alternate surgings, rising and falling rhythmically over them for a distance of ten vertical feet or more. But Marr, undaunted, gave the order to proceed, and crept forward to the bows, where, with the painter in his hand, he eyed the rocks in readiness for a shorewards spring.

We never thought he would make it, but we underestimated his boldness and determination, for from the crest of the swell he suddenly launched himself into the air with surprising agility and landed spread-eagled on the glistening slippery rocks, while the dinghy dropped down far below into the sucking chasm of the lowest ebb. He slithered and slipped alarmingly downwards for some seconds, but finally gained a hold, and swiftly belayed the painter round a knob of rock. Now it was my turn, and I hesitated in dismay for what seemed minutes, rising and falling against the uncompromising rocky mass on which I could see no good, or even relatively unprecarious, place to jump for. Finally, in desperation, I leaped at random, hoping for the best but without the slightest confidence of achieving a happy landing. I came down flat on a smooth sloping rock, slippery with green slime, and felt myself sliding helplessly downwards. Marr made a grab at me from above, but missed, and I pretty well made up my mind to go in over the head in the mercilessly cold water. However, at the last moment my feet found some resting place, and my descent into the depths was stayed. By frantic clawing and wriggling I worked my way upwards, and when the next swell rushed in it submerged me only up to the thighs. Marr now caught hold of my outflung arm from above, and there I stayed as a link in the chain to help Ashton and Back follow us up safely onto the narrow ledge.

A few minutes later, with sighs of relief, the four of us were standing together on the rocks, well above the reach of the tumultuous sea. The dinghy, with the oarsmen backwatering vigorously to avoid being swept up against the ledge, remained a few yards off, while the coxswain made fast the end of a line to the wood-framed Union Jack and sent the other end singing through the air towards us; we grabbed it and as soon as they had pushed the awkward thing over the side into the sea, commenced to haul it in. It plunged and reared ungovernably in the seething waters, sticking up its legs like the arms of a drowning man and catching in the cracks between the rocks;

but eventually we managed to bring it up undamaged out of the yeasty sucking brine and lay it out, dripping but still resplendent, on a ledge to landward of us. After some search we found a cleft where we could jam it upright in a dominant position, facing seawards, and commenced to find and pry out loose rocks to pile round its base and make it more secure.

Here my botanist's instinct got the better of me, and I left the party to make a quick scramble up the slope to the bottom of the sheer rock face itself, some thirty feet above. As I went up, Marr shouted a warning after me to watch out for icefalls from above, but I gained the face without mishap. I was safer there, I argued, embracing the very monolith itself, than the others who stood some distance out from it. But disappointment awaited me, for the face of the rock was completely barren and destitute of living substance, as bare as on the day when it was pushed up, still steaming, from the depths of the sea, and I slithered down again to join my comrades, who by this time had completed their task and were surveying their handiwork with satisfaction.

Some semblance of a ceremony seemed called for, and we doffed our miscellaneous headgear and tried to stand to attention for a second or two on the uneven and pinnacled rocks; it was a feat which would have taxed the skill of a tightrope walker, but after much wobbling and tumbling over we succeeded in getting ourselves into an upright and decorous stance in which we might fittingly salute the hoisting of the British colours on this most southerly outpost of far-flung Empire.

But at that moment we heard an ominous rushing sound from above, and all the military starch went out of our bearing as great clumps and masses of wet snow came cascading down upon us off the cloud-concealed summit of Cape Renard directly above our heads. They burst all around us with a *whoosh* upon the rocks, and we scrambled helter-skelter down the ledge in most undignified retreat.

'Make haste, get aboard, lads!' yelled the coxswain from the dinghy; 'the old man up there doesn't like your visiting card, and he's pelting ye with cream puffs; come on aboard, quick, before he lets ye have the whole works, with ice and all!'

We needed no encouragement, and got back into the dinghy in the most expeditious way possible, namely by sliding down the wet slimy rocks on the seat of our pants; just how we effected the embarkation I fail to remember. As we rowed slowly back to the ship over watery hills and valleys, the brightly coloured visiting card left by us propped up among the rocks, even at a few hundred yards distance formed only an insignificant gaudy speck at the base of the sombre towering pinnacle, and by the time we had clambered up the side of the *Scoresby* and stood on the deck looking at Cape Renard receding in the distance, we were unable to discern it at all without field glasses. We were all pretty well wet through, especially in the basal portions, and gladly descended below to the wardroom, where a grateful fug awaited us, with the steam pipes hissing agreeably and giving out much-needed warmth. We took turns standing against them, until we had dried out sufficiently to be able to sit down in comfort.

*

Doc Back and I were sitting side by side at the baize-covered table; he had found a greasy deck of cards and employed himself with building a house with them, the slow swell being so little felt here on board that it did not seriously interfere with this project. I found a copy of the *Antarctic Pilot* (navigational directions for Antarctic waters)[2] among the logbooks and nautical tables stacked in the glass-fronted wall case, and busied myself in perusing its pages and illustrations.

Doc was holding his breath as he gingerly placed two cards in juxtaposition on top of the delicate structure and covered them with a third. And the thing stood, five stories high. Doc prepared two more cards to place on the very summit in the form of a crowning peaked superstructure. And then the shock came. There was a twice-repeated double clanging of the engine room telegraph, which rang through the ship with the urgency of a fireball. The engines, with an intensified roar, commenced to churn full astern, and we lurched forward almost out of our seats with the sudden cessation of our forward movement. Doc's house of cards fell noiselessly but irrevocably flat upon the table.

After a minute or so with the engines in reverse, the telegraph rang out sharply once more, and we slowly gathered way again in the original forwards direction.

'Iceberg', said Doc, and we both raced up on deck to see what we must have narrowly missed. But it was no iceberg; the wide bay lay clear and ice-free on all sides, right up to the mainland. Fleck[3] came down off the bridge, and acquainted us with the cause of the commotion.

'*Lurking* great jagged reef full ahead, half awash,' he informed us in passing, 'missed it by a couple of yards,' and he vanished down the companionway to seek for indications of it on the charts. We scanned the wake astern for evidence of the sunken rock, but could see nothing, and returned below to our seats at the wardroom table. Back picked up the scattered ruins of his house of cards, and replaced them in the soiled packet. I searched through the index of the *Antarctic Pilot* to see what information I could glean with respect to this notable hazard to navigation right out in the middle of Flanders Bay.

'Surely there must be warning of this in the *Pilot*,' I remarked. 'If we don't find it mentioned there, in the only authoritative guide we've got, what use is it at all? We'd be better off without it altogether. Flanders Bay, an indentation of the Bismarck Strait. Bismarck Strait. Here we are: "rocky and dangerous".

'Obviously. What do they say further? "The RRS *William Scoresby*, in 1930, having passed through Peltier Channel, steered 300° through

Bismarck Strait, passing northward of Wauwermans Islands, with Joubin Islets ahead. No shallow soundings were obtained and no dangers were seen with the exception of a rock, awash, lying about 2½ cables northward of the middle of Wauwermans Islands." That can't be it; the Wauwermans Islands are way out west of where we are now. Then it goes on to say: "Commander Ryder,[4] who was in command of the *Penola*, in 1934–37, recommends, however, that a vessel, having brought the conspicuous peak near Cape Errera to bear 104°, distant one mile, should keep this peak astern on that bearing until clear of Wauwermans Islands, when she should alter course so as to pass southward of Buff Islet ... The only off-lying danger observed in this passage was the reef off Brown Island." Couldn't be that, either: Brown Island's miles away from here. So that, apart from the general statement that the Bismarck Strait as a whole is rocky and dangerous, the *Antarctic Pilot*'s no help to us at all. We might have gone down then with all hands, if we had put our faith in its vague generalizations and ambiguities. Doesn't it go to show, Doc? We can never safely allow ourselves to be guided by the printed word, no matter how authoritative it may claim to be; to do so breeds false confidence, and readily leads to destruction. The only thing that saved us was the fact that we had a good captain to our ship, alert and with sharp eyes for dangers, standing watchfully at the helm; and although, being only human, he may not always be able to see concealed rocks in these treacherous waters, nevertheless he is always on his guard against them, and I put my faith in his clear-sightedness and intelligence at all times a thousandfold more than in this printed compilation.'[5]

And I replaced the *Antarctic Pilot* on the shelf where it belonged.[6]

4

The Onrush of Winter

MUCH HAS BEEN WRITTEN, and probably more spoken, concerning the notorious fickleness of the weather in Antarctica, and justly so, as we soon found out for ourselves. One morning we would be working in our shirtsleeves on and around the house under the rays of a resplendent warm sun (41 °F in the shade, considerably more in the sun), the sky a serene and cloudless blue, not a breath of wind ruffling the glassy waters of the bay, and the mountains around us standing out like rather badly painted stage scenery. Taff Davies even stripped and tried a dip in the sea – certainly tempting in its crystal clearness – but being only a few hundred feet from the glacier face and scattered with floating blocks of ice, the water remained always at about freezing point, no matter how warm the sun, and Taff's sojourn therefore was short. The next day, the face of nature changed completely. A bitterly cold easterly wind, almost reaching gale force, hacked at the rocks and the waters, the sky from horizon to horizon was a uniform unfriendly grey, and the mountains hid their faces behind a blanket of scudding dun-coloured cloud.

On such a day as this outdoor work is unpleasant in the extreme. Care must be taken to load down with heavy stones any loose sheets of corrugated iron, for the stronger gusts can lift them up and fling them through the air like autumn leaves, and an airborne sheet of corrugated iron could easily decapitate any person it might chance to strike in its unpredictable flight. A cold easterly wind is usually the precursor of a blizzard in these parts, and on the evening of the day in question the air began to fill with fine granular snow, coming almost horizontally owing to the force of the wind, and hissing monotonously over the house and the rocks surrounding it. Then indeed we were glad to be on the right side of a good wall, with firmly closed doors and windows to exclude the white searching fingers of the drift.[1]

It was on one of these changeable days, beautifully sunny and promising in the morning hours, that Chippy Ashton and I were deluded into starting to cover the roof with rubberized felt, a job which had been reserved for the first really fine day. When halfway through with this, we were caught out by the elements, and had to finish the operation in the most inglorious weather, assailed by the bitter cold wind and mercilessly lashed in the face by the driving wet snow.

Towards the end of February the main part of the house was quite complete, and work was also far advanced on an extension to one side of it which was being constructed by Chippy with the help of Taylor, Doc Back, and myself. We had progressed so far in our apprenticeship to the building trade that Chippy allowed us to cut, fix and nail up the boards forming the walls. These house walls, as explained above, are double, consisting of an inner and an outer layer of tongue-and groove boards, nailed vertically to a solid frame of upright and horizontal timbers, with a layer of aluminium foil in between. Anybody who has worked with tongue-and-groove boards will know that on one side they have a groove, and on the other side a projecting tongue, so that when placed correctly side by side they interlock; he will also know that not uncommonly they are considerably warped, and it may happen that two adjacent boards, although joining together perfectly throughout part of their length, diverge at one end, and refuse to be united. To overcome this difficulty, Chippy initiated us into a secret procedure; a strong wood chisel is placed alongside the refractory board, and its point buried by several smart mallet strokes into the underlying timber crossbar of the wall; it is then used as a lever against the board to force it into correct union with its mate, upon which the board is quickly nailed into position. This operation became Doc's specialty, and his loud cry 'Chisel!' was often heard above the general turmoil of the building operations. They say that brute force never settles anything, but I know better, having seen Doc unite two boards with their tongued edges together by the application of this method.

One fine day as we were working thus, we were startled by a rumbling as of thunder coming from the Sierra du Fief to the east of our island. Thunder it could not be, we knew, and as we turned our heads in the direction whence it came, we saw an enormous avalanche of snow and ice cascading down the sheer vertical rock face from its summit, well over 3,000 feet high. It came down in a huge dense white cloud, took a minute or longer to reach the bottom, and on striking the piedmont glacier at the base of the range blew up into a tremendous cloud of snow, like steam, which took five or six minutes more to settle and disperse. The height descended was so great that it appeared to be coming down quite slowly, and it was hard to realize that thousands of tons of snow and ice were hurtling and crashing and thundering down the cliff face. We did not know at the time, fortunately for our peace of mind, that some of us were fated at a later date to make a closer acquaintance with this interesting phenomenon.

'Calving' of the glacier face near our island was also of frequent occurrence; there would be a sudden heavy report, like the firing of a cannon, and part of the face of the ice cliff, about a hundred feet in height, would slip down with a thunderous roar into the waters of the bay, raising a tidal wave, seething with ice blocks and brash, which a few minutes later would strike the shores of our island and break far up on its rocky face.

Doc Back, in addition to his medical and constructional duties, was entrusted with the recording of meteorological data at the base, and with the help of Marr, Taff Davies, and myself erected the screen to house the instruments near the summit of the island about 200 feet away from the house. Thereafter, Doc made his rounds every three hours between the house and the screen to take the readings, in fair weather or foul. In early March he began to be preoccupied somewhat with the state of health of some of the members of the expedition, for many of us about this time began to catch various infections, such as sore throats, septic fingers, etc. These complaints persisted for about ten days, then vanished as suddenly as they had appeared, never to return during the whole of our subsequent sojourn in the Antarctic. It is quite true that, as has often been related, uniformly excellent health and freedom from colds is enjoyed in the polar regions once the virus brought in from the civilized world has been eradicated.

The construction of the house now being virtually completed, Taylor and I commenced to cast around for a suitable site for the Nissen hut which we intended to erect for storage purposes, and having selected a fairly level place near the house, laid out a rectangular base for the foundations. Concrete foundation pillars were poured at intervals, brought up to the required level, and the horizontal 'runners' which were to form the base of the structure were fastened into position upon these foundations. In the places where the bedrock sloped away, a gap up to two feet high was left between the ground and the runner, and to close it up we built crude walls of loose stones handily accessible; we had to make excursions farther and farther afield to find these and then carry them in by hand, until one of us, worthy child of progressive civilization, conceived the idea of sledging them in bulk on a curved sheet of corrugated iron, on which they could be dragged in large quantities over the snow patch nearby and even over the rocks and gravel beds. In this way several tons of stones and boulders were transported from all parts of the island and built into the buttressed base of the structure.

Onto the runners were now attached the semi-circular steel girders forming the ribcage or thorax of the Nissen hut, and these had to be guyed up into position with ropes until stabilized by the application of the outer skin of curved sheets of corrugated iron over them. These sheets went on in three sections, one arching over the roof and the other two forming the sides, and were fastened in place with screw nails driven through them into horizontal wooden shafts joining the semi-circular ribs at intervals. The corrugated iron stiffened up the structure, at first distressingly wobbly, to such an extent that one of us was able to clamber up on top of it and drive in the nails while draped over the curving roof in a prone position, gesticulating downwards to the straining caryatids below like the warning angel in Goya's inverted mural at Saragossa.[2] Finally the prefabricated wooden end sections were brought into position, and the Nissen was complete and ready for the reception of the stores, which up till now had been lying in dumps scattered over the rocks of the island.

Many of these store piles had been covered over with tarpaulins for protection against wet snow, and when we went to dismantle them we found that in most cases the edges of the tarpaulins, by repeated thawing and freezing of the surrounding snow, had been frozen in, and were held in the vice-like grip of glassy ice inches thick. Short of waiting for a warm day to melt the ice holding them, an improbable event at this time of year, there was nothing for it but to break up the ice into fragments with crowbars, taking care not to puncture the stiffened canvas more than necessary, and pry loose the edge laboriously, inch by inch. Taff, when previously faced with the same predicament, having been requested by Tom Berry to fetch a case of this or that for the galley on short notice, had resorted to the stratagem of entering under the tarpaulin by the narrowest possible opening and then forcing his way by squirming and writhing under the canvas and over the boxes, up, around, down and about, until he found what he wanted, and finally emerged, greatly flushed and half asphyxiated: 'a job for a bedbug', as he aptly expressed it.

Returning to the house at meal times, we were daily astonished by some new refinement in civilization fabricated by the mind and hands of Chippy Ashton. We now ate our meals at a real table, sitting on proper benches; along one side of the house, partitions had been built to form five separate cabins, each with two cots, and even boasting curtains in each doorway for the privacy of the inmates. Pictures of wives, mothers and sweethearts made their appearance, and were affixed to the walls beside the cots, in many cases side by side with striking studies of a curious race of human females characterized by strongly curved outlines and a quite remarkable length of legs. I was often brought to wonder, in raptly contemplating these, whether there might not be some danger at a later date of a loss of erotic interest *vis-à-vis* the common stumpy-legged form of the species.

The entrance hallway was heated by a small iron army cooking range which bore the inscription in cast iron lettering: '8 OFFICERS OR 20 MEN'; the comments of the twenty men concerned, I could not help thinking, would also be of a cast iron nature. Of the sanitary arrangements, I will content myself with stating that they conformed to the highest standards of hygiene attainable in these latitudes, and were constructed with sufficient duplication to avoid undue competition except in the direst emergency.

By early May there was no doubt that the summer season was finally over, and we could expect only a few more warm days with temperatures at or above freezing point. The bay around our island froze over; the snowfalls, at first intermittent, became stronger and more continuous, and on fine clear days the powdery snow, glittering and shimmering in the sunlight, would be blown by the wind into deep concave drifts around the buildings. Our first Antarctic winter had arrived.

Our expedition being primarily a scientific one, our first care, after establishing the base and making it habitable, was to make preparations for biological, geological and cartographical research. To this end we lost no time in equipping one side of the main living room of the house as a combined biological laboratory and

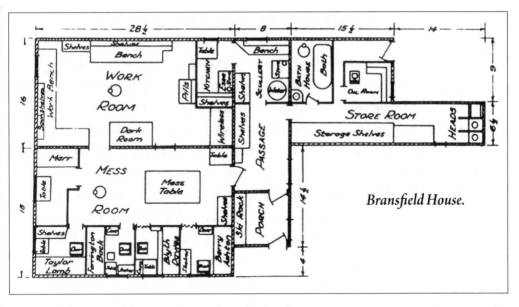

Bransfield House.

surveyor's office. A work bench was erected, shelving put up for books and bottles, surveying instruments stacked in a corner, and the two microscopes taken out, assembled and adjusted for use.[3]

Strictly speaking, the season for biological investigations was already over; the bay was completely frozen, and deep snowdrifts covered our island, except on the higher parts where the strong winds prevented them from accumulating. Nevertheless, I was able to carry out a good deal of work on the flora of the island, this consisting entirely of lichens and mosses, growing on rock faces too steep to permit the lodgement of a snow cover. Most of these plants grow in crustaceous form, as a thin layer spreading over the surface of the rock. Many species occur intermingled, and much time has to be spent with hammer and chisel chipping off representative fragments for preservation as herbarium specimens. In the house I then examined my gatherings under the microscope, classified them provisionally according to their genera, and stored them away in paper packets upon which were written all the necessary data as to locality, date, occurrence, exposure, etc. In this way, working intermittently throughout the winter, I was able to fill several boxes with specimens destined for later study at the British Museum in London.

Ashton and I also erected a photographic darkroom of diminutive proportions against the wall at the entrance to the main workroom. It was a simple affair of battens covered with several thicknesses of stout brown paper pasted over to prevent the access of light, and was provided inside with a working bench and a red safelight operating off torch batteries. We had with us two cameras, a large Sanderson plate apparatus supplied to the expedition, and my own Leica, together with an ample supply of plates and film for both, printing paper, developing and fixing solutions, etc., so that my own lack of skill as a photographer was the only factor limiting the quality of our output. One serious difficulty remained, and could never be completely overcome, except during the summer months: namely the shortage of water in liquid form for washing films and prints. All water had to be obtained by melting snow in buckets on the galley stove, and was hence in short supply, so that I was not in a position to follow the book's instructions with regard to washing for at least an hour in running water. Fortunately, I hit on the method of using a weak solution of iodine, which quickly neutralizes the fixative present in the negatives and prints, and was able to obtain good results with only a few changes of water.

Taylor started at once to make a detailed map of our island with contours, and a plan of the buildings upon it; he also, with the aid of plane table and rangefinder, plotted the main features of the surrounding country, working on clear days from a rocky knoll high up on the island behind the house. It was obvious, however, that for the successful completion of this work more extended trips into the surrounding country were necessary, and so Marr, with the help of Taff Davies, Taylor, and myself, commenced to unpack and make ready equipment for sledging trips.

We were provided with skis of the regulation army pattern, and as these had largely lost their correct curvature in transit through the tropics, they had to be reshaped in a press of Chippy's design, and were then given several coats of a mixture of Stockholm tar and linseed oil. Afterwards, a good deal of our spare time in leisure moments was spent practising on them on the snow slopes behind the house, for we were all novices in this method of locomotion. Our sledges, packed in separate parts, were also brought out and assembled. They were of the Nansen type, with flat wooden runners, some six feet, some nine feet long. The latter size was subsequently found more convenient for travelling, while the former were used around the base for the transportation of coal, ice, stores, and garbage. The individual parts were joined, not with screws or nails, but with strips of rawhide which, previously soaked in water, were threaded through holes bored in the wood, drawn tight with a loop of thin wire, and the ends fastened down onto the wood with small brass screws. The resulting joint is very strong, flexible to a certain extent, and can withstand very rude shocks without breaking. The front of the sledge (or should I say the bows?) is rounded off with a curved 'cowcatcher' made of bamboo covered with a twine lashing, and the top consists of parallel wooden slats to support the burden when loaded.

Not being provided with dogs this season, we were dependent upon ourselves for traction, after the classical manner of Captain Scott; three or four men dragging the loaded sledge along by means of individual canvas harnesses attached to the ends of draw ropes or traces. Marr and Davies spent much time with twine, needle and sail-maker's 'palm', making these harnesses. Contrary to what might be expected, the lack of dogs at this first base of ours was not such a serious handicap, for our projected journeys were all to be made on the surrounding islands, where distances were small. Human traction, by its relative simplicity and by its doing away with the need for extra loads in dog rations, was better suited to the type of terrain which we intended to explore. The human harness consists of a broad canvas belt which crosses the body loosely at the level of the thighs, and is kept up in that position by crossed-over shoulder straps of the same material, fastened to the belt in front by wooden toggles. The two free ends of the belt behind are attached by large eyelets to the end of the rope drawing the sledge. Thus the hands are left free to manipulate ski sticks, which greatly assist in the dragging of the load, whether one be on skis, on snowshoes, or on foot, according to the type of snow being traversed.

The important item of camping equipment now received our attention. Firstly our tents were unpacked, erected on the snow patch behind the house, and thoroughly examined for any possible flaws. They were of the double-walled pyramid type, supported on a framework of four bamboo poles meeting at the apex, the floor space inside being a square just over six feet across. Each one was really like two tents one inside the other, with an air space of about six inches between the two walls for insulation against the outer cold. The inner wall, of light white cotton, had at its base flaps which extended inwards and were covered by the square canvas groundsheet laid down on the snow. The outer wall, of strong green canvas, had similar flaps running outwards, and onto these flaps was shovelled a sufficient quantity of snow to anchor down the tent and form a windproof seal between the walls and the ground. In addition the tent was moored on all sides by guy ropes attached to pegs driven into the snow. Entry and exit is by a tube-like opening going through both the walls, and closed by tying with tapes like the neck of a sack, either from the inside or from the outside as the case may be. At the apex of the tent a short piece of rubber hosepipe running through both walls provides for ventilation and for the escape of fumes generated by the pressure stove inside. Each tent accommodates two men in their sleeping bags, together with the gear needed for preparing their food.

The sleeping bags provided for us were, on account of the wartime conditions prevailing, not of the appropriate polar type, but were those supplied to the British Army for use in temperate European conditions, and therefore, of course, it was very necessary to test them for sleepability under our conditions before embarking with them on a sledge journey. I took it upon myself to make a preliminary test of one of them inside the tent, and one night in early June after supper left the house with a bag, an oil lantern and matches, to spend the night outside. The bag was provided with a canvas cover, and on the snow floor of the tent I first arranged a sheet of waterproof paper under the groundsheet as additional protection against cold and damp from below. Then I wriggled fully clothed into the bag, blew out the lantern, and composed myself for a night's sound sleep, the temperature being 24 °F, with a moderate easterly wind blowing outside. However, I was warm from the house and from a good supper, and after some turning and shifting and smoothing away of hard lumps in the snow, soon dropped off to sleep.[4]

After what seemed to be only a few minutes I was awake again, cramped and distinctly cold. I tried to ignore this, and fell into a fitful and dream-ridden doze, from which at intervals I awoke completely, ever more intensely aware of the cold penetrating through my bag and clothing. Finally, I lit the lantern and got out my watch: 3.30 a.m. In the light of the lantern I could see that the inside wall of the tent had become covered with glistening crystals of hoarfrost from the condensation of my breathing, which rose like steam from my mouth and nostrils. As I learned the following morning, the temperature had gone down to 0.4 °F during the night. Further sleep was out of the question, and I was sorely tempted to get up and make for my warm comfortable cot in the house. But natural obstinacy and considerations of prestige forbade this. Finally things got so bad that I took the oil lantern to bed with me, arching up the sleeping bag over it, and with the help of this feeble warmth was able to pass the weary hours before and after dawn, until I heard Tom Berry moving about in the galley; then I felt that I could retreat to the house without losing face, and entered the galley to greet Tom with a casual air and assure him that I had passed an excellent night.

But thereafter I saw to it that all the sleeping bags taken on sledge journeys were made up double, one being placed inside the other, and from that time onward none of us ever slept cold on sledge journeys except on a few occasions with very low temperatures or when lying in damp clothing.

5

Preparations and Small Excursions

———

FOR OUR FORTHCOMING JOURNEYS, a great deal of time was spent, chiefly by Marr and Taff, in calculating, weighing out, and packeting up sledge rations. Miscalculations may not cause death, but they will produce an unbalanced and monotonous diet. First of all we ascertained from the *Polar Record* and from the accounts of previous Antarctic expeditions, the relative amounts of protein, fats, and carbohydrates, and the number of total calories needed for one man per hard working day. Then the quantities of pemmican, pea-flour, dried milk, egg powder, butter, chocolate, oats, and biscuit were computed and weighed out to cover these requirements and make up a balanced daily sledging ration.[1] These foods were put up in separate packets, each containing the daily 'whack' per man. The pemmican, I should mention in passing, was not the preparation of sun-dried meat to which the name was originally given, but a compound supplied in cans and consisting apparently of a base of beef fat impregnated with meat extract and bone flour, very greasy to the palate and filling to the stomach, especially when melted down together with butter, pea-flour, oats and broken biscuit. Taff also tested the pressure stoves for kerosene consumption, so that we knew how many burning hours we could expect per filling and how many fills were carried in each reserve container of fuel.

As clothing on sledge journeys we were provided with windproof *anoraks* and pants, and *mukluks*, or sealskin boots, imported from Labrador. Both of these are Eskimo names and inventions. The *anorak*, like the seamless shirt of Trèves,[2] is in a one-piece pullover pattern, with an attached hood which can be pulled up over the head when necessary. We had both inner and outer *anoraks*, the outer being of windproof material, the inner of thick fleecy blanket cloth with a trimming of fur around the edges of the hood, not so much for decoration as to prevent fine drift snow from penetrating inside the garment during a blizzard. The *mukluks* are hand sewn with sinew by the Eskimos from shaven sealskin, and on unpacking them we found them to be shrunken, contorted, and hard as a board, a condition to which they are subject when not in constant use. The Eskimos, according to the *Polar Record*, overcome this by thorough mastication. Accordingly, some of us, not to be outdone by the Eskimos, set to work to chew our *mukluks* from toe to top, undeterred by an unsavoury odour and taste with which they were impregnated. At a later date, in another number of the *Polar Record*, we learned that the Eskimos, in default of other available tanning media, use urine for the preparation of the sealskin.[3]

We were all set up for winter surveying and collecting trips, and it was now late July. Our first excursions were not at all ambitious, being merely for the purpose of testing our equipment in field conditions, tying in the cartography of the immediate vicinity, and becoming familiar with skis and sledges as a means of locomotion. Many of them were only one-day outings over the sea ice and up onto the surrounding islands.

To get up onto Wiencke Island, in a bay of which our islet was located, it was necessary to scale the side of a steep snow ridge, which we called the 'Knife Edge', above the now deserted penguin rookery, and guide the sledges carefully for a few hundred yards along the narrow crest until it opened out onto the wide snowfield which gave access to the other side of the island. This snowfield was actually an almost dead glacier, apparently free from crevasses and covered with an even layer of deep snow which offered an excellent surface for ski and sledge travel.

One day while we were up on this snowfield, Taff Davies, in a pause between surveying duties, decided to experiment with an idea for a rapidly constructed emergency snow shelter dug into the snow and roofed over with a few slabs in igloo style. Accordingly he took a shovel and commenced to dig a hole in the snowfield. When he got down about four feet and was pounding away with his shovel at the hard snow at the bottom, he was surprised to see a small black spot, which he at first took for a stone embedded in the snow; but on examining it more closely he found that it was nothing but darkness, a little hole through which lumps of ice fell and could be heard dropping and bouncing down until the sound was lost in some unfathomable cavernous depths beneath his feet. He was in fact digging down through a snow bridge covering a mighty crevasse, and I have never seen anybody jump out of a hole so quickly as Taff did in the moment of that discovery.[4]

After that experience we realized the advisability of roping ourselves together when marching over snowfields where concealed crevasses might exist, and of probing the snow before us with ski sticks in case of any doubt. We devoted some afternoons to 'crevasse drill' at the ice edge on our islet. One man, roped to the others, would throw himself suddenly over the precipice and hang sustained by the rope held fast by the others behind him.

Taff's idea of a snow-hole made me interested in the possibilities of the Eskimo snow house or igloo as a means of emergency shelter in the Antarctic, and during leisure moments I commenced to experiment with the construction of these dwellings on a patch of deep snow behind the house. After a number of abortive attempts I was able, again with the help of instructions given in the *Polar Record*,[5] to erect a passable and weatherproof snow house of the classical type within the space of about one hour, cutting rectangular blocks of hardened snow or *névé* with a saw made for the purpose from a strip of galvanized iron.

First of all a circle of the diameter required, about ten feet, is traced out on the snow, and around it are placed edgewise and end to end sufficient rectangular snow blocks to form a closed wall. Part of this wall is now cut down diagonally to ground level, so that further tiers of snow blocks built on the top of it run up in spiral formation, each block as it is laid being supported by its base and by contact with the end of the one preceding it. In this way it is possible to build the walls with an inward inclination which gradually brings them together at the top in a dome-like formation resembling the old-fashioned straw bee skep, loose snow being used as a mortar to cement the blocks firmly together. When the walls have reached a certain height, it becomes necessary to work from the inside, and a doorway is then cut in the wall at the base, through which the builder enters and pulls in after him the snow blocks cut from the snow patch outside. Finally, the time arrives when the whole structure is complete except for an irregular hole at the apex, and this must be closed with an accurately fitting keystone block which consolidates the whole structure into a continuous dome. The bringing into position of this final block is a somewhat delicate operation, and is done in this way: a block larger than the opening is first gently placed from the outside over the top of the dome; the snow mason then enters the igloo with his snow saw, and thrusts the latter up along the edges of the opening to cut away the sides of the superimposed block to the same shape and allow it to sink gradually into position, fitting exactly into the hole and finally wedging itself down between the neighbouring blocks to the same level. This done, the house is complete, except for the trimming away of any projecting lumps inside or outside, the plastering up of any cracks with loose snow, and the construction of a short tunnel-like entrance passageway running outwards from the doorway.

Such an igloo, when properly constructed, is completely weather-proof, and, provided the temperature does not rise much above freezing point, perfectly stable. It offers certain advantages not to be found in a tent, such as more ample living space and the absence of the disturbing flapping and smacking of the canvas in a high wind. Provided that sufficient time can be spared and suitable snow is available for its construction, an igloo is the perfect answer to the problem of protecting perishable stores and scientific collections without the need of sacrificing a tent for the purpose, and a knowledge of how to construct one may well be of vital importance in the case of any emergency caused by the loss or destruction of a tent.

One calm sunny day when the barometer indicated that we might reasonably expect a spell of fine weather, Chippy Ashton, Johnny Blyth and I started out on a short collecting trip, pulling behind us a six-foot sledge loaded with a tent, sleeping bags, cameras, and collecting equipment. We had some difficulty in traversing the bay separating our base from the Wiencke Island penguin rookery, for the tide was very low and the sea ice near the shore strongly tilted and cleft by gaping cracks. A few hours of sweaty pulling brought us out on the summit of the icefield, and from there onwards we made good time on the downward slopes to the northern end of the island, where we set up camp directly overlooking the Neumayer Channel. Contrary to our expectations, dense cloud and fog began to drift in from the north, and the temperature rose to slightly above freezing point. In spite of the fog, the light reflected off the snow seemed unusually intense, and Ashton and I put on our yellow snow goggles, advising Blyth to do the same.

Next morning the fog had lifted, but a continuous canopy of grey cloud covered the sky from horizon to horizon. Leaving the tent standing, we started out on skis for the northernmost part of the island, later to be named by us 'Blyth Point', and descended the steep snow slope by a series of traverses, although it was difficult to avoid side-slipping on the smooth hard surface, which was like marble, because our skis were not provided with metal edges. At the point, about a hundred feet above the channel, we found considerable areas of bare rock bearing a rather rich lichen flora. I spent several hours making a collection and taking photographs, after which we returned to our camp in the late afternoon.

The following day the temperature had dropped considerably, but the sky had cleared and we felt quite warm in the brilliant windless sunshine. Again we set out along our tracks of the previous day, but after going a couple of miles we branched off to the left around the lower contours of Noble Peak, a small rocky mountain about 1,000 feet high, and made for the rock buttress on its northern side. By the time we reached this place we began to feel the effects of strong sunburn on our faces, especially on the lips, and again Chippy and I advised Blyth to put on his snow glasses, but he had left them in the tent. Removing our skis, we left them stuck upright in the snow at the foot of the buttress, and commenced the ascent of the peak up the spine of exposed rocks. At a height of 800 feet we were confronted by a sharp snow crest about half-a-mile long, the only means of access to another smaller buttress higher up on the face of the mountain. It did not look too good; on the right hand side it dropped off in a steadily steepening slope of hard wind-packed snow which seemed to extend right down to high ice cliffs bordering the channel. To lose one's footing and commence a slippery descent looked easy and fatal. To the left the crest was actually overhanging an almost vertical face of smooth glacier ice which dropped in an unbroken descent for several hundred feet into the snow-filled corrie of the mountain.

After some debate, we decided to make our way cautiously along the right hand side of the slope, well clear of the treacherous overhang, which might collapse beneath our weight. Roping ourselves together with a fifty-foot alpine line, we started along the crest, myself leading and cutting steps into the hard snow with our one ice axe. It took us over an hour to traverse the distance of about half-a-mile, but we did it without mishap, and gained the second, higher buttress. Here we skirted the base of a massive cliff of cracked and precariously hanging rocks, here and there stained a vivid malachite-green by the copper ore contained in them, and climbed up a narrow sloping gully filled with hard snow until we at last reached the small cushion-shaped snow cap covering the summit of the mountain. From what we had seen of this peak from below on previous days, we suspected that this snow cap was to a great extent overhanging and unsupported from below, and so we decided to approach it with caution.

Taking our stance on the highest of the exposed rocks, we joined two fifty-foot lengths of line, and took a turn of one end around a projecting knob; Ashton and Blyth held this free end securely. I tied the other end around my middle and, armed with the ice axe, commenced to clamber slowly up onto the snow cap, cutting holds for hands and feet as I went. The line, when fully paid out, was just long enough to allow me to reach the summit, where I lay flat on my stomach. From this position I could see nothing, as the snow cap sloped away from me on all sides. Cautiously, I rose to a standing position, but hardly had time to raise my head and look around before I felt the snow give way beneath my feet, and the whole expanse on which I was standing dropped with a loud rushing thump. I felt as if the bottom had dropped out of the world, and instinctively threw myself backwards in the direction of the slope up which I had climbed. A moment later I found myself sliding with ever increasing speed head downwards towards the rocks where Chippy and Blyth were standing, horrified. Fortunately I was not altogether unprepared for this happening, and I succeeded in jamming the point of my ice axe into the snow slope, thus braking my headlong rush and allowing me to land on the rocks with my feet instead of my head. As we had suspected, the summit of the peak was an overhanging snow cap, and I made a mental note to tell Taylor on our return to deduct five or six feet from its altitude as previously determined by theodolite from the base.[6]

That night in the tent Blyth complained that some grit had got into his eyes, which appeared to be considerably inflamed. By next

morning he was completely snow-blind. Chippy and I decided to transport him back immediately to the base for Doc's attention. We put all the rations and equipment into the tent, which we then closed up securely, and placed Blyth, enveloped in his sleeping bag, onto the six-foot sledge, his head resting on a rucksack containing our cameras and notebooks. The two of us then started to haul him back over the glacier to the base.

On the homeward run down the snow slope, to make better time, we transferred to our skis, and did the last three miles at speed, making a series of wide traverses. Each time we made a turn, the sledge, with its blinded and motionless occupant, started into a sidewise slither and gained momentum straight down the slope until arrested and jerked into its new course by the tightening of our harness lines. On one occasion, taking too sharp a turn, we capsized it completely, and deposited Johnny like a mummy in its cerements face downwards in the snow. We bundled him on again with scant sympathy, but afterwards I began to think that to be given a Nantucket sleigh ride when you are totally blind cannot be one of life's most pleasant experiences.

On arriving at the slope above the penguin rookery, within sight of the base, we saw that the ice in the bay around our islet had broken up during our absence, with leads of open water between the cakes too wide to take the sledge over. As we came down the slope leading down to the beach, we saw that we had been observed (no doubt by Tom Berry from the galley window), and the motionless figure on the sledge remarked upon. We were still too far away to shout the news across, and enjoyed the confusion and alarm which we could see developing at the base. It was like kicking open an ants' nest. Small gesticulating figures ran hither and thither over the rocks and clustered together in the boat harbour, dragging the dinghy with feverish haste out of the ice into a lead of open water. The boat, with Marr, Taylor and Doc on board, beached on the rookery after a strenuous pull among the ice floes, and they came running up the slope, Doc and Marr bearing a first-aid outfit between them, to find Blyth sitting up in his bag on the sledge enjoying a cigarette which we had lighted for him and put between his lips. We put in strong pleas for clemency, but Tom Berry, as Johnny's immediate superior, promised him punitive fatigue work scrubbing out the galley once he got his *talking* eyes open. It took him all of three days to recover.

6

Snow-Blindness

ONLY A RELATIVELY SMALL NUMBER of this world's inhabitants live in regions where they are perpetually exposed to the inhuman glare of the light reflected by vast expanses of snow and ice – chiefly the Eskimo race, whose numbers little exceed 30,000 by the latest reliable census. In other parts of the habitable globe the eye may be accustomed to the sight of snow, but there are other surrounding objects upon which its gaze may more comfortably rest. Thus the Peruvians do not always need to stare at the gleaming sugary spires of the Andes, nor the Tibetans at the immeasurable white uprearings of the Himalayas: they may turn their eyes aside to softer tints of green verdure and brown earth. When one considers these things, one begins to understand why the affliction of snow-blindness has received so little attention in our literary and scientific records in comparison with the many other diseases to which the human eye is subject.

I have consulted many works in my search for reliable information on this local but distressing ailment, including many meritorious treatises on the science of ophthalmology, and in hardly any of them have I found even a passing reference to it. Your great encyclopaedias – your *Americana*, your *Britannica*, your *Chambers's*, your *Collier's*, your *New International* – pass briskly on their scholarly way direct from *Snow berry* to *Snow bunting*, and even the *Grand Dictionnaire Universel* of Larousse, though giving much interesting and recondite information under the heading of *Cécité** in general, omits all

---

* Blindness.

reference to the *cécité des neiges*; and in the learned Posey's *Hygiene of the Eye*[1] we similarly seek in vain for any specific reference to snow-blindness. Nevertheless, my search for a literary fulcrum on which to erect my enquiries in this respect has not gone entirely unrewarded. I am the fortunate possessor of an invaluable treatise in German entitled *Synoptische Darstellung der Traumatischen Augenentzündungszustände,** which I acquired at one of the boarded bibliophilic oases which dot the banks of the Seine between Notre Dame and the Quai des Orfèvres, at a slightly reduced price on account of the first 482 pages being missing, for which reason I shall never know the author's name to venerate it.[2] In the glossary at the end of this work I found what I so sorely needed, namely a definition of the disease, the nature and causes of which we earnestly seek to elucidate: '*Schneeblindheit: Blendungszustand, welcher von Schnee verursacht wird.*'† Armed, then, with this fundamental definition, we already feel our feet on firmer ground, and proceed with some considerable measure of assurance to the following more detailed considerations.

All agree that blindness is a terrible affliction. The blindness of the snow is above all things insidious, and treacherous in its onset. Eager to get a better view of the limitless white expanse around him, the polar traveller lets his gaze sweep widely from horizon to horizon, and for a time rejoices in his power to take in and seemingly to comprehend the wondrous secrets of the glittering realm which lies spread out invitingly before him. But pain and disillusionment quickly follow, and before he has had time to realize fully the folly of his efforts, he finds himself struck blind and stumbling helplessly in circles, most likely to perish miserably in the snowy wastes unless he quickly manages to reach some known haven of salvation. The eyes feel as if filled with gritty particles, and tears well up incessantly,

---

* *Synoptic Presentation of Traumatic Ocular Inflammatory Condition.*
† 'Snow-blindness: Glare condition, which is caused by snow.'

the lids become inflamed and swollen, and finally the passage of light into the pupils becomes so intolerable that even the weakest rays will cause acute discomfort. These things I have experienced myself, although not to the extent suffered by Johnny Blyth, who disregarded several warnings. There were some among us who at first hardly believed in snow-blindness; we thought of it rationally, as merely a psychosomatic effect, brought on solely by the power of suggestion acting on a superstitiously receptive mind. But in this we were assuredly mistaken. On one of our first local sledging forays, when the brilliant sun shone down out of a cloudless sky over countless square miles of virgin snows, I scorned the cowardly tinted glasses, and let my eyes drink in to the full the glorious panorama bathed in dazzling bluish-white light. If my eyes are not able to look at this (I argued), the most resplendent manifestation of Light which is vouchsafed to us in this world, what good are they at all? And even after the onset of the inevitable affliction, several hours later, I refused to think that it could be due to this cause, and vainly tried to rub the imaginary offending particles of grit out of my eyes. Thus are we often blinded by our foolish attempts to seek simple rational explanations of complicated and profound phenomena.

But there are times when we must penetrate the highest and most inaccessible mountain summits and the limitless snowfields of the polar icecaps. For those whose business takes them there, or who wander into these realms from some inexplicable inner compulsion, human experience and ingenuity has, by repeated trial and error, evolved adequate means of protection in the form of shields or screens to place before the eyes. Such snow spectacles are absolutely effective in preventing the access of the lethal rays which attack, inflame, and ultimately destroy the tissues of the human eye, and with them on we can travel dauntlessly and unharmed over the most dazzling sunlit snowfields of the globe, provided always that we never, in impetuousness or arrogance, let drop the indispensable guard.

Broadly speaking, they are of two kinds, based on two different optical principles, depending largely on the degree of civilization attained by those who use them. The first kind utilizes coloured glasses designed to let through only harmless rays, and hold back the damaging ones which lurk at the extreme limits of the spectrum. Such goggles, with yellow or rose-tinted glasses, were provided by the wise and experienced authorities to the members of our expedition. They were found at all times to be entirely effective, although irksome to wear constantly, because when, from the exertions and excitement of fast travel towards your destination, you get sweaty and steamy-headed, they rapidly cloud up with a misty film, and rob you of anything approaching accurate vision. Only so long as you remain relatively inert do they stay clear and practically useful. The other type, which was devised by the Eskimos depends, as I say, on an entirely different optical principle, that of restricting the area through which the light impressions are received by the eye, without in any way altering their essential quality. This is achieved by the use of goggles provided, not with coloured glasses, but with very small openings, which are just sufficiently large to allow the wearer to see what lies directly in front of his nose, and yet so diminish the sum total of rays entering the eye that there is no possibility of an inconvenience or injury.

I have studied several collections of these Eskimo snow goggles in various museums and private cabinets, and have been much impressed by their workmanship; constructed of wood, bone, ivory, or stone, many of them are true works of art, ornamented with a fantastic diversity of fanciful and not unpleasing carvings representing beasts, men and mythological figures, half human, half divine. I have been told that the exact shape and size of the orifice in them is determined by the shaman of each tribe, an individual by all accounts endowed with supernatural wisdom in these matters and who, being on intimate magical terms with the Sun, can regard it fixedly at any time without any artificial protection whatsoever, and prescribe infallibly the quantity of its rays which should be allowed to enter the eyes of the members of his flock. The double orifices in these goggles, thus determined, are of various shapes, being in the form of a narrow slit, a small circle, a diamond, or a cross, among which the last mentioned is, as I have been given to understand, that most generally recommended.

So, Reader, if your ways should take you over trackless snowy wastes, never neglect to equip yourself with one or other of these indispensable protective contrivances, suiting your own fancy and inclination as regards the choice, and you may rest assured that you will never be subject to the agonies of snow-blindness which are visited on the impious traveller who, with Promethean wilfulness, disdains all artefacts of mediation between his eagerly restless searching eye and the dazzling radiance of the featureless white expanse which he has vowed to expose and strip of all its mysteries.

7

Fifteen-Mile Odyssey

IN EARLY SEPTEMBER Taff Davies and I constructed two light toboggans, which he baptized 'Explorer' and 'Pioneer', and the two of us made a one-day trip up onto the Wiencke Island icecap, dragging them behind us loaded with fifty pounds each of equipment. Even with the sealskins which we had attached to our skis,[1] we found it rather hard to obtain sufficient traction on the steep snow slope above the penguin rookery, but once the summit was reached the going was good. We offloaded our shovels and levelled off the sharp snow crest at the approach to the glacier, in order to make smooth the way for the large sledges which would follow later along the same route.

After traversing a distance of about four miles uphill on the gently sloping snowfield, we reached the summit of the icecap, and commenced to ski down the slope on the other side, in a wide col separating the two mountain ranges. As the slope increased, the toboggans began to make swift rushes to overtake us, but Taff had already thought of this difficulty and overcame it by letting a slack loop of rope drag underneath the front end of each toboggan; this acted as a drag-brake and kept the toboggans behind us at a respectful distance.

As we entered the narrowest part of the col, the towering walls of black rock on either side of us loomed up impressively; the silence was complete, except for the rhythmic squeak and grunt of our skis and toboggans on the hard snow, and not a single living creature apart from ourselves was to be seen. We were making our entry into a dead world of rocks, ice and snow. At the other end of the passage, isolated mountain peaks slowly rose and became visible above the skyline as we proceeded on our way, and soon joined up into an extensive mountainous panorama of inspiring grandeur, extending down to a wide channel or arm of the sea, still open, separating them from our island. This mountainous landscape, covered with untold thickness of ice and snow, was the Danco Coast of the Palmer Peninsula, extending north-east and south-west to a distance which we estimated as approximately sixty or seventy miles.

At this point we made a halt for our midday snack of crackers and margarine, chocolate, and tea from our vacuum flasks; Taff made a panoramic sketch of the landscape before us, while I took photographs at various angles and bearings with the prismatic compass. From where we stood we could see that there was a rock-clear sledging route out to the Nemo Peaks at the north end of Wiencke Island, but it was impossible to tell whether there was a passable way around to the south-east behind the saw-toothed and precipitous Sierra du Fief. We returned to the base at six in the evening after an absence of eight hours.

Our final and most extensive sledge trip of the season was begun on September 22nd. Marr, Davies, Taylor, Ashton and I climbed to the top of the 'Knife Edge' on skis, and made for the place where we had left our ready-loaded sledges on the previous day.[2] We harnessed ourselves up to them, two men to each, with Chippy Ashton as fifth wheel pushing behind on the heavier one, and started on our journey up the slope of the icefield. After making a long traverse around the base of 'Wall Mountain', we found ourselves confronted by a short steep downward slope. Taylor and I, with Chippy guiding at the handlebars, managed to get the first sledge, with the rope brake thrown under the runners, safely, in spite of much side-slipping, around the contour of the slope onto more level ground. The other sledge, similarly braked, was taken straight down the slope. With a short mad rush it reached the bottom, where it suddenly tilted over and sank deeply on one side; it had gone into a crevasse. We attached a fifty-foot alpine rope to the trace line, and all together commenced heaving on the sledge. With a sudden snap the curved cowcatcher parted, and the sledge settled more deeply in the crevasse. The only thing to do was to offload it, and this was done by Marr, secured to the rest of us on the end of the alpine rope. He trod delicately, and removed the ration boxes and tent off the sledge as furtively and quietly as a burglar robbing a sleeping household. In spite of his precautions, the sledge suddenly dropped several inches, and we heard the bang and the rattle of ice blocks bouncing down into the yawning depths below. We took a renewed stance and firmer grip on the line, expecting to see Marr take the drop at any moment, and hoping that the rope would keep clear of his neck. But the offloading was completed successfully, and the empty sledge then shifted to a safer spot where an emergency repair could be performed on it.

Continuing our journey after this interlude, we kept as much along the contour of the snow slope as possible. We were now on our own, Chippy having taken leave of us and returned alone on his skis to the base. Following the contour route took us a good deal out of our intended way, and after two hours we found ourselves directly underneath the sheer cliff of 'Wall Mountain'. Its black sides, variegated with a fine web-like pattern of white lines from the snow lying on its narrow ledges, loomed up oppressively above our heads until lost in a layer of grey fog about a thousand feet above us. A little farther on, our way became impeded at every few yards by scattered blocks of ice from a few feet across to the size of a small house. A skua, the first animal life we had seen all day, swooped down from the black cliff face above us and winged swiftly out over the glittering expanse of the glacier, uttering a hoarse and melancholy screech as it flew; it reminded me of a raven.

Our senses had been dulled by the hours of monotonous hauling, and our thoughts were occupied mainly by visions of food;

otherwise I would be hard pressed to explain the tardiness of our mental reaction to the phenomenon presented to us.

'*Coughing* bastard lumps; where do you think they come from?' shouted Marr over his shoulder as he and Taff strained their sledge around the lee of a particularly large ice-block.

'Must be from upstairs; Taff and I saw some hanging glaciers in this face from the other side last Tuesday when we . . .' My sentence remained unfinished; I was caught back by a sharp jolt as the harness trace tightened, and I turned to see Taylor, stiffened in his tracks, staring up into the weaving fog around the rock face a thousand feet above our heads, his eyes filled with a curious expression of fascinated attention which I had never observed in them before. Elijah must have looked upwards like that when the still small voice came through on Mount Horeb.[3]

The delayed-reaction realization, so beloved of the early screen comics, struck us all at the same moment after a few seconds of standing there, and without a spoken word we began with one accord to travel onwards as fast as we could, straining desperately on the harness traces, towards the far side of the block-encumbered slope.

It was inevitable. Hanging glaciers calve probably only a few times each day, and this was one of those times. First a sharp report like a cannon being fired, the echo almost immediately drowned by a swelling peal of rumbling thunder from above, incessant, and every second increasing in volume until the eardrums were stunned by the supercharge of sound. Our heads jerked upwards, and we beheld thousands of tons of ice and snow hurtling down through the fog like a slowly descending white curtain.

For some time, probably only a second or two, we stood motionless in our harnesses, gazing upwards fascinated at the destruction coming down to overwhelm us. The white curtain dropped with ever increasing velocity, with bouncing and hurtling ice blocks dimly seen in its midst as through a cloud of steam. The noise was like the shriek of a locomotive issuing from a tunnel.

Completely by instinct we accomplished the complicated manoeuvre of struggling out of our harnesses and unlatching our skis, and started running madly down the steep slope, floundering among the ice blocks, stumbling, falling, and getting up again, in a headlong wild rush for preservation.[4] We had gone only a few yards when we were knocked flat in the snow by a tremendous blast of icy wind; everything was suddenly blotted out by fine snow, like sand, forced into our eyes, ears, mouths and nostrils.

*

Everything was still, and at first I thought I had just wakened up in my bed in the morning. Then I remembered. Could this be ...? Certainly I had no sensation of a body. But no, it was all just a joke; I could feel cold water running down my neck, and opening my eyes, I saw my knees sticking up out of the snow, in which I was almost completely buried. I pushed my way out of it and looked around hastily for my comrades. Two snowmen were standing five or six yards away, beating mechanically at the white powder covering them, while a third was pushing himself up out of a small hillock, a large slab of snow falling like a tombstone off his breast. It made me think of an allegorical engraving which I had once seen in the frontispiece of an old Flemish Bible,[5] and I had to repress a desire to break out into extravagant laughter. My cap and mitts were lying half-buried thirty yards down the slope. Without words we climbed up to where we had abandoned our sledges; one of them had been blown over onto its side, and the bamboo cowcatcher of the other, which we had repaired after the incident with the crevasse, had been snapped off completely and was immovably jammed under an ice block of about the size of an automobile. We replaced it with a loop of rope, and eased the sledges, with double rope brakes, straight down the slope until we emerged from the area of danger and demolition.

After travelling on in silence for another half-hour, a rather disturbing feeling of complete exhaustion began to grow upon us. We were trembling visibly, our faces were covered with sweat although chilled to the marrow, and we felt as if we were losing life blood from a severed artery. We decided to make camp for the night before all strength left us, and hastily unloaded and erected the tents, although it was only four in the afternoon. When we had made hot cocoa on the Primus, and rested awhile in our sleeping bags, we began to talk again, and Taff, always practical, suggested the advisability of inventing a quick-release mechanism for casting loose our harness from the draw rope of the sledge in emergencies such as that we had just experienced. We slept very soundly, which is unusual on the first night of a camping trip.

The following day was splendid, calm and sunny, with a strange clearness of the atmosphere, which made the surrounding mountains look almost close enough to touch by stretching out one's hand. We made an early start in good spirits. After four hours of uneventful hauling, we reached the end of the col which Taff and I had reconnoitred previously, and there made a halt to set up tripods and theodolites and make a series of observations. This took up about an hour, at the end of which time we took a hasty mouthful of food (our inactivity had made us very cold), and resumed our journey, descending the rolling glacier slope for a distance of three or four miles to the level icefield above the channel separating us from the mainland of the Palmer Peninsula. By this time we were feeling rather tired, and decided to make camp for the night.

The two tents were pitched on level snow a few yards apart, and we passed our bedrolls, ration boxes, pressure stoves, and other gear through the round entrance flap as soon as Taff inside had laid down the groundsheet and brushed out the powder snow with a clothes-brush which we carried for that purpose. Everything seemed hopelessly muddled and cramped, for we had not yet learned the technique of arranging our chattels so as to exist in comparative comfort in a tent. A few days of practice in this respect brought a considerable improvement.

When you wake up in the morning, the first thing to do is to light the pressure stove to warm up the tent and melt the covering of fine ice crystals which has formed during the night inside the walls from the condensation of your breathing. If you move about or brush against the walls before lighting the stove, a shower of fine ice crystals will descend all over you and your bedding and later melt, making everything unpleasantly damp. When the temperature has risen to a comfortable degree, you extract yourself from the sleeping bag, open up the entrance flaps to have a look at the weather and to fill the cooking pot with fresh snow, large clean slabs of which you have providently stacked within easy reach on the right hand side of the entrance. You then raise one corner of the groundsheet and urinate into a small hole dug into the snow beneath it. Having put the pot of snow on the pressure stove to melt, you open the ration box lying between you and your tent-mate, and take out the makings of breakfast – oats, powdered milk, salt, sugar, margarine, cocoa or coffee powder, enamel plates and mugs, and spoons. When the snow has melted, you add the oats, and porridge results, which is eaten. The pot is then refilled with snow to make cocoa or coffee, after drinking which you return the tins and utensils to the box to get them out of the way.

By this time it has usually become necessary to leave the tent, and you struggle into your sealskin boots, windproof pants and *anorak* with some difficulty, as you cannot rise above a lying or sitting position. Once outside, it all depends on the weather: the worse it is, the sooner you come in again. After a smoke, and muffled communications with the other tent, your bedfellow creeps outside in his turn, and later you can push out to him through the door flap first the ration boxes, then the radio, and finally the groundsheet and the bedrolls; these things he loads onto the sledge and lashes fast. The guy ropes are now cast loose, the tent lifted, collapsed, laid flat on the snow, and rolled into a cylinder, then covered with its canvas sheath and lashed down lengthways on top of the sledge load. You are then all set to start the day's travel.

On this particular morning, however, the wind was blowing great guns, and when I poked my head out through the tent flap I saw nothing but an impenetrable white wall of driving snow. Breakfast over and utensils repaired, we reclined in our bedrolls and smoked several pipes, in the hope that the weather might shortly improve, but for the whole of that day it remained impossible to travel. The hours passed fairly quickly until lunch time, and our midday meal consisted of beef extract in hot water thickened with broken crackers to the consistency of a mush, followed by a chocolate bar. The early afternoon we spent sleeping in our bags, the stove being extinguished to save fuel. The worst time of the day is the late afternoon, when the daylight begins to fade and the night, with its comfortable candle-lit embrace, has not yet arrived; you are cramped, your stomach is slightly upset from the afternoon sleep and too much smoking, and you look at your watch frequently to see whether it might not be time to start up the stove and begin melting snow for supper. You feel lonely and depressed, strongly conscious of your anomalous position in an icy world never intended for human habitation, and the yelling of the wind outside and the creaking and flapping of the tent begin to get on your nerves.

Supper time comes like a deliverance. For this third and last meal of the day, unless we opened a can of beef and carrot stew, we prepared a pemmican mush out of snow water, pemmican, pea-flour, margarine and canned bacon, topped off with several mugs of well-sweetened cocoa. A candle is lit and stuck upright on the top of the ration box in a pool of its own wax. The radio receiver is dusted off, turned on, and used to get the time signal and Morse messages relayed to us from the base seven miles away at this prearranged hour. Taylor improvised a loudspeaker by placing the earphones inside an empty cracker tin, which he suspended from the peak of the tent by a bootlace. A few more pipes and a round of desultory conversation concludes our day, and we relapse into our sleeping bags for another night.

The next day the blizzard continued even more strongly; during the night we estimated the gusts to have reached a velocity of sixty miles per hour. Nevertheless, our tents stood up excellently to the incessant straining, and showed no tendency to lift or shift. Taylor and I spent the greater part of the day practising Morse code. When lunch time came around, I had the misfortune to upset the pot of boiling water over my feet. The pain was intense for a few seconds. I peeled off my socks, a good deal of skin coming with them, and applied Vaseline. The burning sensation kept me awake for the greater part of the night, but by the morning the pain had subsided.

Two more days after this we spent tent-bound, wondering whether the blizzard would ever come to an end. Towards the end of the third day a new problem arose, namely the steadily increasing dampness of our clothes and bedding. Normally the water vapour given off by the body penetrates outwards through the layers of the sleeping bags until it is condensed by contact with the cold groundsheet lying directly on the snow floor, so that the underside of the bag becomes quite wet, but this moisture is kept at bay in the outer part of the bag by the warmth radiating from one's body. But after two or three days without an opportunity of airing the bags, which are made of balloon fabric stuffed with eiderdown, the water gets the upper hand, and soaks inwards until at last one's buttocks are resting uncomfortably in a pool of moisture. Taff made a dash over to our tent to express his dismay over this situation; he was in even worse plight because he had previously waterproofed the cover of his sleeping bag with linseed oil to keep out the damp, instead of which he trapped it inside, some twenty ounces of it each day, this being the normal amount of moisture daily exuded from the pores of the human body.

The storm finally blew itself out on the morning of the fifth day, and we looked out over the top of the deep snowdrifts piled halfway up the tents, the fresh snow packed down and stratified by the force of the wind and glistening attractively in the morning sunshine. We spent the best part of two hours digging out the tents and sledges;

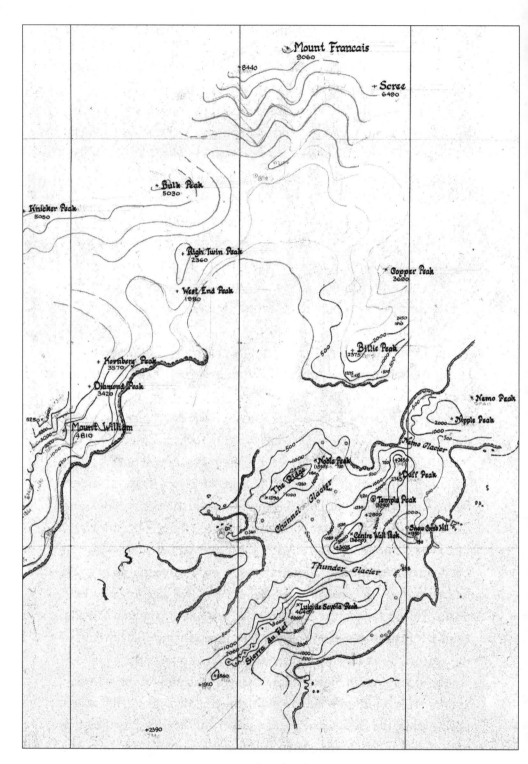

Wiencke Island.

on the windward side an even slope up to their tops, to the leeward a deep trough kept clear by the confusion of the air currents sweeping around the obstacle. When we dismantled the tents, there remained on each side a square of soiled snow, disfigured with garbage and yellow patches, with two deep depressions like graves where our bodies had been lying and had gradually melted their way down into the snow. The remainder of the day was occupied in a detailed panoramic survey with theodolite and plane table of the surrounding features of the island and the peaks of the mainland over the way across the channel.

We were out of cigarettes, of which the four-day blizzard had made for greatly increased consumption, and Marr had gone over to a pipe made from the hollowed-out end of a ski pole fastened to a broken thermometer tube with adhesive plaster. It was high time to return to the base, particularly since we had tied in all the local topography and made sufficient observations for a fairly detailed map of the east side of Wiencke Island. Before starting on the return journey I made a short botanical collecting excursion to a small rocky peak some two miles west of our camp, and climbed up it to a height of about 1,200 feet, with some difficulty as I had sealskin boots on, not being able to wear my ski boots on account of the large blisters on my feet from their recent scalding. On the frost-shattered rocks near the top of the peak I found a considerable vegetation of lichens, mainly the yellow and black shrubby species of *Usnea* which goes by the name of *Neuropogon*.* I was thirsty, and pulled about a bushel of the lichen off the rock, put a match to it, and found as I had suspected that it burned excellently and gave out sufficient heat to melt a can full of snow for drinking water.[6]

Two days later we arrived back at the base, after an epic journey of fifteen miles, and were received with acclamation as hardened veterans of polar travel.[7]

---

* Now *Usnea sphacelata*.

8

Rustle of Spring

———

THE INCREASING STRENGTH of the sun, rather than a rise in the air temperature, was the first intimation which we received of the return of spring. On October 17th, Taylor, Taff Davies, Blyth and myself, taking angles and observations on the exposed icecap of Wiencke Island, shivered in a strong north-west wind which blew the drift snow like sugar over the surface of the glacier. The sun shone down out of a cloudless blue with unusual brightness, but we all felt very cold, and interrupted our work at frequent intervals to do a little war dance and flap our arms frenziedly against our bodies. While Taylor and I were working with the panoramic camera, fumbling with frozen fingers at the refractory mechanism, Taff and Blyth excavated a pit in the snow (this time probing carefully for hidden crevasses) in which to crouch for shelter from the biting wind, but the drifting snow which blew onto them melted on their dark clothing in the strong sunlight, and after a while they were as wet as if they had stood outside in a rainstorm.[1] I turned this observation to some practical use by spreading out a black rubberized tarpaulin and strewing snow over it; within minutes it melted on the dark surface and provided us with all the water we could drink.

Soon, however, we began to feel and appreciate the increasing warmth of the sun on windless days, and would sometimes take our tea outside, sitting on the ribs and vertebrae of whales on the stony beach above the boat harbour. More and more the rocks emerged from the snow, and everywhere on our islet we could hear the musical gurgle of water running down the rocks and gullies from the melting snow patches. The ice in the bay surrounding our base broke up completely and, on one or two days when the wind blew offshore, the floes disappeared entirely and went far out to sea down the open channel, only to return another day when the wind blew in the opposite direction. One floe, on which I had left a broken ski stick, departed and reappeared in this way four or five times before finally leaving us for some destination unknown along uncharted shores to the south.

Radio communication with the other base on Deception Island and with the Governor's headquarters in the Falklands increased daily in volume and interest, and we would crowd around Farrington as he sat at his instrument panel at the scheduled times of these communications; for a few seconds or minutes he would rap off a string of cryptic remarks on the key in an offhand and nonchalant way, then suddenly pause, take up his pencil, and commence to transcribe word by word the message from beyond. We crowded closer, breathing down his neck, and our imaginations took leaps and bounds ahead of the words slowly appearing out of the tip of his pencil. The moving finger writes . . .[2]

On one occasion Farrington indulged himself in a mild hoax by writing down for our benefit a fictitious signal to the effect that we were all to be transferred for three years to a new base on Peter I Island, a small and extremely isolated island lying way down to the south-west of the Palmer Peninsula in the horrifying latitude of seventy-two degrees south. Even the authentic messages were somewhat conflicting, and their laconic brevity nourished a rich crop of rumours concerning our future movements, the latest to date being that the *William Scoresby* would be leaving Port Stanley at the end of October, and would call at Deception Island to pick up Flett and Matheson, then take Marr back to the Falklands for conversations with the Governor regarding arrangements for the coming season. It seemed certain that in any case we should be moving on to Hope Bay to establish a permanent base on the site reconnoitred by us previously, and word came through that two additional members of the survey personnel, Sub-Lieutenant James and Captain Russell, would be coming out from England to join us.

We were now no longer alone in our domain; during the past few weeks the penguins had been returning to their rookery over the bay in ever increasing numbers, defiling the remaining snow patches with squirts of their reddish excrement and filling the air with stench and clamour. A couple of Weddell seals had also made their appearance on the ice floes still attached to our islet, and in due course gave birth to pale furry pups, staining the ice with blood in the process. After a while they used to leave the pups on the ice for long periods while they went off into the water to feed, and during their absence we would pick up and fondle the delightfully soft and appealing little creatures, replacing them hastily and retreating when the mother returned and started to make angry rushes at us, moving swiftly over the ice on her undulating belly like some gigantic slug or *bêche-de-mer.**

A colony of cormorants out on the point returned to their nests, tower-like structures built up from seaweed and old rope from decaying whaling scows left beached nearby years ago; the whole firmly cemented together with their excrement. Their first egg was laid on October 25th.

Concerning penguins I shall have but little to say; their characteristics have been lovingly dwelt upon in a wealth of detail in other accounts of life in the Antarctic regions, notably in H. G. Ponting's classic *The Great White South*.[3] I would only take issue with the common tendency to represent them as little less than human, paragons of sagacity, which is a misconception engendered by their upright gait and tuxedo-like plumage; actually they are among the least intelligent of birds, and any of their actions and reactions in which we may think to discern human traits are the product of

---

* Sea cucumber.

a blind instinct little superior to that manifest in insects. Their eyes are fishy and impersonal. Only in the water can they really be admired, as they flash over the clear stony bottom in a zigzag course, almost too swiftly to be followed by the eye, propelled by their beautifully adapted wing-flippers. On land they are ungainly waddling monstrosities, recalling to mind Baudelaire's lines on the albatross:

> A peine les ont-ils déposés sur les planches,
> Que ces rois de l'azur, maladroits et honteux,
> Laissent piteusement leurs grandes ailes blanches
> Comme des avirons traîner à côté d'eux.[4]

But the most fascinating life was to be found in the rock pools now ice-free and made accessible by the exceptionally low spring tides. By the hour we would wade in our sea boots in the shallows, peering down among the polished stones and under the rocky ledges, every few minutes picking out for inspection some amazing example of the never ending interplay of the life force with inanimate substance. There were small striped bloated fishes, shrimp-like amphipods, sea-urchins, sponges, translucent pink and grey naked molluscs, tube-inhabiting worms, and primitive crayfish-like creatures of the genus *Glyptonotus*, probably the closest related living form to the long extinct trilobites. Most beautiful were the transparent ctenophores, the comb-bearers, like swimming soap bubbles, clear as glass, with iridescent colours playing over their internal organs. Wonderful indeed in life as they rolled and drifted on the bottom of the pool, but when lifted out of the water collapsing on one's hand into a formless mass of slime.

Marr broke out two drums of formalin and spent days going back and forth between the shore and the workroom collecting and pickling this abundance of marine life in quart-sized jars and test tubes. I found him one day trying to pickle a sea-squirt, of the order *Tunicata*, an orange-coloured hollow ball of jelly rooted to a piece of stone. Its simple appearance, he told me, was deceptive; it belonged to a highly evolved group of animals which had elected to give up their free-swimming existence and spend the rest of their days rooted like jelly-plants to the rock, entirely abandoning activity, and living on the microscopic organisms wafted into their hollow bag-like bodies by the water currents. To make sure it was well pickled, Marr filled a syringe with formalin and injected a good shot into its interior through the combined mouth and anus. I could well believe that the animal was more highly evolved than it looked when I saw it squirt the formalin back into his face. It died hard, like the mite which I had taken off a patch of lichen a few days previously, and found to be still alive after being corked up for twenty-four hours in 90 per cent alcohol.

Marr, although a professional biologist, had never lost the unspoiled childlike faculty of wonderment when confronted with these riddles of organized being. 'Why all these myriad forms and structures,' he would say with a sigh, 'when one would serve each purpose just as well?' And on another occasion, 'What's the use of the yellow fluted fringe along the margin of that nemertine worm, and the bunch of striped tentacles planted on the head of this holothurian? Why so many of these useless and senseless ornamentations?'

'Our trouble', I replied, 'is that we don't understand a joke. We can't accept the purely playful variety of lifeforms, prodigal waste of resources in production of egg cells and so forth, and on the other hand mean little niggling economies in the combination of the functions of love and excretion, all that sort of thing, just for what it is: a cosmic belly laugh of the highest order.'[5]

*

It was pretty good to be alive on these rare warm days, with God in his heaven and all right with the world, when one could spend hours getting free entertainment on the seashore, examining every patch of lichen and moss which had emerged, turgid and sprouting life, from the blanket of snow under which it had lain dormant all winter. It was on one of these verdant moss patches that I suddenly came face to face one day with one of the largest land animals of the Antarctic continent, and for a moment stood undecided whether to flee or to face up to it. *Belgica antarctica* was its name, and it stood at least one-eighth of an inch high to its shoulder. It was a wingless gnat, blackish in colour, peculiar to this continent, no blood-sucker, but a blameless browser among the tufts of moss and lichen during its brief existence of one Antarctic summer.[6]

Several other birds, besides the penguins and the cormorants, now put in their appearance, bustling around busily with only one idea in their heads. The most ubiquitous and obtrusive were the sheathbills or paddies (*Chionis alba*), pure white birds about the size of a pigeon, which congregated in crowds on the rocks outside the galley window, feeding on every kind of garbage thrown out to them. Their nests, made in crevices between the rocks, were largely constructed of penguins' cast-off tail feathers, in default of other available building material. Seagulls (*Larus dominicanus*) were fairly abundant along the shoreline, but in numbers and aggressiveness could not compete with the brown skuas (*Catharacta skua*), which plundered freely, driving the other birds off their spoils and, on our approach, watching us truculently out of the corner of a hard and impudent eye, retreating only at the last possible moment and hopping just a few yards to one side until we left them in peace again. Obviously they regarded us humans with considerable contempt, and if we should dare to approach their nests, they would fly straight for our heads with strident cries, deflecting their flight at a distance of about six inches from our faces. To have several of these large fierce-looking birds simultaneously making downward rushes at one's head from all sides was rather intimidating. But the most inspired exponents of the science of dive-bombing were without doubt the terns (*Sterna vittata*); these small, graceful birds with forked tails, grey of plumage, with black heads and bright red bills and legs, defended their stony apologies for nests with great valiance, and were not content with making feint rushes, but would actually strike one's head or face with their wings in their downward flight. When walking through their nesting colonies on my way to take photographs from the point opposite our islet, I used to push the camera tripod down my back inside my jersey, with the legs sticking up above my head, so as to give them something better to rush at than my wincing features. Their small brown spotted eggs, one or two to a nest, were very attractive. Snow petrels (*Pagodroma nivea*) pure white, with black beaks, were hardly ever seen to land, but flew over in droves high up in the air, uttering their thin and strangely plaintive cries.

For sheer repulsiveness, probably no bird alive can compete with the giant petrel (*Macronectes giganteus*), affectionately called the 'Stinker' or 'Nelly'; a large potbellied bird, pale dirty brown in colour, always attracted to any old seal carcass, on which it gorges itself until it becomes too heavy and distended to fly. If you then approach it, it will watch you coming with a shifty anxious eye, and when it deems it necessary to take to flight, it will vomit up all the contents of its stomach before starting to run off upwind, its bat-like wings widely extended, to get sufficient lift to take off into the air. After you have moved on, it will, like the dog, return to its vomit, re-ingesting this before renewing its attack on the rest of the seal carcass.

What a contrast to this incarnation of the fifth deadly sin, then, is the tiny black Wilson's petrel (*Oceanites oceanicus*), hovering over the water with unsteady, lightly fluttering, apparently aimless move-ments like those of a butterfly, their long spindly legs trailing down and occasionally dipping lightly into the waves. I have never seen them come to rest on the surface of the water.

The shags or cormorants were the first to be levied upon for food for our table. Tom Berry had a row of them hanging up under the eaves of the galley veranda, each with an onion stuffed into its gullet to dispel the fishy flavour which they are supposed to have. He disguised them very skilfully before presenting them at the table, so that we might forget that we were lapsing barbarically from civilized diet. The eggs were about as large as those of a goose, and undeniably good eating. I would hardly say the same for penguins' eggs, nor did anybody else think much of them with the exception of Marr, who characterized them as 'bloody good'. Indeed their appearance was somewhat bloody, on account of their red yolks, which, when boiled, showed up uninvitingly through the completely transparent albumen, and I could never eat a freshly boiled penguin's egg without thinking of eyes torn from their sockets. A cake baked by Berry with penguins' eggs came out of the oven bright red instead of the normal yellow colour which would have resulted from the use of orthodox methods of cookery.

Every few days Doc Back and Blyth would go over to the rookery with two buckets each and fill them with penguin eggs. The colony here at Port Lockroy consisted almost entirely of the Gentoo penguin (*Pygoscelis papua*), a fairly large but lazy, indifferent and unaggressive species, which allowed its nests to be plundered without giving much trouble. On the approach of the two human figures the birds would usually vacate their nests voluntarily, only a few obstinate ones here and there requiring the assistance of a boot. Other species of penguin, notably the Adélie, which we were later on to encounter at Hope Bay, are much more difficult to manage, and make egg-collecting quite a strenuous occupation.

On November 9th a signal came through to tell us that the *William Scoresby* had left Port Stanley the previous day, but had come up against thick continuous pack ice about a hundred miles north of Deception Island.[7] This might mean a delay of another week or so, but it would allow us more time to prepare our notes, letters home, and biological and geological collections which were to be taken back by her. Chippy Ashton commenced to lay out the frame and corrugated iron sheets for a more or less completely prefabricated hut which was to be erected at Hope Bay when we got there to serve as our temporary living quarters, so that we should not suffer the inconvenience of having to live in tents during the construction of our permanent base hut. From what we knew about the ice conditions prevailing around Hope Bay, it seemed very unlikely that we should be able to count on living aboard the ship for more than a night or two at the most; probably we should be landed with our building materials and supplies in one quick operation and thereafter left to fend for ourselves.

Intense activity reigned on our islet; out of the open window of the hut could be heard at all hours the chattering of Farrington's radio key as he exchanged signals with Port Stanley and the other base on Deception Island; Chippy on the beach hammering spikes into the timbers of his prefabricated hut; and Davies and Blyth shovelling up the garbage which had accumulated around the base during the winter and transporting it over the rocks to the water's edge in a large wooden box mounted on two handles like a stretcher. Marr had on the previous day found a jellyfish nearly three feet in diameter swimming with gentle pulsations of its umbrella-like body in the clear water of the boat harbour. With infinite patience he guided it into a shallow pool with a boathook and then dumped it bodily into a barrel of formalin. Fortunately, it did not seem to be of the stinging kind. Now he was flensing the blubber off a sealskin hung over a timber frame on the foreshore. The greasy and malodorous layer, about two inches in thickness, parted cleanly downwards under each stroke of his knife. This was the sort of work which we all enjoyed, outside in the warm windless sunshine.

In early December the *William Scoresby* made another dash south from the Falklands, and this time got through to Deception Island without meeting any pack ice. There she picked up Flett and Matheson and continued her voyage southwards towards Port Lockroy. On the evening of December 7th she arrived at last, anchoring in the inlet on the west side of our islet. A boat was lowered, and nine members of the visiting party came ashore, among them the *Scoresby*'s captain, Lieutenant Marchesi of the Royal Navy, Flett and Matheson. With them they brought a canvas bag containing our long-awaited mail from civilization. After the boat had returned to the ship, leaving Flett and Matheson with us, we had a late supper with alcoholic libations in honour of our guests; then, after the tumult and the shouting had died, the watches of the night were disturbed only by the steady hiss of the pressure lamps and the rustling of paper from the cots where the letters from home were being carefully read and re-read.

Among others, the *William Scoresby* had brought down from Port Stanley the army dentist, who the following day set up his whole stock-in-trade, swivel-chair, foot-driven drill, etc., in the alcove next to the galley, and did whatever repairs were necessary to our teeth or dentures. Welcome supplies of fresh foodstuffs, such as mutton, vegetables and oranges, were also brought ashore, and a small live pig was liberated from a crate and soon made itself at home underneath the house.

The instructions remitted by the Governor of the Falkland Islands Dependencies through Marchesi envisaged our final evacuation and transfer, using the *William Scoresby*, the *Fitzroy*, and another newly chartered vessel, the *Eagle*, to Hope Bay in early January. But the prevailing ice that year prevented such an early start, and we remained, together with Flett, on our rocky islet until the first days of February, taking the fullest advantage of our short but interest-packed Antarctic summer.[8]

9

Deception

ON JANUARY 28TH, 1945, we received news that the *William Scoresby*, the *Fitzroy*, and the *Eagle* had arrived at Deception Island. Five days later the two first named steamed into Port Lockroy and dropped anchor side by side in the inner bay.[1] We had spent the last week in feverish preparation for our final departure, packing our equipment and personal belongings, drafting reports of the season's activities, and cleaning up the living quarters so as to leave everything 'shipshape and Bristol fashion', as Chippy put it, for the next occupants to take over.

The prospect of seeing fresh faces filled us with excitement and at the same time a certain amount of misgiving. Would the new members of the expedition who were to join us for the next season at Hope Bay prove as congenial as we found ourselves to be, or would they be of the ultra-serious, know-all, professional explorer type who would throw scorn on our empirical and unorthodox methods of camping and polar travel, and treat us as greenhorns and nincompoops in spite of what we had accomplished during the previous season? The tone adopted by some of the contributors to the *Polar Record* had indicated that this omniscient and self-satisfied attitude was rather prevalent among those who had previous practical experience in polar exploration, and so when Taylor, Chippy, Taff and I rowed out in the dinghy to the *Fitzroy*, we were all very much on our dignity and carrying a lightly-balanced chip upon our shoulder. Among the faces watching us from the rail above as we climbed the rope ladder, only that of Marr was familiar to us, and he greeted us with a new stanza:

Our metaplasm freely wipes
With softe paper
AND SOME CHIPS.

'Chaucer this time', I thought to myself with a chuckle, and felt somewhat reassured, as I climbed over the side, to find him in such good spirits, for this seemed to indicate that he at least had found the newcomers congenial.

We were introduced to the three new members of the Hope Bay task force, David James, Freddy Marshall and Victor Russell, and also to Alan Reece, the new officer-in-charge of the Deception base, Niddrie,[2] the meteorologist at Port Stanley, and Carr, the Falkland Islands customs officer. Our conversation with them was brief but cordial enough, but gave us no chance to really size them up. Later, in the mess-room, we met also 'Jock' Lockley, who was to take over at our Port Lockroy base, Colonel Momber, commander of the Falkland Islands military garrison, and Captain Roberts, manager of the Falkland Islands Trading Company.[3] Lockley had been on the zoological staff of the British Museum, and was an old acquaintance of mine; Colonel Momber had accompanied us out from England the previous year on the *Highland Monarch*, and Captain Roberts we had met a few times at Port Stanley when we were transferring our stores onto the *Fitzroy* before sailing south to establish our base.

On the morning of Sunday, February 4th, we took leave of Lockley, our old colleague Layther, and Frank White, who were to be our successors at Port Lockroy, and embarked in the *Fitzroy's* motorboat to go aboard. Our islet, as we receded from it over the glassy waters of the bay, stood out clear and peaceful against the imposing backdrop of the jagged Sierra du Fief, and I think we all felt a certain amount of regret at leaving the Antarctic home which we had built with our own hands and inhabited for very nearly a whole year. Early the following morning we steamed out of Port Lockroy en route for Deception.

Sixteen hours later, in dull cloudy weather, and in the teeth of a fairly strong wind, we passed in turn through the single narrow entrance passage into the inner bight of Deception Island, picturesquely named Neptunes Bellows, and saw another vessel, the *Eagle*, moored not far from the deserted whaling station. All three ships were soon lying at anchor side by side.

Deception Island seems to belong to another world when you set foot on it coming from other parts of Antarctica. Instead of the clean, hard, glistening granodiorite rocks, capped with virgin and unsullied snow, to which you have become accustomed, you find yourself among endless rolling plains of black cinders; these rise up to grotesquely sculptured red and yellow cliffs of soft and rapidly weathering agglomerate rock. The few snow patches visible are thin and soiled with volcanic dust. I thought I could detect a sulphurous smell in the air, and this proved later not to be wholly imaginary. The greater part of the eastern shoreline is occupied by the ruins of the derelict whaling station, at one time second only to that of South Georgia in importance, but for many years deserted and dilapidated, now that pelagic whaling from factory ships had made the upkeep of land-based stations unprofitable. The whole place reminded one of a huge untenanted gasworks.

In 1911, the Norwegian whaling settlement at Deception, called 'Community City', numbered 711 inhabitants, or 712 when one of the co-partners of the enterprise brought his wife there from Chile. The island is a sunken, almost extinct volcano, with only the rim of the crater, about ten miles in diameter, projecting up out of the sea. The crater basin itself, some five miles wide, is, as one might expect, of unfathomable depth in places, and is connected with the outside sea by the single narrow entrance, Neptunes Bellows, not much over 300 yards in width. No eruptions are known to have taken place since the island was first discovered, but numerous evidences of dormant volcanic activity are seen in the form of hot springs and fumaroles of steam and sulphuretted hydrogen. Being so completely surrounded by the high escarpments of the crater rim, it forms a perfect natural harbour, in which a whole fleet could safely lie at anchor.

A year or two before our arrival, the station had been visited by units of the Argentine navy, and the Argentine flag, of horizontal blue and white stripes, with a golden sun in the middle, had been painted on several of the large, gasometer-like oil tanks at one end of the settlement. Brass capsules containing formal documents of annexation had also been deposited at various points on the island, which is regarded in Argentina as an integral part of the southern dominions of the Argentine Republic.

We landed in the motorboat at the edge of the disintegrating platform of huge timbers where the carcasses of whales used to be drawn up by winches for flensing. All around us were masses of heavy derelict machinery, half sunken in the black cinders, together with iron boilers all eaten away with rust. The factory buildings, some of them of considerable size, were still standing, but many of the sheets of corrugated iron covering their frames had been whipped off by the winter gales, while others, attached only by one end, clanked and groaned mournfully in each gust of wind. Many of the smaller buildings were entirely roofless. The living quarters, not far away up the beach, were constructed of wood, and were now largely dilapidated, with hardly a whole pane of glass in any of the windows, but a central portion of the former dormitories, containing about three rooms, had been renovated by the members of our party the previous year to serve as their dwelling place.[4] The walls had originally been painted dark red, but the high winds, carrying powder snow and abrasive volcanic dust, had scoured away nearly all this coating, and polished the bare grey wood to a smooth shining surface resembling aluminium.

One of the smaller buildings into which I penetrated had apparently been used as a chemical laboratory. Metal retort-holders were still standing on some of the benches, and the floor was strewn with broken bottles, most of which had contained chemicals, but almost as many whisky, and chemical glassware. In a box on the floor nearby I found quantities of small, neatly packed tablets of a substance resembling a hard, reddish-brown jelly, each one stamped on one side with the letters 'S.B.C.' and with the representation of a baby's head on the other. They smelt like cod liver oil, and I hazarded the guess that they might have been some vitamin preparation made from seal or whale livers and intended for sale on the market. But one of the most mysterious and fascinating objects in the room was a large wooden crate bearing the stencilled address 'Mr Dan Jack Williams, Community City, Deception Island, Antarctica'; it was partly broken open, and to my astonishment I found it contained a kind of superlative mechanical juke box containing, behind the glass of its upper portion, an array of small model cats holding tiny musical instruments; apparently a cat-orchestra set in motion when the machine was made to play. Obviously this expensive and useless toy had never been unpacked from its crate, and I left the mysterious building shaking my head in puzzlement over this unusual and unexplainable eccentricity on the part of the former inhabitants.[5]

In the main room of the base, heated by a bogie stove with the smokestack taken out through a boarded-up window, I found Doc Back[6] with our old friend Charlie Smith, the latter as cheerful as ever but now hidden behind a long and straggling beard which gave him a rather saturnine appearance. He regaled us with hot tea, which we drank as Doc gave us a recital of the facts and rumours for which we were equally thirsting. It seemed that Marr, for health reasons, had decided to relinquish his leadership of the expedition and return to England. We were not altogether surprised to get confirmation of this rumour, for he had aged visibly during the past year at Port Lockroy, and had had a very tough spell of arduous service in inhospitable climates, such as Iceland, ever since the outbreak of the war. We would sympathize whole-heartedly with him in this decision.[7]

The second important item of information was that Andrew Taylor was now entrusted with the leadership of the party to be established at Hope Bay. I was very glad to hear this, because Taylor was one of my closest friends, and I knew that any mission entrusted to his direction would certainly be well organized and likely to meet with all possible success. We had all been rather afraid that one of our 'new buggers' might be appointed to a post of leadership over our heads. But nobody would be able to tell Taylor how to do his job, with all the experience of Arctic travel which he had had in the northlands of Canada. Unfortunately, Mr Sheppard,[8] the captain of the *Eagle* and former harbourmaster of St John's, Newfoundland, was suffering from the effects of some broken ribs which he had sustained the previous week, when he had been thrown off the bridge during a gale on the voyage between the Falklands and Deception. He insisted that he would be able to take the *Eagle* into Hope Bay on schedule, but the doctor was somewhat doubtful of the wisdom of letting him attempt this in his present condition.

As we left the settlement to continue our tour of inspection among the ruined buildings, the air was suddenly rent by a spasm of long drawn out, wolf-like howls, and on rounding the large factory building to the west of the dormitory we came face to face with the dogs which had been brought out from Labrador to serve us on our sledging trips during the coming season. They were a scruffy and ill-favoured lot, and we did not like the look of them one bit. We half expected them to rush at us, but they made no attempt to do so; their slanting mongoloid eyes regarded us without any hostile expression. At the time we did not realize that they were far from being at the top of their form, having suffered great hardships of hot weather and close confinement on the long journey down through the tropics, and even now they were not feeling very much at home lying on dirty black cinders. Their natural environment is snow, and only on that can they really be said to thrive.

On our way back to the motorboat, we passed two members of the *Fitzroy*'s crew, carrying cans of red paint and large brushes, making their way towards the oil tanks where the Argentine flag had been painted. I knew what they had been detailed to do, and I hoped that they would do it quietly and expeditiously, without unseemly jest. Not that I was interested in the matter of formal sovereignty one way or the other, and had more than once openly jeered at this business of Antarctic claims and national flagwaggery, but . . . well, a flag is an emblem that one grows up with and which has certain associations, and it should be treated with becoming reverence whether it happens to be one's own or somebody else's. I was carrying with me a little book, the cover torn off and the pages stuck together with damp, which I had found on the floor of one of the deserted sections of the dormitories. It was in Spanish and called *Recuerdos de Provincia*,[9] by Domingo Faustino Sarmiento who, in my ignorance, I did not know at the time had been one of the most famous and enlightened presidents of the Argentine Republic.[10] Any kind of reading matter is a great acquisition in the polar regions, and I carried away my damp little trophy, which had obviously been left by the Argentines during their visit, with great expectations of perfecting my Spanish during the coming season.

That afternoon Taylor, Flett, Ashton, Back and I made up a shore party to forage for usable lumber, nails, bolts, etc. which might be serviceable to us at our new base. As we went from one derelict building to the other, hauling large baulks of lumber and piles of boards down to the beach, it commenced to rain steadily, and we quite enjoyed the remarkable sensation of getting wet to the skin; we had almost forgotten what rain looked and felt like.

I used up the remaining half-hour of daylight in walking along the cinder beach to the nearest rock outcrop, picking up a few mosses and lichens, and noticing a small patch of civilized grass, a species of crabgrass,[11] which had taken root in one place by the doorway of an outside privy, obviously introduced from seeds carried probably in packing materials. It seemed to be thriving quite well and had even produced a few immature flowering spikes. Altogether this place, with its ghost town of buildings and oil tanks, its black snow-free slopes, its rain, and its grass, did not make the impression of being part of the Antarctic at all. It had all the dreariness of industrial civilization, and I did not envy Flett, Charlie Smith and Layther, who had had to spend the greater part of a year there. However, on questioning Charlie concerning this an hour later, as I sat with him in his galley sharing his repast of strong tea and cold mutton, I found that the depressing atmosphere of the place had not affected him in the least, as he passed nearly all his time within the four walls of his galley and the mess room, leaving the house only to fetch ice or water and to dump garbage on the shore; only once had he been even as far as Neptunes Bellows at the other end of the beach.[12]

Having eaten, and dried my clothes somewhat, I returned to the ships with a working party from the *Fitzroy* which had been landing coal from a scow towed behind the motorboat. On boarding the *Scoresby*, I heard voices coming through the port of the wardroom, and went down the companionway to see who was there. Marr, Marchesi and Fleck, the first mate, were sitting at the head of the table with a bottle of gin before them. Marr invited me to join them, and poured me out a glass, which I accepted gratefully, for I was beginning to get shivery in my wet clothing. As I could see that they were in the midst of a confabulation, probably of a private nature, I rose and took my leave after having told Marr of my regret that he was leaving us. When I was halfway up the companionway, Marchesi called after me: 'Oh, Lamb, all the chaps are coming over for a little drink on the *Fitzroy* at twenty hours; I want you to meet the OICS and the CUSCI.' A lot of Marchesi's conversation was unintelligible to me because it was so freely compounded of those initial-words of which such a spate had sprung up during the war years: NOIC, NAAFI, PUS, WAAF, and the like. I had found out that NOIC stood for Naval Officer in Charge; but CUSCI was quite new to me, and I did not like to betray my ignorance by asking for its meaning.[13]

The *Eagle* was moored directly alongside, and I crossed over on the two planks between the neighbouring bulwarks. She was a wooden ship, a sealer from Newfoundland. The rain was running over the decks, carrying with it little streams of coal dust. At first I thought the ship was completely deserted, but up forward I heard some footsteps and a series of heavy bumps, and went up to investigate. The sounds were coming, not from the ship itself, but from a scow and a barge moored alongside. In the light of an electric lamp mounted on the handrail and shining through the drizzle I saw a solitary figure lifting bags of coal and transferring them to the barge over a gangplank extended between them. I climbed down the rope ladder and joined him.

'Are you all alone here?'

He surveyed me for a moment, but vouchsafed no answer. He was quite a young lad, about eighteen years old, very robustly built; his features very coarse and animal-like, stupid but not vicious (for viciousness is peculiar to fully human countenances). His strong jaws moved incessantly as he chewed on a wad of tobacco, which showed up now and then between his teeth as he masticated, and the brown saliva ran down his chin. I had never before seen such a youngster, a mere boy, chewing tobacco, and was intrigued to observe the deft way in which he expectorated the juice in explosive squirts all around him. Seeing that he was not inclined to enter into conversation, I set to work with him, and for some time we heaved the 200-pound sacks of coal in silence, crossing and re-crossing the gangplank. I was glad of the exercise, which warmed me up and began to dry my clothing, in spite of a fine drizzling rain which was continuously descending. After ten minutes or so I ventured to reopen the conversation.

'Are you from the Falklands?'

'Falklands be *drydocked*; come from Twillingate.[14] Come all the *jutting* way down from St John's, see? Captain Sheppard he's a *talking* fine skipper, by Judas. Do your sodden work right, he don't mind ye, give ye a tot of rum afterwards. So long's ye do your bleeding work, that's all right.'[15]

Our conversation was interrupted by a well-modulated voice from above addressing me, and I looked up to see Lieutenant David James coming down the rope ladder into the barge to join us. 'We're shifting this coal onto the barge for tomorrow morning,' I explained to him, and without a word he shouldered a bag and commenced to work with the Newfoundlander and myself. Twenty minutes later our combined efforts had accomplished the task, and we rested awhile standing together in the coal dust in the centre of the empty scow.

After a few minutes of conversation, James and I took leave of the boy from Newfoundland, and returned to the *Fitzroy*, for it was time to go aboard to have that little drink and be presented to OICS and the CUSCI, and other important personages from the Governor's entourage in Port Stanley. Quite a sound of revelry broke forth as we opened the door of the *Fitzroy*'s saloon and found ourselves, blinking in the electric lights, surrounded by distinguished company, all of whom seemed to be having a Good Time. Marr and Marchesi took us in tow, gave us each a glass, and motioned us towards the baize-covered table which was adorned with an imposing array of bottles.

Everybody was talking at once; the din of voices was quite deafening. Marchesi, nearest to me on the other side of the table, was conversing with Niddrie and Marr. I could hear only scraps of what he was saying: 'NOIC wanted us to go over to Col Sec's, and we met MOPS on the way ... Quite a little party that evening.' I poured myself a drink, and gulped down about half of it. In this august assemblage I was feeling distinctly inferior and embarrassed; my hands and face were black with coal dust, and my wet clothes were sticking to my back. Marr came over to me after a few minutes, and steered me over to join Captain Roberts and the CUSCI, who had expressed a desire to meet me. I shook hands with Captain Roberts, but my eyes were riveted on the CUSCI (I never learned his name, nor the transliteration of his title). He overwhelmed me with his magnificence.

The first thing I saw was a splendiferous camera, glittering with chromium, its wide unwinking bluish eye surrounded by a complicated array of flanges bearing concentric numbers, some in black, some in red, suspended in its shiny leather case by a strap and resting on an ample stomach; then I saw a large, flushed and jovial face fringed by the white fur trimming of a spotlessly clean gabardine parka or *anorak*, around the neck of which were hanging, dangling on a cord, two huge mitts of dazzling white sheepskin. I had never seen such elegant polar equipment; the CUSCI looked as if he could walk to the South Pole and back without the slightest difficulty. He shook hands with me most cordially, and looked me up and down with obvious glee as if he were examining some rare and curious specimen; the third eye on his stomach doing its best to stare me out of countenance. His face fairly glistened with goodwill and perspiration. We entered into a lively conversation, during which it transpired that he was an enthusiastic amateur botanist, and had spent a large amount of his time in the Falklands making a collection of the indigenous plants; he wanted to hear from me all about the plant life in those parts of the Antarctic which I had visited. He much regretted, he told me, that the pressure of his duties in Port Stanley did not permit him to join us for a season at Hope Bay, but he hoped during these few days to go ashore at several places from the *Fitzroy* and see everything for himself. The fur-lined parka and sheepskin mitts he had had sent down by air from the Hudson's Bay Company in Canada, made to measure, especially for this occasion. The outfit certainly looked most imposing, but I could not help wondering whether I should not have felt it a trifle too hot and heavy most of the time, especially for drinking cocktails in the saloon of the *Fitzroy*.[16]

Hope Bay Revisited

ON THE MORNING OF Sunday, February 11th, 1945, we steamed out through Neptunes Bellows on board the *Eagle*, with Hope Bay for our destination. At the entrance, skirting the steep red cliffs of rusty scoria washed by the everlasting swell of the open sea, we once again entered the wide, dazzling, blue and white world of Antarctica, and our eyes, accustomed during the last few days to the dark panorama of black cinders and slaggy hills closing us in on all sides, blinked and watered in the clean harsh glare of the sunshine reflected from ice, sea and sky.

Every inch of deck space was crammed with stores and building materials, and the dogs, fastened to crates and stanchions everywhere by short lengths of rope, sniffed the freshening air with relish and set up a concert of wolf-like howling. The members of the crew clambered over the piles of boxes and sacks of coal in the discharge of their duties, and up on the bridge I could see the head and shoulders of Captain Sheppard over the canvas windshield as he scanned the horizon for pack ice and directed the helmsman on his course. Undoubtedly, the ship was greatly overloaded, and I did not like to think of the possibility of our running into foul weather with our top-heavy and not very well secured deck cargo.

Marr had already left on the *Scoresby* for the Falklands and home two days ago, and our Hope Bay party, consisting of Ashton, Back, Berry, Blyth, Davies, Donnachie (the new radio operator), Flett, James, Marshall, Matheson, Russell, and myself, was now under the leadership of Andrew Taylor. Farrington, who had been with us at

Port Lockroy, also accompanied us to help Donnachie in the task of establishing the new radio station, after which he would return to Deception for the coming season.[1]

Fortunately the weather remained fair, and at eight o'clock that evening we were favoured with one of those remarkable sunsets which fascinate all travellers in the polar regions, the western half of the sky flaming blood-red, with lambent wisps of rose-pink cirrus cloud radiating like luminous tentacles across the darkening firmament. The conical outline of Astrolabe Island, off the northern coast of the Palmer Peninsula, was sharply silhouetted against the horizon about twenty miles distant on our starboard side.

After darkness had fallen, Taylor called me into the wardroom, where he had spent the greater part of the day working out the details of organization in connection with our landing and the establishment of the new base. From a leather case bulging with notebooks and papers he took a bound volume and tossed it onto the table. It landed with a satisfying thump, for it contained nearly 600 printed pages. I picked it up and examined the title page: *Antarctica or Two Years amongst the Ice of the South Pole*, by Otto Nordenskjöld and Gunnar Andersson, published in the year 1905. It was the account of the Swedish South Polar Expedition of 1901–1903, which, under the leadership of the first-named author, had spent two seasons on Snow Hill Island on the west side of the Weddell Sea, to the south-east of Hope Bay.[2]

'Nordenskjöld landed at Snow Hill on the 12th of February 1902, from their ship the *Antarctic*, and built their base hut there,' Taylor explained to me. 'Six of them, Nordenskjöld, Ekelöf, Åkerlundh, Bodman, Jonassen, and Sobral, stayed there over the winter of 1902 while the *Antarctic* returned to Ushuaia in the Magellan Straits. They had made arrangements for the ship to return and pick them up the following spring and take them back to civilization. We believe that their house at Snow Hill is still standing, and one of our main objectives on our first sledging trip will be to visit it and report on its condition. But there are some interesting historical associations at Hope Bay too, and that's what I want to talk to you about.

'You see, the *Antarctic*, according to schedule, started south from Ushuaia in November of 1902, but was stopped by thick pack ice a little to the south-east of Hope Bay, a long way off from the Snow Hill base. Captain Larsen, in command of the ship, decided to try to get farther south by skirting the pack ice farther east in the Weddell Sea, but before doing this he set ashore three members of the expedition, Andersson, Duse, and Grunden, at Hope Bay with a tent, a sledge, and provisions for about three weeks. The idea was that they should try to reach Snow Hill on foot over the tip of the Palmer Peninsula and the sea ice to the south. It was arranged that the *Antarctic* should call back at Hope Bay on a certain date a couple of weeks later to pick them up, together with Nordenskjöld and the others from Snow Hill if they had been able to make it back there by the overland route. So Duse, Andersson and Grunden landed with their tent and sledge at Hope Bay, and next day, when the ship had left them, they started off south over the top of the peninsula, dragging their sledge with their three weeks' provisions behind them.

'Well, when they got down the other side, they found to their surprise that the way south to Snow Hill was barred by open water. It seemed as if the pack ice was all concentrated farther to the north, forming a barrier. So they turned around and pulled back to Hope Bay, put up their tent, and settled down to wait for two weeks for the return of the *Antarctic*, which they hoped would have been able to skirt the pack farther east and take Nordenskjöld and company off Snow Hill.

'That's where things began to go wrong. In January of 1903 the *Antarctic* got a little too involved in the pack ice out in the Weddell Sea, and was crushed and finally sank. Captain Larsen and everybody else on the ship piled all the stores they could into the ship's scow and started to haul it on wooden runners over the sea ice, making for the nearest land, which happened to be Paulet Island, about twenty-five miles away.' Taylor pointed to the Admiralty chart pinned up on the bulkhead. I could see Paulet Island marked as a tiny spot to the south-east of Dundee Island, north-east of Hope Bay, and a long way north from Snow Hill.

'They made Paulet Island all right and built a sort of big stone igloo to live in over the winter. There's a picture of it here.' He thumbed through the book and found the illustration to show me. The photograph was not very clear, but showed a squat structure built of flat stones at the bottom of a snow slope beside a penguin rookery, with two small boarded-up windows on the side towards the camera. It looked desolate enough. 'They spent the winter there, living on seals and penguins. But it's the three guys marooned at Hope Bay that we're immediately concerned with. You can imagine their feelings when two weeks, three weeks, four weeks passed by without any sign of the ship, their tent getting worn out by the gales and their provisions running out, and the winter coming on at that. They made the best of it, and built a stone hut round their tent near the shore at Hope Bay; the site's marked on this map they give here. You can read for yourself what they say about it.'

I read: 'We soon came to a perfect agreement respecting the plan of work for the building of a winter-hut. Solid walls of blocks of stone should be built up to the full height of a man, the frame of the roof was to be made of the sledge and some poles and pieces of plank we had brought on shore with us, and over this we intended to spread the old tarpaulin, hitherto used to shelter the provision-depot. Then we meant to raise the big tent inside this hut, after flattening the top (of the tent) and lessening the size of the floor so that in shape the whole would be something like a cube. This arrangement would give us a two-fold shelter against cold and storm.

'As the site of the stone-hut, we chose the level and comparatively dry piece of ground near the large tent, which was to remain standing to serve as a provisional dwelling until we could move into the hut. Fortunately there were plenty of blocks of stone and large stone slabs very suitable for our purpose, lying about the camping-ground.

'On the 11th of February we began the work by bearing down several stones and, two days later, Grunden made a kind of hand-barrow of a couple of tent poles and some pieces of plank, and we took it in turns, by pairs, to carry on this the blocks of stone which the third man broke loose from the somewhat frozen earth. On the 17th, we laid all the foundations of the walls, which were considerably more than a yard thick near the ground, and which afterwards daily rose slowly in height; the holes and crannies being filled with masses of fine gravel from the shore.' Facing the next page was a photograph of the stone hut nearing completion; two men were standing outside the square structure, which was already powdered with frost and snow; a barrel and two packing cases were lying near the entrance. A group of the ubiquitous white paddies could be seen scavenging in the foreground. I thought of the picture resting undeveloped in their camera all that long winter, probably in the foot of a sleeping bag inside that dark and narrow stone cell.

'First thing tomorrow when we land, Mack, I want you to go over to that site with your plate camera, before anybody else gets there, and examine what remains of the hut, photographing it from all sides, and prepare a report on its state of preservation and on everything you may find there. As far as we know, nobody has visited the place since they left it in 1903, forty-two years ago. This will be one of the most interesting historical relics of polar exploration.'

'What happened eventually to them?' I replied. 'As I understand it, there were at that time three separate parties stranded in different places, each without any knowledge of the others' fate; Nordenskjöld and his party at Snow Hill, Andersson, Duse and Grunden marooned at Hope Bay, and Captain Larsen and the others on Paulet Island, and their ship lost in the ice. Looks like a miracle would have to happen to get them all safely together again.'

'Well, it wasn't far off a miracle, the way things happened. Andersson and the other two made a second start south on foot from Hope Bay in September of 1903, as soon as the worst of the winter was over; this time they had clear going over solid sea ice. When they got about half way, opposite Vega Island, they met up by purest accident with Nordenskjöld and some of the others from Snow Hill, who happened to be out on a sledge trip at that time. At first they mistook each other for penguins in the distance. They gave the name "Cape Well-Met" to this point on Vega Island where they ran into each other. So they joined forces and all went back together to the house at Snow Hill.

'About a month later, Captain Larsen and five others set out from Paulet Island rowing in their open boat, and made first for Hope Bay, to see what had happened to Andersson, Duse and Grunden. There they found the deserted stone hut with a note telling them that the occupants had spent the winter there and had left for Snow Hill a second time on September 29th. So Larsen and the boat party started rowing south towards Snow Hill. Just about this time, the Argentine Government, not having heard anything about the Swedish Expedition, now a year overdue, sent down a naval vessel, the *Uruguay*, under Commodore Julián Irízar, to investigate. Irízar made a spectacular voyage south, cleverly dodging and skirting the pack ice, and hove to on November 8th at the edge of the ice only a few miles away from the house at Snow Hill. I bet Nordenskjöld and the boys were glad to see him when he came knocking at their door. The only thing that had them kind of worried was what might have happened to the *Antarctic* and those on board her. But they didn't have to worry long, because that very same evening Larsen and the five others from Paulet Island landed at the ice edge about twelve miles away, and walked the remaining distance to Snow Hill, arriving at ten o'clock that night. Nordenskjöld and company sure had some surprises that day!

'Every member of the expedition finally got back to Sweden safely, apart from one, Wennersgaard, who died during the winter on Paulet Island.[3] Considering the hazards confronting them,

I think the Swedish Expedition must be one of the luckiest ones in the whole history of polar exploration. It could so easily have turned out the way it did with Franklin in the Northwest Territories.'

*

Flett appeared in the doorway. 'Andy, Mack, come and have a look at this.' We followed him up on deck. A small group was assembled on the main deck, standing and sitting on crates and timbers, intently observing something that was going on there in the harsh light of two electric lamps mounted on the bridge rail. As we joined the outside of the group, I looked down and saw that I was standing in a stream of blood that was running along the deck. 'Christ, an accident!' I said to myself, and elbowed my way frenziedly through the crush. But it was only the bosun of the *Eagle*, Tom Carroll, known to all as 'Skipper Tom', giving a demonstration of how they flay a seal in Newfoundland. Everybody had a different estimate of his age, the average being around ninety years, and the fact that he had been with Peary on his North Pole expedition of 1908–1909 certainly proved that he must at least be well up in years, although he was as active and agile as a man of thirty, and a lot more hard-bitten. Only his toothless mouth, set in a firm indented line as he concentrated on his task, gave him the appearance of old age; his body was upright and wiry. Oblivious of the increasing cold, he worked on the seal carcass with bare hands, laying it open with a razor-sharp flensing blade, and his movements had the economy and precision of a professional surgeon. The skin, free from blubber, seemed to fall away like a shed overcoat on all sides, right down to the tips of the flippers, and the whole operation was completed within the space of four or five minutes. I remembered how Marr and I had spent hours mangling a seal carcass on the beach at Port Lockroy, getting the oily blubber all over ourselves and ending up finally with a skin in several pieces that looked as if it had been blasted with a charge of buckshot.[4]

Before retiring for the night, I looked over my photographic equipment and packed it in a rucksack, together with a steel measuring tape, a compass, a notebook and pencils, in readiness for tomorrow morning's investigations. That night we slept two to a bunk on the *Eagle*, which had probably never before carried such a crowded complement of passengers and crew. A great deal of noise and shouting came from the foc'sle until a late hour, and I began to wonder whether a mutiny was under way, until I picked out the faint strains of an accordion among the general uproar, and realized that this was the normal conversational tone of the *Eagle*'s crew during the off-watch hours.

As soon as it got light the following morning, I went up onto the bridge, determined not to miss any interesting or photogenic happenings on our entry into Hope Bay, and also with the intention of studying the formation of the coastline as it appeared from some miles out to sea. The weather was clear and very bright, with a strong cutting south-east wind. All around us, and right up to the rocky coast, the sea was open, with only small and widely scattered bergs and floes. Spray was flung high over those which we passed, and as we entered the bay the wind seemed to increase in force. By 6.30 a.m. we were in the bay, about half-a-mile off land, and cruising around in circles until the wind should moderate. Taylor took advantage of this delay to call together all members of the expedition for consultation, reading out to us the text of all signals sent off to Port Stanley concerning our operations (part of his success as a leader was due to the fact that he kept no secrets from the rest of us), and formulating by free discussion an organized plan for the landing and the selection of a suitable building site. Each of us was allotted a certain duty, and several parties of two men each were detailed to proceed to certain locations indicated on the map in Nordenskjöld's book and come back with a report on any suitable sites found.

In due course, towards the middle of the forenoon, the wind abated, and Doc Back, Tom Berry, Vic Russell and I rowed ashore in one of the dinghies. The others landed soon afterwards. The ship's siren was to be the signal for our return to a prearranged spot on the shore. I had with me a tracing which I had made from Nordenskjöld's map the night before, showing the location of the stone hut, and as soon as we landed I set out, guided by my compass, over the undulating stony terrain in the direction indicated.

As far as I could make out from the map, the hut should be about a mile away in a straight line from the spot where we had landed. I counted my steps, and after about half-an-hour's walking judged that I should be immediately in its vicinity. I was now on top of a rocky knoll with an unobstructed view of the stony slopes right down to the water's edge, but I could see no sign of the hut. More than once I turned my footsteps towards what looked like a square stone structure, only to find as I drew nearer that it was merely a large cubical block of rock. Suddenly I saw it, only a hundred yards away, but not in the direction in which I had expected to find it. I broke into a run, with feelings like those the archaeologists must have had when they first discovered the tomb of Tutankhamun.

The hut was standing there in a wonderfully good state of preservation, and looked almost exactly the same as in the photograph of forty-two years ago which Taylor and I had studied the previous evening. The walls, about six feet high and between two and three feet in thickness, enclosed a living space about twelve feet square, from which, through the middle of the north wall, led a small passageway ending in a doorway on its left. The structure was now roofless, as it had originally been covered over by the sledge and tarpaulin, which of course had been taken with them by Andersson, Duse and Grunden when they left on their final journey to Snow Hill. In the centre of the west wall there was a small window opening, with a bottomless wooden box let in between the stones as a frame. The threshold was formed by another box, partly imbedded in the penguin muck surrounding the hut. Several barrel staves and hoops lay around outside, and also a round pole about nine feet long. The floor of the entrance and passageway was paved with a few wooden planks and barrel staves, and the interior was half full of melting ice and snow, covered with penguin feathers and excrement. Dried-up bunches of seaweed were still to be seen in the interstices between the stones of the walls, where they had been stuffed by the occupants to keep out the drifting snow. About thirty yards to the north-west of the hut, some wooden planks were wedged in the form of a St Andrew's cross on top of a small knoll of rock, presumably as a marker to indicate the position of the hut to ships entering the bay.

I took photographs from all sides, and then proceeded to make a closer examination of the interior, jotting down in my notebook all measurements and information on the exact location of any objects before disturbing them. Under the snow I found masses of clotted and decaying penguin feathers, from which I surmised that the occupants had probably laid down numbers of penguin skins on the floor to form an insulating layer. Among these, several interesting relics came to light – a leather shoe, pieces of string, remains of tin cans, a crowbar, a piece of soot-blackened woollen cloth, and a round can filled with a black substance smelling strongly of blubber, obviously one of the 'smoker' stoves mentioned by Andersson as the means by which they heated and lighted the hut and cooked their meals of seal meat and penguin soup. A few yards away from the hut I discovered, barely projecting from the frozen ground, several iron tent pins in their original position about four yards apart, marking the site where the tent had been erected before and during the building of the stone hut.

I sat down on the ice and penguin filth inside the hut and fell to imagining the life of the three polar Crusoes during that dark and lonely winter of 1903. I tried to put myself in their place and think what their daily conversations must have been about, their hopes and fears concerning the fate of the *Antarctic*, and their chances of getting through to Nordenskjöld at Snow Hill on their second attempt. Many a time they must have thought that these four rude stone walls would form their tomb. But they were destined to be spared, and the aura surrounding the place was a happy one.

My reverie was shattered by a thrice-repeated blast of the *Eagle*'s siren, and I started to make my way back to the appointed meeting place to find out what luck the others had had in their selection of a building site.

The Birth of Base 'D'

ANDREW TAYLOR WALKED back and forth a few times, his eyes fixed now on the ground, now on the distant panorama of the rocky slopes around us; once or twice he pushed over a stone with his foot, and examined the underlying subsoil. Finally he raised the steel-pointed surveying staff which he carried and plunged it upright in the ground like a spear. 'Build it here,' he said to Chippy.

We all admitted to ourselves that, insofar as human foresight and intelligence can guide one, his choice of a building site for the future hut and meteorological station of Base 'D' was an excellent one. The level bed of morainic stones and gravel on which we were standing was only a hundred yards from the shore (here formed by a thick ice-foot) and was about twenty-five feet above the highest water-mark. It was well drained and sufficiently extensive to accommodate all the buildings which we proposed to erect, and was well removed from the nearest penguin colony, and lastly, it was at this time provided with a supply of clean fresh water in the form of a small stream running through a channel in the snow patch beside us and fed from the melting of the unsullied ice slope above.

Early next morning the first load was landed from the large flat-bottomed scow, which was towed ashore by the *Eagle*'s motorboat and run up on the gravel beach below the ice foot. We laid a number of stout planks across, and commenced to unload and carry the cargo up the slope to the building site. This load consisted chiefly of the timbers and corrugated iron sheets for the 'tin galley' which Chippy Ashton had previously prefabricated at Port Lockroy, and two hours later the framework of the walls had been erected. By this time the tide had ebbed about five feet, and we would have to wait another three or four hours until it again rose sufficiently to allow a second scow-load to be landed at the ice foot. Some of the *Eagle*'s crew took advantage of this delay to embark on a seal-hunt in the motorboat; they cruised all around the bay, landed on several icebergs stranded in the shallows near the entrance, and every now and then a sharp report rang out in the distance as they added a further Weddell or sea-leopard to their collection. After a while, the motorboat came in sight around the point, making for the shore. It was moving very slowly, although the engine was churning and labouring at full throttle. I saw, spread out in the wake of the propeller, half-a-dozen dark glistening blobs barely emergent above the surface of the water, the heads of the slaughtered pinnipeds each made fast by a hangman's noose to the stern of the boat. The dogs, which had been pegged out along the ice foot nearby, set up a frenzied yelling at the sight of the approaching feast, and turned somersaults at the ends of their chains.

Tom Berry had set up two iron bogie stoves among the rocks nearby, and soon his welcome cry of 'Come and *barking* get it!' summoned us to line up and receive our rations of hot beef stew, ship's biscuit, cheese and tea. Shortly afterwards the second scow-load came ashore, and we continued on the construction of the tin galley until nightfall, by which time the whole framework, right up to the rooftree was erected, the door and both windows were in place, and the structure was standing ready to receive its coat of corrugated iron sheeting.

That was February 13th.[1] The following day we completed work on the tin galley, which was a square structure eighteen by twelve feet with a low-pitched roof supported at the peak from the inside by several pillars of 'four-be-two'. It was admittedly only a temporary dwelling place, intended to house us during the time that we were working on the main building, and had been put up as a rush job without any great regard for strength or durability; very little concrete had been poured below the floor joists and the base of the walls, and the corrugated iron sheets had been nailed to the wooden frame with ordinary wire nails, instead of the spirally twisted screw-nails commonly used for this purpose. (These nails rotate like a screw as you hammer them into the wood, and cannot be extracted by any force on earth unless they are simultaneously turned in the counter direction). We carried in six double-tier iron bedsteads taken from the derelict hospital building at Deception and, in the small remaining space at one end of the hut, fixed up a small galley stove for Tom Berry to cook on.

Stores were now arriving not only in the big scow, but also in the *Eagle*'s dinghy and motorboat, and the crew, to whom the landing operation was solely entrusted, worked like galley slaves. Soon a number of very respectable piles had grown up on the rock slopes around our settlement, in places indicated by boards stuck upright between the stones and marked 'House lumber', 'Nissen hut parts', 'Food stores', 'Hardware', etc. The bags of coal were dumped along the shoreline, and formed a sort of castellated rampart on top of the ice foot.

That night, in order to relieve the congestion on board the *Eagle*, Berry, Blyth, Flett, Back and myself unrolled our sleeping bags on the double-decker bedsteads in the tin galley and made it our head-quarters. I climbed up into my upper berth, using Doc's prostrate form in lieu of a stepladder, and eased my way into my bag. Every bone in my body was aching from the unaccustomed toil of carrying heavy crates and boxes all day long up from the waterfront. The low tin roof was exactly ten inches above me, and the underside of the rafter directly above my head was ornamented with the pointed ends of the nails which had been driven through from outside to attach the corrugated iron sheets. Some of the nails had missed the beams entirely. I dropped off to sleep hoping that nothing would wake me up with a start.

At noon next day we put on a special luncheon party in the tin galley in honour of Captain Sheppard, whom we seated in our only folding chair at the head of the table. The rest of us drew up empty boxes and bedrolls, and we enjoyed a two-course banquet including fresh bread baked by Berry in the little oven the previous evening. This was the first opportunity which I had had of meeting Captain Sheppard at close quarters. From what I knew of the *Eagle*'s crew, I had assumed that he would prove to be about as tough as one could possibly imagine a ship's captain to be, and so my astonishment was considerable on finding that, on the contrary, he was amiable to a degree, soft-spoken, and possessed of charming manners. His orders to his crew were given quietly, without profanity, but with unmistakable authority, and each and every one obeyed him instantly with the deference of well-trained manservants. However, he made no attempt to restrain their conduct in any way during their off-duty hours. I asked him about the injury which he had sustained two weeks previously, and he assured me that the two broken ribs had more or less healed up and now caused him no inconvenience, but at times I could observe him give an almost imperceptible wince and raise one shoulder as if to seek relief from a painful sensation in his chest and back.

Aided by the favourable weather, which had remained relatively calm and sunny, we got all the remaining stores landed off the *Eagle* by the end of February, and Ashton, with several helpers, finished the concrete work and the foundation piers of the permanent hut, laid the joists, and put down the greater part of the flooring. Flett, James and I were entrusted with the erection of the Nissen hut to house our perishable stores, and we would have made good progress on it if a sudden gust of wind had not caught the structure at a critical moment, just when one of the ends had been brought up into position; the whole framework of semi-circular steel girders collapsed end-on without warning, flat to the ground, the ribs shearing the bolts by which they were attached to the concrete foundations. We had to start all over again, clearing away the tangled mess of metal and cementing in new foundation bolts.

The *Eagle* was due to make another round trip to Deception on March 1st to bring over a second load of stores for our base. On the evening of the last day of February, all the land-based members of the expedition transferred to the tin galley, which could barely hold the thirteen of us, and we lay and sat on our iron cots indulging in desultory conversation after a hard day's work. That day had seen the first heavy snowfall of the season, and the foundations of the permanent house and the piles of stores surrounding it were covered with a six-inch layer of light powdery snow.

Jock Matheson, for the last two evenings, had been sitting on the foot of his cot in the far corner of the hut sewing yards of canvas with waxed twine and a sailmaker's 'palm'. At first I thought he was making a sail for our dinghy, but as the work progressed I could see it was taking on an altogether different, rectangular, sheath-like form. I asked him what it was, and he replied in his slow musical Gaelic voice, looking up at me quizzically from a corner of one of his blue eyes: 'It's lucky we have been so far, but there's no saying what will be happening to one of us soon. Fifteen pounds of stones in the foot of it, and the Union Jack draped over it, and it's splash, wheesh, bubble and sink, and you're way down into the depths, bound for your eternal rest.'

Jock was rather addicted to such grim and deliberate jokes. Actually, he was making a canvas sledge-cover which could also be used to convert the sledge into a boat; an excellent idea for spring travelling over the sea ice, when the chances of becoming suddenly marooned on a drifting ice pan are quite considerable. Next morning he put the finishing touches to it, lashed it onto one of the twelve-foot sledges, and launched it off the ice foot below the hut. We congregated on the shore to watch him put it to the practical test, as he climbed carefully into it and pushed it offshore with a single paddle. 'You've forgotten the fifteen pounds of stones and the Union

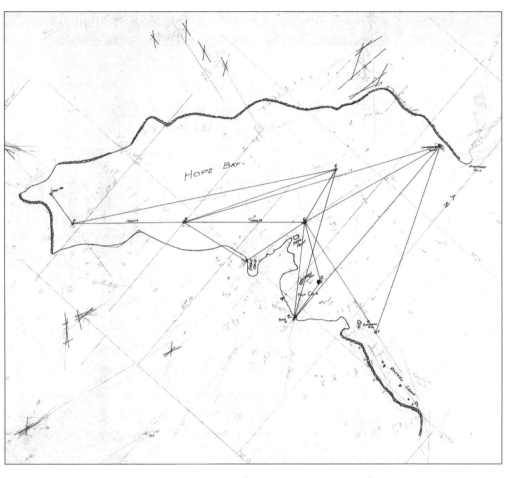

Base 'D', Hope Bay (original scale: 1:10,000).

Jack,' I called after him. 'Hold on a moment, Jock, while I nip back to the hut and get the Burial Service for you.' But he navigated the frail craft in perfect safety out to a distance of about fifty yards from the shore, and brought it in again triumphantly farther down the beach.[2]

Two days previously, during an hour's break from housebuilding duties, I had been studying the lichen vegetation on the large rocks on the hillside about half a mile above our base. One patch of a crustaceous lichen growing on the smooth vertical face of a prominent cubical block attracted my attention by its excellent development, with numerous small black fruiting bodies (apothecia).

The idea occurred to me that it would be interesting to study the seasonal variation in its spore-production by removing these bodies at intervals throughout the coming winter and preserving them in formalin for subsequent microscopical examination. With this end in view, and in order to mark the exact patch under investigation, I painted a red arrow on the face of the rock pointing directly towards it. In doing so, I little realized that I was precipitating a first-class Antarctic mystery.

The following Thursday at dinner time, Flett returned from a geological collecting trip in a state of suppressed but obvious excitement. Up near the foot of Mount Flora, he told us, he had found a red arrow painted on a large rock. He had immediately deduced that it must be a sign left by the Swedish expedition over forty years ago to mark the position of some important cache, depot or document. Out of malice I kept my mouth shut, and let him expound at length a variety of theories to account for his discovery. That evening he spent several hours carefully reading Nordenskjöld's *Antarctica* in the hope of finding some reference to Red Arrow Rock. Early next morning he left for the site carrying a theodolite with tripod and a steel measuring tape, in order to take exact bearings on the direction in which the arrow was pointing. After some hours of painstaking observations on the exposed hillside, he came to the conclusion that the arrow was pointing directly to a large cubical block of stone about fifty yards away, and he was convinced that beneath this stone there must be deposited something, perhaps documents of the greatest historical and even political significance. 'For all we know,' he said, 'the Swedish expedition may have claimed this territory on behalf of the Swedish or Argentine governments, and deposited documents of formal annexation under the rock marked by the Red Arrow.' I opened my mouth with the intention of telling him the truth before the affair grew to uncomfortable proportions, but it had already gone so far that I did not know how I could break the news to him without precipitating an unduly violent reaction.

The whole business had got completely out of hand, and when Flett left again for the site next morning, armed this time with a large crowbar and a shovel, I accompanied him in the hope of being able, if not of telling him the whole truth, at least of convincing him that the Red Arrow was just some routine marker left previously by somebody or other for some quite insignificant purpose, and not worth any further investigation. On arriving at the spot, Flett insisted that I help him in levering up the rock with the crowbar, while he carefully excavated the gravel beneath it with the shovel. His enthusiasm was so infectious that even I half expected him to unearth a brass cylinder, an old camera, or something of the kind. The fruitlessness of our investigation did nothing to damp his ardour, and on the way back to the base he unfolded a new plan to excavate a continuous trench along the line marked by the arrow for a distance of fifty yards or more. I decided that by one means or another he must be told the truth that very evening.

After dinner I joined Tom Berry and Johnny Blyth with an offer to help with the dishes. By degrees I steered the conversation around to the subject of alcoholic beverages. 'This Navy rum we're supplied with, Tom,' I asked, 'is it good stuff, would you say?'

'*Talking* good stuff,' replied Tom. 'There just ain't no finer. A good glass of that, and you don't mind what *freezing* well happens.'

'Could you give me about a couple of glassfuls in a bottle, Tom? I think I ought to have a supply of it on hand for sledging trips, in case one gets chilled, or falls through the sea ice, or something like that.' Tom complied with my request willingly, and I returned to the berth occupied by Flett with a bottle three-quarters full of the dark reddish-brown liquid.

Flett was sitting on his cot making a tracing of Nordenskjöld's map of Hope Bay, drawing a series of concentric circles around the site of Red Arrow Rock.

'Feel like a little spot of rum, Flett?' I asked, and without waiting for a reply poured him out a generous tot of the undiluted liquid in a tooth glass. He took it from me mechanically, and sipped it without thinking as he bent over his task. As soon as his glass was empty I quickly replenished it. His eyes began to sparkle and a flush spread over his countenance. I had to refill his glass several times before it appeared in my judgement convenient to broach the delicate subject.

'That red arrow, Flett,' I commenced. He nodded dreamily, his lips wreathed in a beatific smile. 'Couldn't it be that it's just a marker painted on the rock by some botanist, such as myself for instance, to show the position of a certain patch of lichen or moss or some other plant growing there?'

'Aye, it could be that, Lamb, it could be that. Thass thing I never thought of, myself, come a think of it. *Crimes*, thata be funny thing, wouldn't it now, after you and me go alla way up there and lifting all those stones looking for relics and dog-dog-documents.' He began to laugh softly, and lay back on his berth with his eyes half-closed. 'If thassa way it is, then you an me been pretty well made fool of, eh, old man? But who could have done it, d'you think? Eh? Who done it?'

'I did it,' I replied softly, and gently drew the blanket over him, for his eyes had closed completely and he was fast falling into a state of blissful and dreamless slumber.

From that day onwards, no reference was ever made again in our company to the subject of Red Arrow Rock.

Phenomena

THE MONTH OF MARCH was ushered in by a further and much heavier snowfall, which lay over a foot deep on the floor of the unfinished house and transformed our carefully located and marked piles of stores into amorphous excrescences on the white surrounding landscape. Ashton and Flett plied their brooms vigorously, and called for more helpers to nail planking over the framework of rafters so that the structure should be roofed over completely as soon as possible, even though doors and windows had not yet been fitted into the walls. James and I, having done all we could on the Nissen hut alongside (we still lacked one end wall, which was to be brought over on the *Eagle*'s second trip, and had covered the opening temporarily with a large tarpaulin),[1] transferred our services to Chippy and were set to work on the floor and roof. The galley at one end of the house had already been planked over, and Taylor, as on the previous occasion, helped Tom Berry to assemble the 'Esse' range, this time disposing in one way or another of all the parts supplied for it. I could hear their voices arguing bitterly over it down inside as I crept to and fro across the sloping roof above on hands and knees, a hammer in my hand and my mouth full of nails.

As I straightened up once in a while and supported myself against the wire guys attached to the smoke stack, I could take in from this vantage point the extensive panorama which here surrounded us on all sides. Out to sea the vista was closed by a dense fog bank running across the channel at the mouth of Hope Bay, and through it dimly seen the ghost-like outlines of three large tabular bergs grounded in the shallows; a wan sun, like a grease-spot on grey paper, struggled feebly to penetrate the snow clouds and heightened the vague and Turneresque quality of the distant view. Closer in to shore, the waters of the bay were saturated with the snow which they were too cold to digest, and had taken on a milky white colour and a degree of viscosity which subdued their waves to a slow, snake-like undulation accompanied by an audible hissing due to the snow crystals jostling against each other in the semi-fluid matrix. A slight further lowering of the temperature would now freeze the whole surface solid, and might be expected anytime within the next two weeks. The freeze-up at Port Lockroy the previous year had occurred in a somewhat different manner; winds and currents had broken up and dispersed the half-solid sheets of snow and sea-water, and these, by a series of constant gentle collisions, had assumed a rounded form, with their edges turned up in a rim all around, so that they reminded one very much of the leaves of that giant Amazonian water lily which William Jackson Hooker, in honour of his sovereign, named *Victoria regia*.[2] Later on, after countless buffetings and interslidings, they lost their mobility and fused into a solid and continuous crust of sea-ice.

In the other direction, inland and to the south, the land rose in a series of moraine-covered hills to the base of the stratified mountain called Mount Flora by the Swedish expedition on account of the abundance of plant fossils which they found on its slopes. Farther to the south-east, and just visible over the plateau ice cap, could be seen the tilted and very regular pyramid noted by us on our first visit the year before, and named, as you would rightly expect, 'The Pyramid'. Otto Nordenskjöld had described the location very well in one of his diary entries, reproduced in his published account, and which I now knew almost by heart:

> It is a spot of special beauty, very suitable for a wintering-station; I called it provisionally, 'Depot Glacier', as I pointed it out specially to Duse and Larsen, in the event of my afterwards

determining that a depot should be established here after I had left the vessel. You see a magnificent and extensive valley, amphitheatrical in form, and with precipitous sides, but one's interest is chiefly attracted to an especially well-individualized glacier possessing a couple of beautiful lateral moraines, the only ones I have yet seen in these regions. In conclusion, I ought to mention the broad snow-free foreshore.

My eye followed the snow slopes receding in a succession of planes up to and beyond the mountain, and I looked forward to the day when we would have all this house-building behind us and would one morning set off with our sledges and dog teams up those slopes and down the other side, following in the footsteps of Andersson, Duse and Grunden, and making, as they did forty-two years ago, for the house on Snow Hill. Yes, the way south lay wide open to us from here, but . . .

It was the dogs that worried me. Not one of us had any previous experience in dog driving, and although I was inclined to jeer at the complexities and refinements of dog team travel as described in the *Polar Record*,[3] I fully realized that this was not something that could be learnt in one day. Up till now the dogs had been in the sole charge of James and Russell who, aided by Matheson, had spent the greater part of the previous week in hunting and slaughtering sea-leopards to accumulate a supply of dog food which would last through the winter. From where I stood on the roof I could see the three figures about half a mile along the shore, dragging a huge and flaccid carcass towards a grave which they had dug in the snow to preserve it in cold storage. I made a mental note to raise the matter of training (ourselves more than the dogs) at supper time that evening.

We continued our hammerings on the roof until it got too dark to see the heads of the nails. During the last hour of daylight the temperature rose considerably, the air became completely still, and

more snow began to fall, this time in huge feathery flakes larger than any I had ever seen before; they were loosely-knit aggregations of fine-spun crystals, and some of them were over two inches long. I asked Doc Back, in his capacity of meteorologist, what this unusual type of snow might signify. He shook his head; 'Not good,' he said, 'barometer's been falling steadily since midday. Chippy! Ixnay[4] on roofing felt tomorrow!' Ashton had suggested that we might take advantage of this warm and windless spell of weather to accomplish the somewhat delicate task of laying and nailing the rolls of tarred felt on the now almost completely planked-over roof.

At the supper table in the tin galley that night, the conversation on dogs got started off on a rather unfortunate footing. It so happened that two days previously three of the dogs, temporarily released from their chains on the wire cable, had run out on an ice floe after a Weddell seal, and had drifted off out to sea before their absence had been noticed. We had hoped that a turn of the wind might bring them back to shore again, but there had been no sign of them since then, and in the present conditions of complete calm no hopes of their return could be entertained any longer.[5] James remarked regretfully on their loss, and the irresponsible Doc had to come out with a classroom tag from Ovid's *Amores*: 'Ossa quieta, precor, tuta requiescite in urna, et sit humus cineri non onerosa tuo.'* 'I think we'll have to dispense with the urn in this instance, Doc,' I laughed. '"Coelo tegitur qui non habet urnam,"† if I may quote Lucan in preference to Ovid.' The levity of these ill-timed remarks obviously did not please James and Russell too much, and I hastened to make amends by straightening out my face and saying how much I really regretted the loss of these three valuable animals from our teams. But sometimes, as you yourself have probably noticed, a conversation, once started off on the wrong tack, tends to keep veering round again to unfortunate topics, and Doc and I seemed quite unable to steer clear of controversial remarks and displeasingly high-flown quotations.

'Cats', said Doc pontifically, 'are in every way superior to dogs. No arse licking there, no false humility, no craven fostering of the master's egotism by fawning servility and submission.'

'Kant,' I observed in my turn, 'in his *Observations on the Feeling of the Beautiful and the Sublime*, remarks that "in submissiveness there is not only something exceedingly dangerous, but also a certain ugliness and a contradiction, which at the same time betrays its illegitimacy." Need I say more?'

'And the sexual behaviour of dogs,' added Doc, 'their unconcealed and impudent lubricities . . .' he covered his face with his hands in well-feigned embarrassment.

'You don't seem to think much of dogs', said James, 'but I saw you take a piece of Spam off your breakfast plate this morning and slip it into your pocket. It wasn't for old Rover, was it, by any chance? I saw

---

* Roughly translated: 'The bones of calm, I pray you, rest in safety in an urn, and may the earth lie lightly on your ashes.'

† Lamb's reply is from the Roman poet Lucan (Marcus Annaeus Lucanus): 'He is covered by the heavens who has no sepulchral urn.'

you giving him something later outside by the front porch.'

'I was only straightening out the chain on his collar,' I replied.

And that was how I started out with rather a bad reputation regarding dogs, and one which it took me quite a long time to live down.

*

At 6.30 p.m. Doc donned his naval greatcoat,[6] thrust his feet into sea-boots, pulled his balaclava helmet well down over his collar, and set off on his meteorological round, swinging in one hand a buzzing clockwork contraption known as a psychrometer, the function of which, if I remember rightly, was to record the relative humidity of the air. Five minutes later he returned to the galley, replaced his instrument on its hook, and started to divest himself with a thoughtful and serious expression on his face.

'Snow stopped, Doc?'

He nodded, and a moment later said: 'Go outside and look at the moon.' Considerably surprised, we crowded out through the doorway and stood shivering in the snow outside looking up at a sight which none of us had ever seen before.

Paraselene is I believe the correct scientific name for it; 'mock moons' is the more common and expressive term by which I had previously heard of the phenomenon. The sky in the zenith was quite clear, and up above our heads there was the bright half-moon, forming the centre of a complex system of arcs and haloes of brighter or fainter light. Two concentric rings ran right around it, and the inner of these was touched tangentially by two broken arcs, one on each side. In addition, the whole figure was bisected by a broad band of fainter light, obviously a segment of a very large arc, for its curvature was slight and its ends passed out of view behind the mountain masses of inky black cloud which were rising from the horizon on all sides. At each of the six points where the arcs intersected could be seen a faint but quite distinct image of the

Ivan Mackenzie Lamb working in his laboratory at Operation Tabarin's Base 'A',
Port Lockroy, Antarctica, July 1944.

Unloading stores on Goudier Island, February 1944.

Bransfield House under construction, 12 February 1944.

Above: Base 'A' on Goudier Island, photographed from the north with the Sierra du Fief in the background.

Right: The completed Bransfield House, Lamb's first Antarctic home.

Left: Base 'A' from the east, showing the Nissen hut.

Left column, top to bottom: Andrew Taylor, James Marr, Lewis 'Chippy' Ashton, Gwion 'Taff' Davies; *right column, top to bottom:* Tom Berry, James 'Fram' Farrington, Eric 'Doc' Back, John Blyth.

Midwinter's Day celebrations, 21 June 1944.

Ivan Mackenzie Lamb, with a lichen-covered rock, Base 'A', 1944.

Returning from a seal hunt, 2 July 1944.

Setting a fish trap at Port Lockroy.
During the first year of the expedition attempts at fishing proved all but futile.

Lamb emerging from his igloo, 14 August 1944.

A roped-up Marr gingerly unloads his sledge, caught in a crevasse
during the early days of the Wiencke Island survey, September 1944.

Above: Surveying at the foot of the Wall Range, Wiencke Island.

Left: Lamb at a drifted-up Camp 'A' during the Wiencke Island survey, October 1944.

Right: Lamb and his tent during the Wiencke Island survey.

Far right: The miniature 'garden' planted by Lamb in December 1944. By January 1950 all the vegetation had succumbed to the elements.

Above: The ruins of the stone hut built at Hope Bay in 1903 by members of Otto Nordenskjöld's Swedish Antarctic Expedition.

Right: Base 'D' under construction, Hope Bay, February 1945.

Below: The derelict Hektor Whaling Station, Whalers' Bay, Deception Island.

Below right: Lamb dog-driving in the vicinity of Base 'D' – perhaps during the 'embarrassing episode' described in Chapter 14.

Above: Interior view of Eagle House, Midwinter's Day, 21 June 1945.

Right: Eagle House after a heavy snowfall, October 1945.

Below: Dog-sledging across the 'Bay of a Thousand Icebergs'.

Below right: Dog team and a packed sledge.

Top and above: Distant and close-up views of Nordenskjöld's hut on Snow Hill Island.

Assorted artefacts recovered from the Swedish base on Snow Hill Island. The steel tent pegs (bottom right) would prove particularly useful.

The 'Odds and Sods' gorge themselves on seal meat towards the end of the first survey journey from Hope Bay, 9 September 1945.

Ivan Mackenzie Lamb with Dainty.

The end of the first sledge journey from Hope Bay:
(*left*) Victor Russell and David James; (*right*) Andrew Taylor and Lamb.

moon itself.

Such unaccustomed prodigies of nature, when seen for the first time, invariably give rise to a certain feeling of uneasiness and dismay, even though the physical operation of the underlying factors be perfectly clearly understood. It almost seemed to us as if the moon, deprived of other means of communication, had surrounded itself with all these cryptic circles and watery figments of its own substance in a mute but frenzied gesture of warning in the face of some imminent catastrophe, much as a person on the other side of a soundproof plate glass window might try to convey to you by a wealth of extravagant and horrific gesture that something standing behind you was lifting its bony knuckles to encircle your throat . . .

Inside the galley, Doc gave a low whistle of amazement. 'Not very much over 686 millimetres,' he said, looking round at all of us in turn, as if he suspected that we might be personally responsible for this phenomenal fall in the barometric pressure; '686 *steaming* millimetres! That's about the lowest pressure ever recorded in all time! You only get pressure as low as this when you're right in the eye of a cyclone! But we don't get cyclones down here!'

'You sure of that, Doc?'

'Well, yes . . . but . . . Chippy, we're in for something; I don't know exactly what it is, but if I were you I'd do something to strengthen this galley if that's at all possible.'

'The only thing we can do is to pass lines over the roof and fix them to something heavy at starboard and port,' Ashton replied. 'There's nothing we can do about the bulkheads if we're in for a blow. Wait, though, yes, I could jam some of those heavy baulks from Deception up against the leeward side if I knew what bearing the wind was going to come from; you know what side it will blow, Doc?'

Doc shrugged his shoulders. 'Can't say a thing as yet, Chippy. It's still perfectly calm outside, not the least breath of wind. It's quite possible it may not come to anything after all. But I don't know; this low pressure, the mock moons, those pitch-black clouds rising up all round on the horizon . . . there's something on the way, not much doubt about that.'

Several of us went outside to help Chippy bear up the heavy baulks of lumber from the shore, and hastily to fill some empty wooden boxes with stones; three lengths of stout rope were then thrown over the roof of the galley and made fast by the ends to the weighted boxes on each side. The timbers were laid outside the door, ready to be used immediately for shoring up the walls from outside once the direction of the wind became manifest. There was a curious heaviness, or I should say lightness, in the air, and breathing seemed difficult, as if half the oxygen had been used up; even the brief exertion of carrying the lumber up from the shore made us gasp for breath and left us running with perspiration.

These things having been done, there was nothing further we could do but go inside and wait to see what would happen. Tom Berry and Johnny Blyth, after clearing away the supper table and washing the cooking pots, brought out a greasy pack of cards and started slapping them out on the table for one of their interminable and vociferous games of cribbage. Doc Back, Freddy Marshall and I, seated at the other end of the table, embarked on one of those discursive conversations, apropos nothing in particular, which might range all the way from Cole Porter to Kierkegaard and then back again. Taylor, impassive, lay on his back in his lower berth, his head propped up on a pile of books, calmly puffing on his pipe and leafing through the *Antarctic Pilot*; I knew him well enough to know that he, too, was seriously worried about our situation, but with the realization that at the moment there was nothing more that we could do about it.

It was nearly eleven o'clock at night before anything happened to give us some inkling of what we had to expect. During the preceding hours, the black cloud banks had mounted the sky steadily from all sides and finally fused in the zenith to form a continuous gigantic cupola, in which the earth and all upon it was enclosed in a blackness as of the pit. Even the blanket of snow on the ground did little to relieve the unusual darkness. Then the wind came at last; not an open, angry, rushing, blustering gale, the hearty wind that roars through the beech forests on the English downs in early spring, but a furtive, complaining, spiteful movement of the air which moaned, hissed and sighed, now outside the window, now at the door, as though it were quietly seeking out with invisible fingers the weak spots in our armour, so that it might later return in the full panoply of its might and then destroy us.

Through the window, in the radius of the lamplight, we could see the fingers of the wind now made manifest by the fine snow which it carried with it. The white tendrils flickered over the window panes in an ominous caress. A slight lull, as if the forces outside were holding a brief consultation, and then they returned to the attack with colours flying. The voice of the wind ceased to be a moan and intensified itself into a steady shriek; the drift now raged and danced over the window panes like white fire. At the same time the temperature fell so quickly, even inside the building, that Doc thought for a moment that the bulb had broken off his thermometer and the mercury was draining out of it. I picked up an iron pot-lifter that was lying on the floor in a corner of the galley, and it stuck to my fingers as if it had been smeared with glue. Fine snow sifted unceasingly into the hut through every unseen crack and crevice, and commenced to pile itself up along the framework and between the floorboards in miniature snowdrifts. Even the air inside was filled with tiny falling ice crystals which had been forced in through the finest cracks in the roof and walls by the intensity of the wind.

To go outside now would be suicide, and quite a quick death at that; it would be like plunging into a raging cataract of ice-cold water, and the powdery drift would be forced instantaneously into your eyes, ears, mouth and nostrils, right down into your lungs, in a matter of seconds. Fortunately we had all the supplies we needed inside, including eight or nine bags of coal stacked up at one end of the galley; it looked as though we should probably need plenty of it, as the stove, although closed up completely and with the damper pushed right in, was roaring up its red-hot chimney flue like a blast furnace in the intense suction of the draft.

Indeed, there was nothing more one could do about it but go to bed and hope for the best. Chippy and Taff had shored up the leeward wall of the galley from the outside with the large baulks of timber, and the three ropes over the roof were weighted down on each side by the wooden boxes containing in all well over a ton of stones. Nevertheless, when I had climbed up into my upper berth and had wriggled down into my sleeping bag, and lay listening to the fury that was separated from my head by a poorly fastened iron sheet one-sixteenth of an inch thick, I was gripped, understandably, by a spasm of cold fear. Nature, which I knew perfectly well was quite blind and impartial in its operations, took on in this moment an amazingly realistic semblance of personality, a much more impressive counterfeit even than the angry speechifying and flashing frenzies of the thunderstorm. It was imitating, in fact, with a fantastic degree of similitude, the maniacal ravings of a homicidal psychopath. That continuous yelling and buffeting of the wind, by its very inflections, produced in one's mind exactly the same reaction of distress and fear as would an incessant stream of threats and vile abuse poured out upon one by a demented person with that dreadful intensity which, happily, only the staffs of mental institutions know can be produced from the human throat.

The snow-filled air must have been rushing round and over our galley at a speed of ninety to a hundred miles an hour, at least. Picture yourself inside an aeroplane travelling at this speed, and then imagine its fuselage to be constructed, not of stout aluminium plates fastened to a steel framework by regular rows of rivets an inch apart, but of loosely overlapping sheets of corrugated iron doubtfully attached to the wooden beams by ordinary wire nails, many of which had missed their mark entirely.

Hour after hour I lay listening to the inferno raging on the other side ten inches away from my head. The whole galley was shaking and vibrating like a furniture van driven at top speed over a road full of potholes. Then I heard another sound that made my blood run colder still. It was the rending screech that a nail makes when it is being drawn forcibly out of the wood. I hastily grabbed the flashlight which I kept inside the sleeping bag and focused it on the rafter above my head. The sound was repeated, and this time I distinctly saw the pointed end of the nails retreat about half-an-inch into the wood. I do not know how long I gazed upwards in fascination at this performance, repeated by one or other of the nails every few minutes during the more particularly intense blasts; it might have been for minutes or it might have been for hours. Once all the nails had been drawn out of the beam, and the wind got under the loose edge of the corrugated iron sheet . . .

*

I awoke in complete stillness. The interior of the galley was suffused with a strange greenish light, as if it were lying at the bottom of the sea. The windows were in fact completely buried in solid snow, which filtered out the red and yellow parts of the spectrum of daylight. Tom Berry had just risen, and boldly opened the door of the galley; he walked into a solid white wall, on which every joint between the boards, and every screw-head, was faithfully reproduced in reverse as on a plaster cast.[7] The hut was completely buried in one huge snowdrift.

I lay on my back looking up at all the nails; then I commenced to laugh, silently. I laughed until the tears streamed down my face.

Those nails . . . last night . . . I could have clinched them on the inside. I could have clinched them on the inside . . . *I could have clinched them on the inside . . .*[8]

13

The Meteorology
of the White Expanse

TAKEN AS A WHOLE, many of the atmospheric phenomena such as I have described in the previous chapter, and which we encountered not only on that occasion but on many others, are so portentous that they may well strike terror into the souls of those given to superstition or to an anthropomorphic or animistic view of nature; the voice of the shrieking snow-laden blizzard, in particular, seems to express inscrutable malice directed against the cowering bodies and minds of its victims. Sir Douglas Mawson's terrible experience of the polar tornadoes in Adélie Land led him towards a similar view. The world of Antarctica then seemed to him 'a void, grisly, fierce and appalling. We stumble and struggle through the Stygian gloom; the merciless blast – an incubus of vengeance – stabs, buffets, and freezes; the stinging drift blinds and chokes'.[1] Note well the animistic overtones. Our own experiences were mild in comparison; we were only on the outermost approaches of the great high continent, on the beckoning finger of the Palmer Peninsula which leads up to it like a Jacob's ladder from the brisk but habitable lands of Tierra del Fuego. And yet our reactions to these meteorological phenomena were much the same. Their very unpredictability made us feel always vaguely apprehensive.

And yet few things can be more certain than that such a state of things as I have here described, and others have described before me, cannot be altogether meaningless. It is in the nature of man to try to elucidate their meaning on a rational basis. With a view to approach the root of this matter, I have examined with some care all the accounts available to me of the manifestations of Antarctic meteorology. Comparatively meagre as they are, there is enough in them to afford me some assistance in my undertaking, especially the monumental work of Professor Meinardus,[2] and the weather reports included in the scientific accounts of the various expeditions which have visited this icebound region. The *Antarctic Pilot*, too, in places has furnished pointers which, if rightly interpreted, might contribute in some measure to a satisfactory explanation. But at the end of it all I have come to the conclusion that the task which I intended to set myself, namely a clear and succinct account of these puzzling phenomena, is well-nigh hopeless of fulfilment. Here we walk by faith more than by sight; and many among us, too often, shall stumble and fall. For try as we may, we cannot fully understand the mysterious spreading of the clouds, or the whirlwind that comes out of the South; we cannot enter into the treasures of the snow, or even into the springs of the sea that laps the outermost shores of the White Continent, for the waters are hid as with a stone, and the face of the deep is frozen.[3]

The recorded data are indeed inadequate. Most of them have been collected, not in the heartland of the continent itself, but on outlying coastal bases and islands, and from ships haunting the glaciated and inaccessible shores; comparatively few are available from the interior, compiled during inland sledging journeys. Nevertheless, some sort of coherent picture begins to emerge, although different authorities may interpret it differently, according to their own meteorological training and background. All, however, seem to agree in assigning to the Antarctic continent a position of extreme importance as the one great centre of influence in the climatic features of the Southern Hemisphere, and perhaps of the world as a whole.

To begin with, Antarctica is very different meteorologically from the corresponding latitudes in the northern half of the globe. The Arctic has a summer which permits the existence of an abundance of plant and animal life and, at least in many places, of human habitation; the Antarctic has no summer at all in our sense of the word, and has never been colonized by man, or for that matter, any other terrestrial mammal. It is essentially dead, frigid, and aloof from the world of the living. Here we are presented with a picture, and not a very entertaining one, of the whole earth aeons hence, when the sun will have lost its splendour and contracted into a dull red ball in the blackness of the firmament, and our planet becomes a whitened sepulchre idling aimlessly through all eternity. How one thrills then, when one's fingers extract a tiny tuft of moss or lichen from a crevice in these icebound rocks, and hold before one's eyes the proof that something living, something of our own nature, has managed to cling and persist in the face of this outrageous icy onslaught! But the tiny cryptogam toils not, neither does it seek explanations of its presence there.

Of all the phenomena, the wind is the one that impresses most, because it has activity and movement, and hence the spurious appearance of life. For this reason the wind, perhaps more than any other meteorological phenomenon except the thunder, has always left the deepest imprint on human imagination. 'Behold, a whirlwind of the Lord is gone forth in fury', laments the prophet Jeremiah;[4] and in the Gospel of St Matthew we read how Jesus of necessity arose on one occasion and rebuked the wind which threatened to capsize their little craft.[5] A landscape without a breath of wind seems half dead already; even the recesses of a completely still tropical forest, although teeming with the highest and lowest forms of life, may nevertheless bear the clear imprint of death, with the motionless fronds hanging down like the tattered banners of antiquity in the hushed and gloomy aisles of a great cathedral. The wind speaks to us, in all tones from a soft warm whisper to the yelling shriek of a maniacal rage. And in the White Expanse it usually speaks in fear-compelling tones, and brandishes in our faces its uncomforting rod sharpened with spicules of ice.

Indeed, Antarctica is without doubt the windiest spot in our experience; both in frequency and in velocity its winds outstrip by far those of any other continent of the globe. What is the underlying explanation of these savage winds which tear down screaming from the high plateau above as if seeking to devour and annihilate all life up to its very fringes and beyond? Dr Bernacchi,[6] who took part in the *Southern Cross* Expedition of 1898–1900, writes as follows: 'The prevailing east-south-east and south-east winds at Cape Adare, which is within the area of abnormally low pressure, tend to prove the existence of a great anticyclone stretching over the Polar area, which in its turn necessarily implies the existence of upper currents from the northward, blowing towards and in upon the Polar regions to make good the drain caused by the surface out-blowing south-easterly winds.' This idea gives us a very clear and comprehensible mechanical picture to work with, and appears to be confirmed by the observation made by subsequent expeditions in the same area, that the smoke plume of Mount Erebus, Antarctica's active volcano, would frequently be blowing off the lofty summit in a southerly direction, while the surface winds, as usual, were blowing from that very same quarter. In other words, an anticyclonic circulation of the air from the north at high levels, turning on itself at the Pole, and rushing outwards on the surface from the south.

The existence of an anticyclonic system over the Antarctic does indeed seem certain from the researches of Meinardus and Hepworth;[7] both demonstrate conclusively the presence of a peripheral ring of higher pressures around the margins of the continent. And the parties of Amundsen and Scott, the only mortals who up to now have been privileged to set foot on the Pole itself, both report the almost complete absence of wind on that awesome spot. A very important observation, this, as tending to support our circulationary anticyclonic theory, according to which the Pole, as the centre from which the winds originate, the veritable eye of the great Anticyclone, should logically be a point of absolute rest and calm.

But alas! The researches of later investigators seem to overthrow completely this simple meteorological hypothesis of constant circulation of the atmosphere at different levels and the existence of a great permanent anticyclone at the Pole. According to Palmer,[8] among others, the mechanism is entirely different; there is no permanently centred anticyclone, but a migratory one, forever shifting and elusive, and it is to be sought, not over the Pole itself, but originating in the middle latitudes, often utterly removed from the Polar Continent. In this matter of the winds, therefore, we find ourselves treading on peculiarly thorny ground, and I, as a mere layman in these matters, must leave the tangled skein of conflicting evidence in the capable hands of our trained meteorologists to unravel as best they can.[9]

Let us then pass on to consider another aspect of Antarctic meteorology: that of precipitation. This is naturally in the form of snow, but there are exceptions; rain sometimes falls on the milder oceanic west side of Palmer Land, and in the South Shetlands and South Orkneys to the north. During our own visit at Deception Island, which belongs to the former group, we had an afternoon of heavy rain. In milder and more habitable latitudes, we are accustomed to see snow falling gently downwards from the grey sky above, slowly and softly mantling habitations, fields and forests, and lending peace and tranquillity to the scene. There is something sacred, touching and ineffable in its silent and increasing benediction. Why, if it were otherwise, should it be almost universally represented on the Christmas cards, as a fitting vesture for their glad tidings of peace on earth and goodwill to men?

But those acquainted with snow only in this mild and beneficent form of the habitable latitudes can have no conception of the snow encountered in Antarctica. Crystallographically and chemically, it is true, there is identity, but there the resemblance ends. Read again the accounts of those who have faced it in those desolate regions; without exception, they speak of it in terms of horror. For it comes in hard abrasive particles, impelled on the wings of the furious wind, and brings annihilation to all living things which have no place to hide their heads. It cuts, it lashes, it stifles, it benumbs. The only men who ever yet set foot on the Pole and returned alive to tell the tale round their firesides bore its scars on their faces to the end of their days.[10]

However, do not think that the snow is nothing but affliction and distress, the leaden tips of a myriad-tailed scourge. Like other things which cause us suffering and grief, it benefits us in the end by furnishing a surface and a pathway on which we may attain our final destination. How could we travel on these vast and trackless wastes, were it not for the deep overlying layer of wind-packed snow, over which the runners of our sledges, and the skis on our feet, so effortlessly glide? For, depend on it, the underlying surface beneath this white bland cloak must be hopelessly stony, jagged and involved, an impenetrable Gehenna[11] of jumbled rocks. But the snow, filling in as it does the yawning chasms below, prepares a pathway for our feet, and that which is crooked below is made straight superficially, just as the tortuous ways of this world shall also, we trust, be made smooth to our sorely tried souls when we finally reach the Great Destination above.

Another point: because the Antarctic snow comes, as I said, almost invariably on the wings of the wind, it is well-nigh impossible to be sure of its origin. It may be direct from the skies; but more likely to be off the land, whipped up, whirled about, and thrust in our faces by the force of the wind. In both cases it rushes on its way horizontally, and nobody who encounters it can usually tell whether it is coming direct from above or is spread over the face of the land from a place perhaps hundreds of miles away. This I saw for myself on several occasions on our sledge journeys, when, although we might be battling our way painfully through clouds of stinging drift, the sky above us would be cloudlessly blue and serene. But what difference does it make, whether this invaluable medium of transport and communication comes to us directly from the sky above, or at second hand, after serpentining over miles of barren and tortuous wastes? In both cases it serves us equally well to get where we are going, wherever that may be.

Together with snow, we must consider ice. Now ice may be formed in two ways: either directly by freezing of water, or by compression of snow. The former method furnishes the sea ice over which we travel in our skirmishes around the approaches to Antarctica; the latter the glaciers and polar icecap of the interior. One is formed directly under our feet; the other comes originally from the skies in the form of snow crystals and is consolidated into a vast ice landscape under unspeakable pressures. It is hard to realize that the glassy blue ice, which obtrudes and breaks off in bergs where the glaciers come down to the sea, has originated from the fluffy and exquisite powder of immaculate new-born snow. The one is soft and gentle, fit for babes to play in; the other forms icicles of steely hardness, any one of which might serve as a dagger to one's heart, but they are both the same, and one is the necessary outcome of the other.

I once made some slight investigations into this matter myself, by digging a shaft down into the snow on the surface of the Wiencke Island glacier. Of course, I found nothing which was not well known or at least surmised before (for much work has been done on such aspects of glaciology, this being really a branch of meteorology), but then I did not go very deeply into the matter, for I was afraid of concealed crevasses. The first foot or two, the superficial layer, is light, innocent, woolly stuff, playsome to work with, and is shovelled aside with hardly any serious exertion at all; but then one comes to an underlying layer, varying in depth according to circumstances, which gives more resistance to one's delving. It is called *névé*, and is an intermediate condition between snow and ice, in which the six-starred crystals of the original snow have lost their shape, and taken on other and less predictable crystallographic forms, under the weight of the overlying mass, which is already not inconsiderable.* We can call it an expression of the primary condition of snow. It resists our efforts to cut into it more strongly, but can be excavated with the shovel, and its greater hardness and compactness fits it well for certain purposes. We can use it, for instance, to build an igloo which, for a time, will shelter us against the elements more efficiently than any other more convenient but flimsier habitation, such as a tent. But now, at the bottom of our shaft, we strike against the third and lower layer, against which our poor tools clang in vain, glassy solid ice, interspersed with myriads of tiny bubbles trapped from the upper air, but otherwise completely structureless. Under the blows of our pick it merely splinters into infinitesimal fragments and tires us out unrewardingly, for it is of stony, almost metallic hardness. And so we climb out of our shaft, exhausted, and still have not reached bottom. And yet that stuff moves, and creeps onward imperceptibly but surely over its rocky foundations. What dark and inexpressible trials of force must take place in those depths, forever concealed from human eyes! If, when digging your shaft, you should by any chance see a little unwinking eye of blackness open up under your feet, let neither curiosity nor obstinacy impel you further in your investigations, but get out into the air and sunlight while you can, for you have caught a warning glimpse of the chaos beneath waiting to swallow you up.

All the foregoing meteorological phenomena are, of course, taken at their source, manifestations of the effects of low temperature. Without sufficient cold, there can be no ice or snow, and whatever ultimate explanation, if any, may eventually be forthcoming to account for the baffling and often lethal winds which sweep down off the continent, we may be sure that conditions of temperature

---

* The powdery snow on the surface weighs from 5 to 12 pounds per cubic foot, but when compacted by the overlying pressure, as in the case of *névé*, it may weigh anything between 15 and 50 pounds per cubic foot. (IML)

will play an important part in it. And the White Expanse is cold, colder than we may be inclined to think. We are accustomed to hearing picturesque reports of the effects of extreme cold in the Siberian town Verkhoyansk, which is popularly represented as being the coldest spot on Earth;[12] how, when a house catches fire, the occupants of the upper stories slide to safety down the frozen jets from the firemen's hoses; how spoken words freeze in the air, and become audible only when the thaw sets them free in spring; how dogs and hydrants become joined and are with difficulty put asunder; and other more extravagant matters, some of which we might indeed be foolish to take for gospel truth. But I, for one, suspect that Verkhoyansk and Antarctica are poles apart in the matter of cold, and I have not only good circumstantial evidence to support me in this, but also the opinions of an eminent meteorological authority, whose utterances *ex cathedra* do much to bolster my own admittedly fallible suggestions. On the Polar Plateau, Amundsen, in December, found the mean temperature to be −9 °F, and Scott, who traversed the same region in January, found it to be then already ten degrees lower, −19 °F. What temperatures are these for the months of midsummer, and what unspeakable depths must we expect them to plummet down to in midwinter in these ghastly wastes? Listen to what Dr G. C. Simpson[13] said in his Halley Lecture, delivered to the University of Oxford in the year 1923: 'We know nothing about the conditions at the South Pole during the winter, but I think we should be safe in saying that it is far and away the coldest spot on the surface of the globe. A region which has forty degrees Fahrenheit of frost during its midsummer month must be pretty frigid during its midwinter month.'[14] We may suspect 'pretty frigid' to be something of an understatement.

Of clouds, the visible expressions of strange transactions in the air above our heads, I cannot say much that is likely to be original or of general interest. True, I saw many different types during my two years' sojourn in Antarctica, from the black and frowning nimbus which blotted out the sun in wrath, to the ethereal windswept cirrus which decks the firmament in herringbone wisps and slivers at incalculable heights above the earth; but in the regions where we dwelt, the relatively more congenial threshold of Antarctica, the cloud formations are more varied, on account of the close proximity of open waters, than over the great continent itself, and more akin to those occurring in inhabited latitudes. From all accounts, the cirrus is most characteristic of the great plateau, and consists, not of water droplets in suspension, but of tiny spicules of ice, like diamond dust, floating in the thin and unimaginably cold upper reaches of the atmosphere. Captain Scott, while on the Polar Plateau, noted very frequently that the air was filled with minute ice crystals, which we may perhaps interpret as a cirrus cloud formation descended to the surface; and he furthermore remarked that under such conditions optical phenomena, such as brilliant haloes and mock suns, were commonly encountered.

Mock suns and mock moons: who can repress a feeling of wonder and vague uneasiness on first sighting these celestial mockeries? Even if we relegate them to the catalogue of known phenomena under the more comforting titles of parhelia and paraselenae, and explain away their optical mechanics according to the textbook, we still cannot entirely rid ourselves of a superstitious dismay in regarding them. The sun and the moon, we feel, being fundamental parts of our Solar System (erected indeed to the rank of deities in many of our religions), should be inviolable and not subject to those mocking duplications, in which the eye has difficulty in distinguishing the true orb from its spurious vapoury rivals; and to make it even more confusing, the whole deceptive image is often surrounded by a bright halo in the heavens, which further heightens the illusion of actuality and substance.

Mirages, too, another deceptive vagary of nature, occur in the Antarctic. Shackleton observed them frequently over the Weddell Sea and elsewhere, and describes such as *'Fata Morgana'* in his book *South* (1919). This is a spectacular type of mirage in which multiplied images of terrestrial objects are seen floating high in the air, sometimes inverted. The objects represented in these loomings, as they are sometimes called, often appear larger than reality, and so solid as to inspire complete belief in their existence. Naturally, they are magnified expressions of the true objects of our environment and immediate experience; in the desert, one sees mirages of palm trees and oases, and in the polar regions, of ships, islands and icebergs. The images seen, therefore, usually have every appearance of reality, that is to say, in relation to the geographical situation of the onlooker; but no matter how solid and satisfying they may appear, they are ungraspable phantoms, produced by the chance interplay of air currents at different temperatures, and not to be treated as anything but a harmless and interesting atmospheric diversion. On one occasion, while voyaging in the *William Scoresby* in foggy weather off the west coast of the Palmer Peninsula, we discerned at no very great distance the vague outlines of two huge tabular icebergs directly in our path, shrouded mysteriously in fog. As we turned off course to avoid them I was able to take a photograph, but as we skirted them at a safe distance to starboard, they rapidly wavered and diffused away to nothingness before our eyes, and in their place was only the vacant rolling sea; for all their awe-inspiring and portentous visible form, they were fictions of the air, a mirage, and we could have steamed at full speed right through them without coming to the slightest harm. Be that as it may, the experienced navigator turns his prow aside from such appearances; for what human eye can always distinguish such loomings from reality?

Such, briefly stated, are some of the main aspects of the weather in the White Expanse. I have only scratched the surface, and I could go on, filling page after page with further observations, and expand this chapter into a whole book by itself, weighty with the erudition and the evidence, one way or the other, of universities of scholars. But enough! I despair; I am whelmed with contradictions; I grow weary and faint beneath the intolerable burden of complexity; and bashing my well-bitten quill to the ground, I relinquish these studies to those whose greater piety or wit qualifies them to deal more fittingly with this vast and fabulously intricate domain of Meteorology, and I leave them to probe further into its murky and inconclusive profundities.

A House Built on Sand

BY SOMETHING OF A MIRACLE, it seemed, the Nissen hut and the uncompleted base house had withstood the hurricane without suffering major damage, and we ourselves had been saved for something better than a quick death under a snow pile. This was partly attributable to the fact that the first few hours of the storm, before the wind had attained its maximum velocity, had been accompanied by an exceptionally heavy snowfall, which had formed a protective rampart around the buildings. The framed-in walls of an extension to the front of the house, intended to house the gasoline-driven generator and the latrine facilities, had been blown flat to the ground and buried under several tons of snow, but the main part of the house, which by good fortune was at this stage entirely closed in, had held fast against the maniacal onslaught of the gale. If the storm had occurred a week earlier, when one side of the house was still open, it would have been a different story; the structure would have exploded into a whirling, skyrocketing mass of planks and rafters, which the force of the wind would then have scattered over a radius of several miles.

Taff Davies and I were working two days later on the newly erected walls of the porch; he was nailing on the rolls of aluminium foil, while I was puttying panes of glass into the two window frames. The weather was perfect for this kind of outdoor work, and we could distinctly feel the warmth of the sun's rays reflected back into our faces from the shining aluminium surface. The landscape around us, 'amphitheatrical in form', as Nordenskjöld had put it, basked serenely in the sunlight, and the shadows on the snow slopes leading up to Mount Flora took on deep and subtle tones of indigo and violet. On this day it was easy to forget the savage mauling which we had experienced forty-eight hours previously, and almost to think of Antarctic nature as essentially benign and as dear to us as the cwms and corries of our own Welsh and Scottish homelands. But even in moments such as these a small voice inside each of us was saying: 'Do not be deceived; you were never meant to live here; go hence before the greater wrath is visited upon you.' At last I gave expression to my thoughts as I rubbed a ball of putty between my palms and transformed it into a long dangling snake. 'This rock looks solid enough, doesn't it, Taff? And yet I have a feeling all the time that this house is somehow being built, not on solid rock, but on something shifting and impermanent, like sand. Remember? "A foolish man, which built his house upon the sand; and the rain descended, and the floods came, and the winds blew, and beat upon that house; and it fell; and great was the fall thereof."'[1]

Taff nodded in perfect comprehension; the same thoughts must have been coursing through his mind also. I have never made any claim to the Highland faculty of second sight. My ancestry is too mixed and impure for that, but Taff Davies was at home in the world of Celtic visions and folklore, and may well have been endowed with it. However that may have been, we both undoubtedly felt some kind of shadow descend over our spirits as we worked side by side on the construction of that house at Hope Bay. Even Tom Berry, who was by no means prone to extravagant flights of fancy, perhaps sensed something similar, for that same morning, in the galley, he had remarked to John Blyth and me: 'Funny, don't seem so much like home here like it was at Port Lockroy; don't know, something missing, like.'[2]

'Maybe you're missing the smell of penguins,' Johnny had suggested.

'Penguins be *side-tracked*,' said Tom. 'It's just like it don't feel the same, somehow.' It was a general feeling in the air, perhaps just homesickness for our snug little island habitation on Port Lockroy.

On March 12th the *Eagle* arrived again on her second visit, bringing the remainder of our stores and equipment from Deception. At first, on account of the persistent south-east wind, which was bringing in quantities of drift and floe ice through Antarctic Sound from the Weddell Sea, Captain Sheppard thought that he might have to beat a retreat at any time during the next twenty-four hours, and so he offloaded about fifteen tons of coal and kerosene drums at the nearest point to the ship's anchorage, a small rocky promontory at the edge of the snowfield about a mile from our settlement. The other stores, as before, were towed in scow loads behind the motorboat into the inner part of the bay and unloaded on the ice foot immediately below our base.[3]

Outside work on the house being now virtually completed, Ashton could proceed at leisure, aided by fewer helpers, with the interior construction and furnishings, and this freed several of us for other duties. Taylor decided that Davies, James, Marshall, Russell and myself should start transporting the coal and oil by dog team over from the point where it had been deposited by the *Eagle*, this not only for the convenience of having these fuels near at hand, but also to give us some initial experience in the art of dog driving.[4]

Then the fun began.

James, Marshall and Russell, with commendable foresight, had made a harness tailored for each of the dogs during the long voyage south through the tropics. Some of the dogs having since died, we were supplied with a surplus of harnesses. They were made of thick tubular cloth lamp wick, and fitted over the dog's shoulders and across the chest in front, somewhat in the manner of a brassiere, the two ends at the rear being each supplied with a large metal eyelet whereby they were attached to the rope trace drawing the sledge.

Lengthy debates had taken place as to the most suitable arrangement of the traces for Antarctic travel. The *Polar Record* went into the subject in the most profuse detail, listing numerous Eskimo methods by their native names, as well as the host of modifications named after the seasoned explorers who each dogmatically upheld their method, and theirs alone, as suitable for polar snowfield travel. Also, the authors of these articles informed us, we must take into account the exact consistency of the snow surface to be traversed (many Eskimo, French and German technical terms here) in our choice of the best trace-arrangement to be adopted. Above all, they impressed upon us most strongly, we must never allow the dogs to change their relative position in the team and thus tangle the trace lines. We could certainly see the logic of this admonition, but as to the method of preventing the dogs from doing it, the *Polar Record* was disappointingly silent. Eventually we decided on the fan formation with traces of unequal length, the longest trace being for the leader of the team.[5]

As every reader of Jack London's stories knows, husky dogs are far from democratic in their dispositions. In fact, they adhere strongly to the *Führerprinzip*,[6] which they apply among themselves with a ruthlessness often shocking to one accustomed only to the civilized, indoors, cushion-by-the-fireside, slipper-bringing strains of caninity. Their naked violence and savagery is particularly repellent to us because it is exactly the kind of behaviour which we ourselves would indulge in if the veneer of moral training and civilization were to be scraped off us, as indeed it has in many parts of the world today.

The animals had been brought from various settlements in Labrador, and after a series of bloody mêlées on the southward voyage, had finally segregated themselves into three distinct tribes or gangs, each with its autocratic and usually undisputed leader. We had therefore to make up our teams from the three gangs as already constituted, for any attempt on our part to transfer a dog from one group to the other would have led to furious uproar and butchery. The three teams consisted of seven working dogs each, not including a few surplus animals kept in reserve or excluded for reasons such as old age, injury or pregnancy. Two of the teams were good ones, of strong, upstanding beasts, but the third was an agglomeration of scruffy and ill-disposed individuals who had been brought together in a mutual defence pact by a common inferiority complex and anti-social feeling towards all the others. I suggested that they should be known as the 'Debased and Insulted', after Dostoyevsky,[7] but commonly they were called the 'Odds and Sods', a more succinct epithet with much the same meaning.[8]

By all accounts, the entire pack had been most rigorously disciplined on the outward voyage by the largest of the dogs, one called Rover, who was the size of a small bear and must, in his heyday, have been a magnificent specimen of doghood. But during their sojourn in the Falkland Islands a series of misfortunes had assailed him and robbed him of his supremacy, turning him into a pathetic, broken-down has-been. Firstly, he had a bout of sickness which had enfeebled him considerably; secondly, he had lost some of his teeth; and thirdly, on one unlucky occasion he had got his head stuck in a tin can, and his rivals, seeing him thus temporarily incapacitated, had used the opportunity to give him such a sound going-over that he was left partially crippled, and could never again from that time on make any pretence to authority or leadership. He retired into solitude nursing his wounded pride in his refuge on top of the galley roof, which he reached by climbing up the snowdrift against the wall of the house. I felt sorry for old Rover, as one does even for the blackest of tyrants when they fall into utter ignominy and degradation, and always made a point of visiting him in the morning after breakfast to straighten the chain on his collar.

His place had been usurped by a bristly, yellowish/brown dog known as Captain, who used to make the rounds of all the other dogs daily to make sure they knew their place; if they rolled over on their backs and whimpered before him, well and good, but if not, we had to be quick to break it up and restore order before serious

injury or death ensued. The smugness and arrogance on Captain's face was superb; only Honoré Daumier,[9] had he decided to extend his studies to canine physiognomy, could justly have depicted it. I hated his guts.

We assembled three twelve-foot Nansen sledges, laid out the traces and harnesses on them, and pulled them ourselves over to the other side of the bay where the *Eagle* had deposited our oil and coal. We were not taking any chances on the dogs running away from us with empty sledges, we thought. There we loaded each sledge with a large drum of kerosene or two or three bags of coal, and later in the day returned from the base with two of the teams turned loose and following us. I was interested to observe that, as soon as we fastened up the traces and produced the harnesses, the dogs came milling around us in great excitement, and eagerly allowed us to put the harnesses on them without giving any trouble. Obviously this was something they were quite used to in their native Labrador, and after being harnessed up they danced madly around in the snow, yelling discordantly and just raring to go.

James and Russell took off first with their team and three bags of coal on the sledge. In spite of the heavy load, the dogs got the sledge moving almost at once and set off towards the base at a brisk speed, both the drivers hanging on to the handlebars at the rear of the sledge and steering it around exposed rocks and ice hummocks; at times on the downward slope they had to stand on the rear runners to brake the speed of the descent. A few minutes later they disappeared out of sight round the side of the rocky hill between us and the settlement.

Heartened by this auspicious beginning, I shouted my team up onto their feet and prepared to start off in pursuit. I had the 'Odds and Sods', and since they were to all appearances a punier lot than the other team, I had loaded the sledge with one forty-gallon drum of oil only.

'Huit!' I yelled (Eskimo word for 'Get going!', courtesy of the *Polar Record*), at the same time giving the sledge a lateral wrench to free the runners from the frozen surface. With one accord, all seven dogs leaped forward in their harnesses, and the main trace whipped taut with a report like a pistol shot; the sledge shot forward, and I had just time to grab the handlebars and hang on for dear life, dragged prostrate in the snow behind the speeding chariot. It took me a few seconds to regain my feet and start running at full pelt alongside, heaving desperately at the handlebars in an effort to guide the sledge into the tracks left by the other team. By this time I realized that the 'Odds and Sods' were not by any means so odd and sodden as their name implied, and I began to wish that I had loaded a second or even a third drum of oil onto the sledge.

Yipping and yelling, my team, instead of following the tracks to the right around the rocky hill, started to run straight up the snow shoulder towards its summit. What was the word for 'right' in the *Polar Record*? God, I could not remember it. 'Right! Right! Droit! Destro! Pravo! Derecho! Rechts!', I screamed desperately, delving frantically into half-forgotten linguistic depths in a vain attempt to make them understand and obey me. But it was all to no avail; up they shot to the brow of the hill, and commenced a headlong descent down the other side with ever-increasing speed, in spite of the fact that I was hanging on to the sledge with all my weight, my feet firmly planted on the rear ends of the runners.

There down below, about a quarter of a mile away, lay the settlement, and I saw James and Russell just pulling up to an orderly halt with their team at the side of the Nissen hut. The sight of the downward slope which we had commenced to traverse filled me with dismay; most of it was smooth snow, but there were considerable patches of smooth glassy glare ice, and right across our line of travel extended an outcrop, about fifteen yards wide, of bare rocks and stones, part of the deserted penguin rookery.

I wish I could draw a discreet veil over the rest of this embarrassing episode, but having started to recount it, I am duty bound to record the disastrous and ignominious conclusion.

I suppose we were travelling at about twenty miles an hour when we hit the rocky patch; immediately, with an awful rending sound, the sledge began to disintegrate. First the cowcatcher snapped off and was left by the wayside; then the front end of one of the runners struck a projecting rock and flew away with a bang. Moments later its broken end dug in, the whole left side runner tore off with a splintering crash, and the sledge continued, with unabated speed, careering lopsided on its foundering superstructure. Just before we reached the snow slope on the other side, the other runner split into a fibrous mass of kindling and scattered on all sides, accompanied by the right-hand upright and the top-piece off the handlebars. By this time, acting on the blind instinct of self-preservation, I was draped over the oil drum, clinging to its rim and sides with hands and legs. In this condition we reached the snowdrift at the foot of the hill, just in front of the settlement. I have a vague recollection of hearing confused shouts and seeing figures rushing up from all sides, but my only distinct memory is that of being pulled out by the feet from a snowdrift in which I had been buried head-first. Eye-witness accounts agree that the dog team, the oil drum, the remnants of the sledge, and myself all parted company at this point and went our several ways; the arc which I described through the air before hitting the snowdrift being, by all accounts, most gracefully executed.[10]

As a self-imposed penance for this exhibition, I spent the next two days assembling a new twelve-foot sledge from the stores; James and Davies, impressed by the spectacular mishap, now fitted out all the sledges with an ingenious footbrake consisting of a ski fastened fore-and aft-beneath the sledge, its rear end free for some distance and equipped at the tip with an ice-crampon which dug firmly into the snow when the ski, pedal-wise, was depressed with the foot.[11] These sledge-brakes proved very effective and from that time onwards we never had any trouble in curbing the exuberance of the dogs when travelling downhill or with lightly loaded sledges.

On May 14th, house building operations could be said to be completed, apart from minor interior fittings. Our new dwelling was considerably more spacious than the one we had left behind us at Port Lockroy. This time I shared a cabin with Flett, who proved a most congenial companion, although I consistently avoided putting his humour to the test by any reference to Red Arrow Rock. Our cabin was so filled with geological and botanical specimens and collecting equipment that it took on the appearance of a junk shop, and Chippy heightened this resemblance by manufacturing a fitting of three brass knobs (the Lombard sign of a pawnbroker in England) and attaching it above our doorway; by the same token we were affectionately known by the sobriquets of Lipschitz and Finkelbaum.

Taylor decreed that on this day we should rest from our labours, and hold an 'At Home' or housewarming party in the evening in cele-bration of the successful establishment of Base 'D'. As the weather was fortunately fine, most of us spent the day outside exploring the vicinity and skiing, and returned in the evening with outrageous appetites to sit down to an excellent holiday dinner prepared by Tom Berry and his faithful acolyte, Johnny Blyth. After supper, a

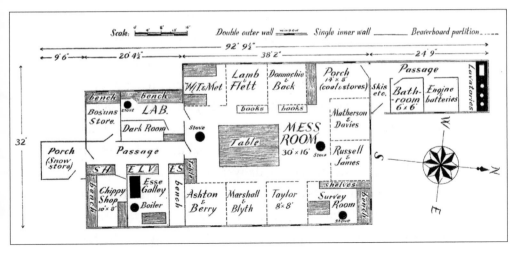

Eagle House.

hot punch was brewed and pleasurably discussed; then the table was pushed to one side to clear the floor for a theatrical performance.

We were not without indigenous talent at Hope Bay; Blyth, who modelled his vocal style with great success on that of Bing Crosby, first gave us a beautiful rendering of that heart-warming classic entitled 'When the Gold of the Day meets the Blue of the Night', after which Ashton, Berry and Davies obliged with a full-dress turn-out of the 'Hope Bay Dog Catchers' Union', enlivened by copious references to runaway dog teams, and culminating in a rendering of 'Don't go down the Snow Mine, Daddy'. Doc Back then favoured us with a pseudo-scientific lecture on 'The Symptomology and Treatment of the Common Cob' (a purely polar term for a temporary attack of moroseness and unsociability), in which he recalled that 'the first symptom is an increased irritability, especially noticeable in the early morning; appreciation of practical jokes is lost at an early stage; and all types of attack are liable to be precipitated by the bites of *Anopheles blythoides antarcticus*', but concluded with the assurance that 'fatalities are fortunately unknown, and all types will resolve with judicious treatment, such as dousing the patient with ice water or bopping him on the beezer'.

Finally, a clamorous demand arose for the 'French Inspector', and I went out to the galley to get my props, which consisted of Tom Berry's uniform cap and a piece of wire which I bent into the shape of a pince-nez. The term referred to an act which I had put on at the time of a similar celebration the previous year at Port Lockroy, in which I portrayed a French government inspector of *maisons tolerées* making his rounds in the course of his official duties. Judging by the uproar which greeted my sallies, delivered in a thick foreign accent, the travesty was successful, but my heart was not in the fun as it had been a year ago at Port Lockroy, and a feeling akin to foreboding began to grow upon me, until suddenly, after a quip in which I pretended to ring up the Paris fire brigade as a last resort, I stopped, involuntarily repeating the words: 'Fire'; 'Flames'; 'Burning'. I looked stupidly around me, then broke off the act and sat down. For the barest moment I had distinctly seen a curtain of flames separating me from my listeners; the hallucination was vivid in the extreme. Of course, I had had too much to drink. All the same . . .[12]

Later that night, as I lay in my berth, I found myself repeating, over and over again, the words: 'Which built his house upon the sand; and it fell; and great was the fall thereof.'

Some Southern Horizons

OVER TOWARDS THE ROCKY TONGUE of Grunden Point,* at the edge of the frozen sea, James, Marshall and Taff were reopening a grave in the deep snowbank, at the place where the first of the sea-leopards shot by us had been buried. Four feet of easy shovelling brought them to hard ice upon which the shovels clanged fruitlessly, and below this glassy sheath, clouded with innumerable tiny air bubbles, a dark extended form could be vaguely discerned. The departing bodily warmth of the freshly killed mammal had melted the snow heaped upon it, and cased it in a glassy coffin several inches thick. On this they went to work with pickaxe and crowbar, and shovelfuls of tinkling ice splinters were thrown up before the mountainous glossy carcass was fully exposed to view and pried loose with poles and stanchions from its bloodstained bed. With all of us heaving on two lines, it was hauled laboriously up the snow ramp and finally lay fully exposed on the surface, hard and rigid as an oaken trunk.

The huge bulk of frozen flesh would feed the dogs for many days to come, but first it had to be dismembered into sizeable portions. To this end a crosscut saw was brought into play, and the carcass, like a conjuror's lady assistant, was sawn into transverse slices about six inches in thickness. Reddish-brown 'sawdust' of frozen flesh particles flew from the narrow cuts as the saw worked back and forth, but the blade cut silently, without the singing and rasping of

---

* Now Grunden Rock.

its customary passage through wood. As the sections were sawn through and fell sideways with a dull thud into the snow, I picked them up and carried them to one side; arranging them in an orderly sequence, I was fascinated by the almost diagrammatic lesson in anatomy which they afforded. All the organs, liver, heart, stomach and viscera, were beautifully displayed in their natural variegation of colour, firmly compacted and frozen together; and it was with reluctance that I interrupted my examination of them to fetch from the hut a couple of large axes, with which we proceeded to split the segments into triangular portions, like slices of cake, and subdivide these into blocks of the right size for a dog's daily ration.

'Knob Nunatak',* a small projection of bare rock on the summit of the snowfield to the south of our settlement, was selected as a suitable site for the first depot to serve our forthcoming sledge journey. The steepness of the slope leading up to it made it necessary for us to sledge our supplies up in small instalments, and the first trip for this purpose was made on May 25th when, with two teams, we hauled up and deposited a tent, some sledge boxes containing pressure stoves, kerosene and some rations, and about 400 pounds of dog pemmican. The same journey had to be repeated several times during the following month, until the greater part of our food, utensils, camping and surveying equipment, and fuel was finally deposited around the rocks in readiness for our final departure for the South. In returning to the base from these trips, we released the dogs at the summit, and after they had scampered down the steep mile-long slope back to the settlement, we would ride the empty sledges back straight down the hillside at an exhilarating pace, one man lying prone on the lattices, the other riding the handlebars at the rear and guiding and braking the vehicle in its downward rush by means of the ski-crampon lever. A joyous and light-hearted plunge through the cold rushing air after the sweaty toil of the ascent.

---

* Now Nobby Nunatak.

Towards the end of June the dogs and ourselves had had considerable experience in local sledge travel, what with the almost daily trips up to 'Knob Nunatak' and over to Eagle Cove for coal and kerosene. Our relationship as drivers and driven, in the early stages somewhat ill-defined, had crystallized, and in both canine and human heads a concrete idea had become established as to what should, should not, could and could not, be done in each particular set of circumstances. Notions of direction had been inculcated, at first with the eighteen-foot whip, later simply by word of mouth: 'Ille!' (right) and 'Yuk!' (left) being the formulae employed, out of deference to the *Polar Record*. Some of the bitches in our company had already been blessed with progeny, and we had several husky-looking little puppies gambolling under Tom Berry's feet in the darker parts of the passageway outside the galley. They showed promise of growing into fine draft animals, and we had hopes of incorporating them in our teams, or even of making up a third team with them, by the end of the season.

Chippy Ashton had attached the cyclometer, a device for measuring distance traversed, to one of the sledges. It was actuated by a bicycle wheel which trailed behind the sledge on a long arm hinged at the base so as to allow it to ride freely over the irregularities of the terrain. On a calm afternoon in late June, with the temperature slightly below zero Fahrenheit, Taylor, Russell and I took the sledge, empty and drawn by two dogs only, several times over a measured course of about one and a half miles on the sea ice of the bay, in order to calibrate it, this distance having been laid out the previous day with the aid of a steel measuring tape in 200-foot stages. On the third and last run, however, the internal mechanism of the cyclometer broke down, and we returned with it to the base, disgusted with its flimsy and inferior construction.[1] Chippy, resourceful as always, replaced it with a ship's log which he happened to have in his box of odds and ends, and this, with its more massive and weatherproof construction, served us well throughout our future journeys, with

150 The Secret South

the aid of a special table elaborated by Taylor to convert its dial reading of knots into miles and kilometres.

On these trips over the bay ice we would pass and repass a solitary figure standing motionless by the hour at the side of a hole in the ice half way across the bay: Jock Matheson, embodiment of patience and eternal hope, with a line let down for fish which only he believed existed. At teatime, time and time again, he would return to the hut chilled to the marrow, and put down his ice-encrusted line on the shelf inside the doorway; our enquiries became daily more ironical, and his answer to them never more than an ambiguous grunt. On the afternoon of June 14th he came in and sat down at the tea table as usual, slowly drank four saucersful without saying a word, then rose and bought in from the porch a canvas duffel bag from which he shot a slithering mass of good-sized fishes out across the table among our cups and plates. The *Notothania* season had begun, as he always knew it would.[2]

Notothania is a genus of fish proper, I believe, to the Antarctic regions, similar in size to a mullet, of uncouth and angular form, with head and mouth disproportionately large, but very fine eating, even allowing for blunted polar palates, as we duly discovered that evening at supper time. Jock's success initiated a feverish rivalry in ice hole fishing between Blyth and Donnachie, and by July 9th we calculated that over 500 of these fish had been raised from the depths and consumed. Like all Antarctic life, they were uninitiated, and could be caught with merely a red rag tied to the hook, or even on the bare hook alone;[3] on occasion two together would be brought up, one on the hook and the other clinging to the line, a dream-fulfilment for the casual angler, but surely anathema to the expert, who expects to ply his art against a creature more worthy of his shifts and wiles.

The dissolution and final death of dog Rover, long impending, took place on the night of July 1st. His only remaining vassal, Widgeon, was heard to utter a repeated wailing lament from the rooftop, and we emerged to investigate. At the place where the 'Odds and Sods' had been tethered, I found three of them, Mutt, Jeff and Sydney, loose, hovering shiftily like wolves with guiltily careering eye and muzzles soaked with blood. It did not take me long to find the body of Rover alongside one of the sledges. Curiously enough, Doc's post-mortem examination failed to reveal any wounds serious enough in themselves to have caused the animal's death; it would seem as if this very old dog had perished of a seizure brought on by the panic of the vile onslaught, in which he had not only his bodily substance, but also his honour to defend. He had been an old tyrant, an apostle of the reddened tooth and claw,[4] a priest of the bloody faith; but, as Shelley wrote in that connection, always he stood

> On the brink of that mighty river
> Whose waves he had tainted with death.[5]

And now he himself had taken the final and inevitable plunge, and his rule was ended. I felt that already in the closing months of his existence he had more than paid the price of his transgressions, and we buried his remains in a snowdrift with feelings bordering on affection and tenderness, not unmingled with respect.

For some time past we had been intending to make a visit to the upper part of the Depot Glacier, that 'exceptionally well-individualized glacier' noted with admiration by Nordenskjöld, for the purpose of laying out a series of markers on it to measure its rate of movement. One day in the latter half of July, the weather being agreeable, calm, bright and not too cold, we resolved in the morning to carry out this project. Taylor, James, Russell and I set out after breakfast with the 'Big Boys' team, towing a nine-foot sledge loaded with surveying instruments and stakes, and made our way up the ice slope past 'Knob Nunatak', where our sledging provisions now formed an imposing pile. From there, passing the tilted Pyramid Peak on its eastern side (its base and ourselves in blue shadow, its upper half bathed in the resplendent rays of the rising sun), we headed south-west over a small saddle between two low rocky hills, and finally came out on the brow of the Depot Glacier. Taylor set up the theodolite in position on a rock outcrop on the east side of the glacier, while Russell and I, on skis, with the steel tape extended between us, marked out distances of 100 yards on the glacier. James, following, stuck the stakes into the *névé* snow at the intervals indicated, while Taylor aligned their position with the theodolite from his vantage point. As a precaution we were roped together, but the crevasses were few and narrow in this part of the glacier. We took turns at relieving ourselves over the base of the stakes to freeze them in, but the last few were, unavoidably, somewhat poorly anchored. Returning to the dogs and sledge, the latter upturned and anchored with an ice axe during our absence, we ate our sandwiches and then set off homewards along the morning's sledge tracks, and arrived at the galley door an hour later after a pleasant, mostly downhill run.

I had taken a photograph of the glacier from its upper end with my Leica camera, and decided in the late afternoon to walk over the sea ice of the bay in order to make another picture of it from the base, showing the lateral moraines and ice cliffs. Accordingly, I started out in a beeline from Grunden Rocks towards the vast iceberg lying shoaled at the entrance to Hope Bay, not far from the tongue of the glacier. The subtle effects of light and atmosphere were indeed remarkable that evening of the late Antarctic winter; the sun had already disappeared behind the massive slopes of Mount Bransfield, and the sky above it was streaked with radiating segments of delicate colours, fine as those on the lip of a seashell: from roseate through orange-pink to pale sea-green, merging into dark violet-blue at the horizon; and above the place where the sun had recently set, a column of golden light extended vertically without limit into the higher reaches of the stratosphere. Even the dense dark shadow near sea level had a curious luminous quality, as if it were filled with a haze of tiny golden particles, and the blocks of the talus slope spilling down into this shadow at the shoreline nearby were like out-thrust cubes of black velvet.

Had these atmospheric conditions been less exceptional, and myself less absorbed in their contemplation, I would not have stepped into Jock Matheson's fishing hole, which, although lightly frozen over, had been conscientiously marked with a small wooden stake. As things were, my downward plunge into the depths was sudden and precipitate.[6]

In one second I was out of the familiar daylight into another world, of which, strangely enough, I can now remember nothing, except that it was a fiery cold embrace of green-black night and seemed to be of infinite duration. My only clear recollection is that of reaching upwards for a faintly shimmering and wavering pale green moon above my head, and of finally grasping it by the edges and pulling myself into it. My head broke through the surface into the orange daylight once more, and seconds later I was standing beside the hole with salt water cascading from my garments. It took only a few minutes to race back to the hut, strip off my freezing clothing which was fast hardening into armour plate, get into every dry article which I possessed, and put down half a tumblerful of neat rum which Tom Berry solicitously brought me. Apart from a tetanus-like clamping of the lower jaw which lasted for an hour, no ill-effects or complications were apparent, and my mental condition remained unperturbed except for the feeling of annoyance at my Leica camera having been damaged by salt water. After all, one does not usually fall through a hole in the sea ice more than once in a lifetime. My only real preoccupation was the attempt to remember, unsuccessfully, what I had seen and felt during those few moments in the depths, for I had a vague feeling that they had been significantly populated.

On the afternoon of July 24th, the temperature being low for the season (−20 °F),[7] Taylor and I pitched one of the pyramid tents on the snow patch behind the Nissen hut and installed our bedrolls and a pressure stove inside it, for it was our intention to make certain that our equipment was adequate for the forthcoming journey, on which we could expect to encounter much lower temperatures than we had had the previous year on the milder oceanic western side of the Palmer Peninsula. We wriggled into our sleeping bags at 9 p.m. with no great degree of confidence, and promised ourselves that no false pride would hinder us from beating a retreat to the warmth of the hut if conditions should become too uncomfortable. But our equipment had now been so improved by past experience and modification that it served us well even on this exceptionally chilly night, and we slept quite soundly until well on in the morning hours. Reassured, we brewed ourselves a pan of coffee on the pressure stove before returning to the galley, where Tom Berry and Flett feigned exaggerated surprise at seeing us return alive and walking.

Now we could put the final touches to our preparations, which had lasted these many weeks. It was only a matter of waiting for reasonably settled weather. The programme of our journey consisted in crossing the tip of the peninsula to the south of our base, descending to the 'Bay of a Thousand Icebergs'[*] on the other side, and thenceforth travelling on the sea ice down the Crown Prince Gustav Channel[†] between the mainland and Ross Island,[‡] making a running survey of both shores as we went; then rounding the southern end of Ross Island to gain Snow Hill, the base of the Nordenskjöld expedition in 1902–1903. The suggestion was discussed that on our arrival at Snow Hill, provided that the Swedish base should be still standing and habitable, James and I should remain there for some weeks to make a thorough examination of the site, making also meteorological observations and scientific collections there and on the neighbouring Seymour Island, while Taylor and Russell

---

[*] Now Duse Bay.
[†] Now Prince Gustav Channel.
[‡] Now James Ross Island.

continued their travels along the coastlines in the vicinity in order to complete the topographical survey. We would then finally reunite at the Snow Hill rendezvous and journey back home together via the eastern side of Ross Island and Vega Island. We had provisions for a trip of one month's duration which, with only two dog teams of seven animals each, meant rather heavy loads, considerably more than 100 pounds to each dog. In order to travel lighter and faster, we decided to offload a considerable portion of our stores at some point on or near Vega Island, where a depot could be established within easy reach of the Snow Hill base, across Erebus and Terror Gulf.

At last we started off on the morning of August 8th, in dull and overcast but otherwise good travelling weather, with a comfortable temperature of seven degrees below zero. James and Russell got off first up the steep slope with the 'Big Boys' team, Davies and Marshall accompanying and helping with the uphill hauling. Twenty minutes later Taylor and I, assisted by Back, Donnachie and Matheson, took the other sledge with the 'Odds and Sods' up to join the others at 'Knob Nunatak', where we took on our full loads and said goodbye to our helpers. Now we were on our own, four men and fourteen dogs, and laboriously we began to plough our way southwards, mile by mile, over the level summit of the plateau towards the top of the long slope which from there descended once more to sea level in the 'Bay of a Thousand Icebergs'.

By late afternoon we had covered a distance of eight or nine miles from Hope Bay, and although the snowfield still presented a level appearance to the eye, running out to a blank horizon on all sides, we knew by the slightly easier going that we were entering on the first stages of the downward grade, which would increase in steepness from here onwards. The last familiar landmark, Pyramid Peak, finally sank below the snowfield to the north behind us, and we continued onwards between the two equally blank expanses of snow and grey sky, into a land where only three human beings before ourselves had penetrated. From a distance, our slowly moving sledges, half a mile

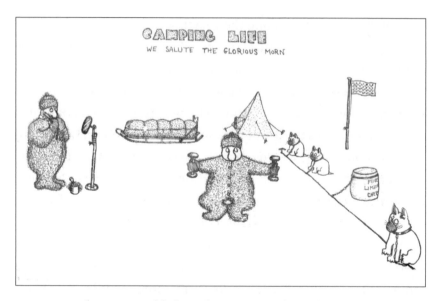

apart, must have resembled, in their canvas shrouds, the carcasses of maggots being dragged along by ants.

We made camp that night on the snowfield, still without sight of any landmark. Our last glimpse of the landscape through the tent flaps before retiring to rest was insignificant, consisting mainly of heavy grey clouds hanging from the vault of the sky in stalactite-like shreds and tatters. It looked as if perhaps bad weather might be on the way, and we resigned ourselves to the possibility of a day or more spent inside the tents up here on the roof of the Palmer Peninsula. But the following morning, when I poked my head out of the tent once more, reaching for clean snow to fill the cooking pot, I was dazzled by the sunlight, and my eyes watered from the glare off the snowfield and the crisp cold wind whipping briskly along its surface.[8] Some radical meteorological change must have occurred during the night, and now the weather gave every indication of being settled fair. So we lost no time in striking camp and loading up, and within the hour were once more on our way, making good progress southwards over the now visibly declining slope.

And then, quite suddenly, the new horizon cut the even line of the snowfield and lay extended before us in the blink of the sun, in a wide magnificent sweep, taking the eye minutes to traverse. The immediate foreground was of course concealed, but at a distance of some five or six miles lay the wide expanse of the sea ice strewn with innumerable icebergs of every shape and size. Andersson, Duse and Grunden must have stopped at this very spot forty-three years ago, when they, the first to sight the bay, gave it its obvious name, the 'Bay of a Thousand Icebergs'. To left and right of the bay the escarpments of the mainland ran southwards until lost in remote distance, consisting partly of blue-fissured hanging glaciers, immobile in the distant atmosphere of sunlight but, by their contortions and manifold tumblings, conveying the unmistakable impression of bursting, cascading movement; and, in the rear of the scene, in various depths of blueness, rocky islands, large and small, leading finally up to a gently rising distant snow dome of obvious immensity, which we recognized as the summit of Mount Haddington on Ross Island itself. These new horizons opened up their arms to us, and we sped onwards to merge ourselves into their virgin purity.

Smooth Running and Food for Thought

AFTER A COUPLE OF HOURS' exhilarating downhill run, we reached sea level once again on the southern shore, where the bay indented the mountainous peninsula in a wide sweep about thirty miles across. It was going to be a glorious day; the brilliant sunshine washed the entire landscape in its pure light, and some of the reddish rock islands ahead of us in the distance seemed to change their shape from minute to minute in the wavering heated air. On one occasion I observed one of these islands, by the effect of a mirage, to taper away at the base in the form of an inverted cone, and finally to rise suspended completely above the level icefield on the horizon. Already I could feel my lips and eyelids tingling with the promise of considerable sunburn. For a moment the phrase 'the friendly Antarctic'[1] seemed to lose a good deal of its absurdity, and the intrusion into the virgin frost-locked landscape of the two slowly moving trains of four-footed and two-footed mammals a less incongruous effrontery than usual.

It took us over half an hour to negotiate the tide crack where the land slope met the bay. The sea ice was here piled high in overriding blocks with deep and wide crevasse-like clefts between, and the sledges had to be almost completely offloaded in order to gain the level sea ice on the other side. Once offshore, however, we found ourselves on a wonderful surface extending limitlessly in any direction in which we might choose to travel. The ice was almost as smooth as a skating rink, in places bare and glassy, in other places covered with a thin layer of windblown powder snow. The sledges shot forward in arrow-like flight, and although the dogs' feet slithered unavailingly on patches of glare ice, the momentum of the sledges carried them on gaily and with unabated speed. We could ride on the sledges or run alongside them, as we chose, and found our Eskimo *mukluks*, soft as chamois slippers, excellent footgear on this variegated surface.

We set our course towards a reddish island of peculiar shape lying due south of us, at a distance of approximately ten miles. High and precipitous, it seemed from where we were to run up in a spiral to a jagged conical peak, not unlike those wooden towers at the fun fairs, down the outside of which, in our youth, we used to make the exciting spiral descent on jute mats onto the sand pile at the base; I called it mentally 'Vortex Island', undoubtedly an apt name, whether or not it may have subsequently been officially approved by the Committee of the Royal Geographical Society.[2] The hummocks formed by frozen-in 'growlers' were so sparsely scattered that it was easy to steer a course between them. The temperature, although fairly low, was pleasant for this kind of travel; the dogs were in excellent spirits, and altogether one could say that this was polar travel at its best.

Only one untoward incident disrupted the even course of our steady run, when, shortly after leaving the shoreline, my dogs sighted a lone Gentoo penguin which was grimly plodding its slow way over the sea ice a hundred yards away to our left, coming from who knows where and headed for some destination known only to itself. With a chorus of furious yelping, my dogs threw themselves off in its direction, and I barely had time to leap onto the rear runners of the sledge as it accelerated to a speed of about twenty miles per hour. I did not even shout at the dogs, for I knew that any attempt to check them in their exuberant rush would be futile. As the yelling band bore down on it, the bird glanced quickly backwards over its shoulder and then, like the wayfarer in Samuel Coleridge's *Ancient*

Mariner, 'having once turned round, walks on, and turns no more his head; because he knows a frightful fiend doth close behind him tread', without however appreciably hastening its pace. Seconds later the foremost dog reached it and tossed it into the air, and by the time the sledge came to a halt all that remained was a patch of blood on the snow and a few tail feathers. The dogs licked their bloody muzzles with relish and grinned up at me with lolling tongues to see how I appreciated their joke.[3]

The morning wore on, and the sun climbed higher in the cloudless azure sky. Vortex Island was now much closer, and we could see the variegated reddish and brown stratification of the rocks composing it, with a conical talus slope skirting its base down onto the sea ice. The pleasant and monotonous running on a good surface frees the mind for all kinds of reveries and entertaining speculations, and soon I found myself once again considering with a kind of pride the wonderful remoteness and expanse of this icebound continent, and its freedom from human encroachments until quite recent times.

This enormous land mass, five and a half million square miles in extent, that is to say about as large as the whole of Europe and Australia put together, was separated from the rest of the world at such an early epoch of geological time that it was never reached and colonized by man or any of the other higher terrestrial animals. Nevertheless it would have been entirely hospitable, for during millions of years it enjoyed a temperate or even subtropical climate, and must have been covered with lush and stately forests; this we know for a fact from the fossilized plant remains found at many places on the continent itself and on its outlying islands.

But about twelve million years ago, in the Pliocene period, the catastrophe began. Every succeeding winter became a little colder and a little longer, every summer a little cooler and a little shorter. After a while the seedlings of the forest trees succumbed before they had reached a few inches in height, and none was left but the ancient giants, now without hope of progeny and every year depleted in number, crashing down in the winter gales and rotting away in crisscrossed piles of fallen lumber. As the severity of the climate increased, the forests of rustling green foliage turned into barren tracts of dead trunks and withered branches, blackened by decay as if licked by the tongue of fire, and finally all was prostrate, a dead mass of woody corruption.

Over the punky rotten wood grew a carpet of green mosses, more resistant to the increasing chill of the air, and the rocks of the forest floor, now exposed, became covered by the multi-coloured patches and fronds of lichens whose growth had previously been inhibited by the dark canopy of branches overhead. During the fleeting summers, still warm enough to melt the ever-accumulating snows of winter, cataracts of ice water gushed down the mountain slopes, carving them into gullies and bearing down the last remnants of the higher vegetation into low-lying lakes and swamps, or even to the sea. In one of these swamps, one day twelve or thirteen million years ago, a twig with four small leaves on it, split from the parent branch, was thus washed into a muddy creek, and there covered with fine black silt before it had time to wither and decay; in the fullness of time it was changed into a carbon imprint between two layers of rock, until one day, on the side of the mountain not far from our camp, it was split out of its resting place by my hammer, and lay exposed once again, in my hand.

All was now given over to desolation, as the snow and ice fastened its grip more and more firmly on the doomed continent. The heavy snowfall, now remaining at all seasons on the higher ground, began to clog the mountain valleys and, converted into solid ice by its own weight, to move downwards and outwards in all directions with inexorable force, scoring and plucking at the solid bedrock in its slow descent. Later, only the highest and steepest mountain summits were left free of the all-pervading ice sheet. The pitiful remnants of a once proud vegetation, now reduced to a little band of hardy lichens and mosses, clung desperately to the few surfaces of bare rock still exposed above the grinding chasms of the glaciers. Lowly organisms though they were, they kept the flag of life flying in the frozen continent, and not only persisted, but in the course of countless years even evolved into new forms, some of them more highly developed than their near relations in the warmer regions of the world.

Some authorities, such as Paul Siple,[4] consider it improbable that plant life persisted in any form in Antarctica during its maximum glaciations. But to me, the high grade of evolutionary development manifested by many of the lichens – peculiar genera, subgenera and sections – seems unaccountable if they are to be regarded as post-Pleistocene immigrants. I would not deny, however, that many of the species comprising the present flora may have immigrated later from the surrounding austral continents.[5]

After the worst of the ice ages had come and gone, and the ice caps of the northern hemisphere had retreated to their present extension, Antarctica remained still a vast ice plateau devoid of higher native life. The animals now inhabiting its coastal fringes all came from the more temperate lands to the north, by sea or by air: seals, birds, and even a vegetarian mosquito, which lost its wings after arriving on the Antarctic continent, and settled down to a terrestrial and blameless existence among the scattered moss-patches. Only the penguins, perhaps, were a purely Antarctic stock, forced to the open water at the edges of the continent and farther north, and there slowly adapting themselves to the marine existence in which today they so conspicuously excel.[6]

Even though the climate of Antarctica has become somewhat less austere in the lapse of the last few million years, its extreme isolation has continued to act as an effective barrier against the immigration of higher terrestrial organisms. It is, in fact, the most isolated continent on our planet, separated from the nearest land masses by over 500 miles of notoriously tempestuous ocean. Not until about the middle of the eighteenth century did the continent catch its first glimpse of the species *Homo sapiens*, in the form of a few desperate mariners clinging to the shrouds of their storm-tossed barques, driven far south of Cape Horn by dreadful gales, and gazing with wide-eyed wonder at distant snow-capped ranges rising into view momentarily through the scudding and blinding drift. It was not, in fact, until 1773 that the Antarctic Circle was crossed by man, by Captain Cook with his two ships the *Resolution* and the *Adventure*. The peninsula alongside of which our sledges were now so smoothly running was first sighted by Captain Nathaniel B. Palmer of Stonington, Connecticut, in the early decades of the nineteenth century, and now appropriately bears his name.[7]

The large tabular icebergs, frozen into the solid bay ahead of us, showed that in some seasons at least this was an open waterway. Who knows but that, one or two hundred years ago, one of those sailing ships, 'lost off Cape Horn with all hands', may have drifted down this very passage, after days and nights of chartless running before a northerly gale, and become welded here into an icy grave? What would we have said if we had come up with the wooden ribs of a huge ship's carcass partly embedded in the sea ice, with tattered shreds of canvas still flapping from the broken spars? What happened to Nordenskjöld's *Antarctica* and Shackleton's *Endurance*, both lost in the icy grip of the Weddell Sea to the east? Did they go to the bottom, or did they drift, clamped as in a vice, farther and farther southwards or westwards to reach finally a permanent dry dock in the shelf ice of some deserted bay? Or to be sighted finally perched high on top of an iceberg drifting back into temperate waters, as some accounts would have us believe of the *Erebus* and *Terror* many years after the disappearance of Franklin's last Arctic expedition?

We, sledging on the sea ice towards the entrance to the Crown Prince Gustav Channel, and our companions at the base, were, so far as we knew, the only human inhabitants of the continent of Antarctica. (At Port Lockroy the previous year there had been rumours among us, of completely unknown origin, of the presence of Japanese whalers in the vicinity, and one of our practical jokers had given considerable verisimilitude to this suggestion late one evening by blowing across the mouth of an empty bottle down by the boat harbour.[8]) Our Antarctic population therefore worked out, if my mental arithmetic be correct, at approximately 0.00002 inhabitants per square mile. We have our *Lebensraum*,[9] but unfortunately there seems no chance of its ever serving as an outlet for the increasing pressure of population in the temperate and tropical lands where the average density of inhabitants per square mile ascends to nearly 700, as on the island of Java. The Eskimos could undoubtedly make a good thing out of it, with the inexhaustible supply of easily obtainable food and fuel in the form of seals and penguins, but overpopulation is not one of their problems.

It is often said that isolation in the vast uninhabited wastes of the world's surface enables a person to see things in a truer perspective. This hypothesis may hold true for inanimate nature and the cosmos outside of man (if such a separation is possible, which I very much doubt), but it certainly does not in the sphere of human affairs and relationships. Continued isolation in a small cooperative group, cut off from daily intercourse with the rest of humanity, blunts the sense of competition and oversimplifies the overall picture. Each of us tends to consider himself the highest authority in his own particular specialized line of activity, and becomes correspondingly dogmatic and assertive in his judgements and utterances. Our very success in getting along together amongst ourselves, and our increasing mastery over the simple technical problems of survival and travel in these inhospitable regions, breeds in us a contempt for all forms of bureaucratic procedure and organization, and for the way in which the outside world is being managed in general. Hence the many gripes heard at the base against the 'bumbling and incompetent' organization of the expedition from 'armchair' positions in White-hall and Port Stanley.

In our sublime self-centredness we seem to have forgotten that we form but a tiny particle, the smallest of the least, in the grandiose and complex structure of the world-wide concerted activity now going on. Not only our isolation from other human beings, but also from the other forms of higher animal and plant life, intensifies in us this restricted philosophy. In an environment of dead rocks, ice and snow, we lose sight of the intimate ecological relationships between ourselves and the rest of nature, and become unjustifiably self-sufficient in our mental attitudes. We forget that our mode of life, far from being a small-scale working model of what human society should be like in general, is completely artificial and atypical, and that its roots are irrevocably fixed in that highly competitive and complicated society of which we have become so contemptuously critical. Just as the germ-free air of the polar regions gives us the spurious appearance of immunity against all ills except mechanical injuries, so does the absence of competition against our fellows, and of the struggle against the more complex forces of nature, induce in us a self-confidence which is quite illusory. In reality, we are steadily losing our immunity against the testing forces of human existence, both bacterial and ideological, and this we shall certainly come to realize when the time comes for us to return to the natural human habitat; we shall fall easy victims to colds, jaundice and dysentery on the one hand, and to a desperate incomprehension of the complexities of modern civilization on the other.

However, these very thoughts are in themselves salutary, and we may be thankful for the chance of our sojourn in the barren regions which produce them in us. Certainly we shall retain for the rest of our lives a truer and better conception of nature and our relationship to it than could ever have been acquired in a climate more tempered to our physical frailties. We have the opportunity of seeing nature as it really is, neither hostile nor friendly, but simply indifferent, and can never again fall into such maudlin and nauseating nature-romanticism as that expressed by Rousseau in his *Confessions:*[10]

'I climbed through a neighbouring orchard on a beautiful path that led through the vineyard ... During the middle of my walk I offered up my prayer, which was not the idle stammering of the lips but a genuine elevation of the heart toward the Author of that friendly nature whose beauties lay before my eyes.' A thousand pities that the Extravagant Shepherd never had the chance of doing his philosophizing while driving a dog team across the polar wastes as well as while sitting in the warm sun on his comfortable bench beside the vineyard in Geneva.

*

When sledging, such long and discursive trains of thought were usually, and somewhat rudely, interrupted by an olfactory incursion, due to one of the dogs in my team relieving inner stresses. Which brings me to think that the only aromas in the Antarctic are the bad ones. By far the greatest contribution in this respect is made by the penguins; a walk through a large rookery is an unforgettable olfactory experience. But away from the coastal fringe, unless one is closely accompanied by dogs, there is a total lack of any aromatic excitement in the air. After a season one longs for the smell of fertile earth and vegetation after rain and for the pungent scent of smoke from leaves burning in garden bonfires. By this deprivation one's sense of smell is heightened to a surprising degree, and I remember in this connection how on one occasion, several weeks previously, on returning to the base from a trip up to 'Knob Nunatak', I caught distinctly a compounded whiff of kerosene, seal blubber and freshly baked bread from the settlement, while still a good quarter-mile distant from it. All the more does one here appreciate the evening pipe of good tobacco, which brings in a dried and concentrated form something of that richness of the lush plant life of field and forest for which one comes to long in these aseptically sterilized surroundings.

The windless atmosphere and the intense sunshine, even though the temperature was well below zero ('nine degrees below

Degreedigrade', as Marr used to say), made the continued jog-trot alongside the sledges a very warm occupation, and when at midday we made our halt for the usual couple of biscuits and drink of Nescafé from our vacuum flasks, we were all steamed up considerably and wet with streaming perspiration. We opened wide the necks of our tunics and fanned the cold air down into our sweaty bosoms, and it was pleasant in the first few minutes to lie down in the snow and rub one's face and hands with it. But it does not take long for the excess of bodily heat to become dissipated, and after ten minutes of standing still a sensation of increasing chilliness made us button up once more and prepare to get moving again. In this environment, practically every waking minute outside the tent and sleeping bag must be occupied with physical exertion to maintain a comfortable body temperature. Enforced inactivity means frostbitten hands and feet within less than an hour. And – what must never be forgotten – to doze off in a state of overheated exhaustion leads to the sleep from which there is no awakening: an easy and most painless farewell to the world, by all accounts, but not to be desired prematurely.

We finally reached Vortex Island in the early afternoon, and decided to make camp there for the night, so as to have a few hours of daylight for reconnaissance and collecting. The dogs were tethered out along their cables, the sledges unloaded, and the tents set up on a more or less level part of the snow slope at the base of the scree, above the tide crack. Taylor and Russell adjourned to one of the tents to plot the day's run and survey, while James and I started out on foot to circle the island, which was approximately a mile in diameter. After we had been walking for twenty minutes or so, I stopped suddenly.

'Listen,' I said. We stood motionless. 'There it is again. Penguins. Hear them?'

'Yes. They must be round that bluff ahead of us.'

Sure enough, there were penguins, a small colony of them, Gentoos, some twenty or thirty birds, on the lower scree slope round the other side of the rocky buttress. Some were standing idly among the rocks, others were wandering aimlessly from group to group, or making short circular excursions out onto the sea ice and back. The ground on which they were standing, largely free of snow, was undoubtedly a rookery; several saucer-shaped nests of stones were to be seen, and abundant tail feathers and a few dead mummified chicks were scattered among the rocks nearby. It was of course too early in the season for breeding, and the presence of the birds at this time in this inaccessible and icebound locality all the more inexplicable. To get here, they must have walked a distance of more than twenty miles over the sea ice from the nearest open water; and now they were here, what did they propose to do and what was their means of sustenance? A brief examination of the tide cracks convinced me that there were no openings wide enough to allow a penguin to slip through into the water below the sea ice, and on examining their droppings I found them to consist of a thin greenish mucus, devoid of any undigested particles. The inescapable conclusion seemed to be that these birds, whatever the reason for their being here, were cut off completely from food supplies, and were undergoing starvation with complete equanimity and with no apparent desire to move off in search of open water. As it was reasonably certain that we would be coming this way again on our return journey, James and I caught two of the penguins and ringed them by tying a strand of red cloth around one leg of each, so that we might be able to identify them on the subsequent visit.[11]

As I avidly gulped down spoonsful of scalding pemmican broth in the tent that evening, I was glad not to be a penguin.

17

Snow Hill

———

THE FOLLOWING MORNING, at Vortex Island, we made a depot, leaving a large part of our loads, including four days' supplies of man and dog food, kerosene, and our skis ('We won't need these'), securely wrapped in a large tarpaulin at the base of some rocks near the shore. As circumstances were to show later, this decision proved to be a more momentous one than we imagined at the time.[1] With loads thus lightened, we sped swiftly forward on our south-easterly course, leaving behind us the towering landmark of Vortex Island, with its reddish-brown agglomerate rock seamed with dykes of black andesite, and made for what appeared to be a passage between two fairly large islands lying directly athwart our route. The weather was bright and calm, and we looked forward to a good day's travel.

On arriving at the space between the two land masses, which lay across the northern end of the Crown Prince Gustav Channel, we discovered that the passage was actually a low col, probably a raised beach, connecting them, and to get across this, with its cover of deep snow, we were obliged to offload the sledges and relay our loads in two trips. On the other side, the frozen sea extended widely before us, offering a good surface on which we could travel without hindrance towards the beetling dark cliffs of Vega Island, some twelve or fifteen miles distant. By lunch time we had traversed approximately half of this distance.

At noontide a cover of high cirrus cloud had commenced to extend itself across the eastern horizon, and shortly after our midday halt it had covered most of the sky above us, accompanied by fluctuating gusts of wind and small tornadoes, which raised phantasmal pillars of spirally whirling powder snow all around us. These would come silently gliding towards us, like gesticulating sheeted forms, at times dissolving before they met us, or passing over us in an icy gust which left us shrouded in white powder, soon melting into water and running down our necks. Later these inconstant airs were blended into a steady south-easterly wind, sending the drift snow scurrying in sinuous lines, like snakes, across the surface of the sea ice, concealing our feet and the lower parts of dogs and sledges. As the wind increased in force, and the mantle of drift became thicker, we would occasionally lose sight altogether of the other team fifty yards ahead of us. After a while it became increasingly difficult to get the dogs to head into the blinding drift.

At 2.30 in the afternoon the wind had attained gale force, and we realized that we were in for a blizzard, and would have to make camp immediately. Unfortunately, we had left this decision a little too late, and were now faced with the problem of getting the tents pitched in a fifty miles per hour gale. As soon as the tent was extracted from its canvas sheath, it started to flap and struggle madly in our frozen hands, and all four of us had to throw ourselves upon it bodily to prevent it from taking off like a kite into the air.[2] As soon as we attempted to raise it into an erect position, a violent gust would catch it and pitch it on top of us. Blinded and freezing with the icy drift, we wrestled desperately with it like starved rats attacking an eagle. Finally we succeeded in getting both tents set up after a fashion by the expedient of hitching a loop of rope over the peak, upon which two of us hauled while the others quickly spread and made fast the walls and basal flaps with guy ropes and piles of snow. When we were able finally to crawl inside, half frozen, we barely had space enough to crouch in a sitting position, with the windward wall pressing in on us under an increasing load of heavy drift snow. In this uncomfortable position we spent the night, having that day covered a distance of only about six miles.

The following morning was calm, with a temperature of 13 degrees below zero, and we spent the better part of two hours digging out the tents and sledges from banks of drift snow up to five feet deep. Of the dogs, the only trace to be seen was a series of low mounds along the site of their tethering wire; on observing these attentively, faint puffs of condensed vapour could be seen rising from a small hole in the summit of each mound, and on scraping away the snow, one would disclose a shaggy snow-encrusted face, and be met with the gaze of a reproachful brown eye.

We now entered the northern end of the Crown Prince Gustav Channel, down which our course lay between Ross Island and the mainland of the Palmer Peninsula. To describe in detail the daily events of our subsequent journey by this route, around the southern tip of Ross Island, and so finally to Snow Hill, would take up more space than I feel justified in allotting to this part of these memoirs, and accordingly I now revert to the time-honoured expedient of transcribing verbatim a few of the laconic entries in the daily journal which I wrote up by candlelight in the tent at the end of each day's journey, and of which the grease-stained pages, squared with blue lines and covered with my crowded and almost illegible pencilled script, now lie before me as I write.

> *Aug. 16.* Overcast. Make for Church Point on mainland, run into deep snow. Very heavy going; Taylor pulling with dogs. Cold (–25 °F), ice over faces makes eating difficult. Head out again to mid-channel; surface improves. Make camp in lee of frozen-in tabular. Weird complaining sounds under ice; Taylor says seals.[3]
> *Aug. 18.* Sea ice becomes undulating, from glacier tongue from mainland pushing out for miles and buckling up sea ice; morainic stones scattered over ice everywhere. Attempt to get close to mainland again frustrated by deep soft snow. Head away towards SW corner Ross Island. Sledging rations, at first too filling and greasy, now barely sufficient to satisfy hunger.

Aug. 20. James and Russell pick up radio message from base that Japanese war over. At last!!! But what next? To win wars one thing, to establish peace another. Wonder why Japan collapsed so quickly.

Aug. 23. Wonderful day. Left camp standing, went out on reconnaissance with sledges loaded with sleeping bags, shovels, equipment only. Taylor and Russell to the S, James and I make for Cape Longing on mainland. T. and R. climb up land ice to 1,320 feet, get good view of Robertson Island and Seal Nunataks to S. Returning by compass bearing in deepening twilight; full moon, flattened-ellipsoid, like huge orange sailing in sky low down over horizon; beautiful, peaceful, lonely. (Later) – dogs got loose on sea ice at 2 a.m.

Aug. 25. Cold! My God! –34.6°, outside tent last night! Hoods, bags, walls encrusted with rime, had to handle utensils with gloves on. Never had it like this before. Spent night shivering in bottom of bag. Russell's feet frostbitten, but still walks. Pass Lockyer Island today. Mirage of ice cliffs to S.

Aug. 26. Warmer later (–18 °F), but strong cold wind. Snow streamers off mainland and Ross. Run into heavy deep snow offshore, have to give Ross wide berth. Russell's feet with open blisters, socks all bloody, but never said word about it. Dogs seemed a little feeble today, time we got a seal. Expect get Snow Hill tomorrow.

And we did. On the morning of August 27th, we split into two parties: Taylor and I to press on to Snow Hill, James and Russell to search for the Swedish depot at Depot Point on the east side of Ross Island. We separated and went our ways with our respective sledges and teams, and in a south-westerly following wind soon lost sight of the others in the scurrying drift. The depot for which James and Russell were searching was that which had been left by Nordenskjöld behind a projecting promontory, a little south of Cape

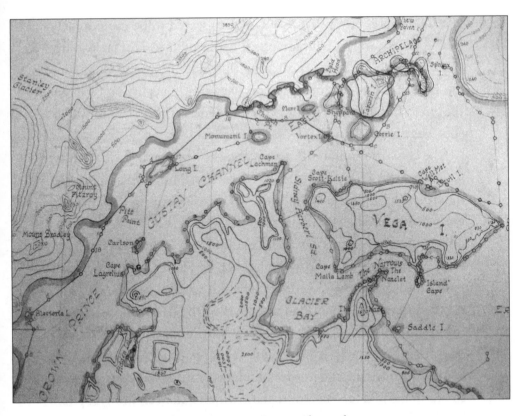

Crown Prince Gustav Channel,
detail from the surveys of August–December 1945.

Hamilton, in March 1902. The position, about opposite Lockyer Island, was meticulously indicated in Nordenskjöld's book, and so they had quite a good chance of finding it. Taylor and I, in the early afternoon, caught our first glimpse of the steep escarpments of Snow Hill Island through the intermittent drift, and Taylor went ahead of the team to prospect the route which would lead us to the little cove in the northern part of the island where the Swedish base hut was, or had been, situated. The sea ice was here very bad for sledging, rifted and hummocky, and on two occasions I was unable to prevent the sledge from capsizing when it ran up on the sides of the high shoreward side of the little bay. And there was the house directly ahead of us, on top of a small stony mound about a hundred yards from the shore. From that distance it appeared to be quite intact, just as shown in the photographs illustrating it in Nordenskjöld's *Antarctica*. My feelings on catching this first glimpse of this mute monument left by our predecessors, steadfastly persisting through the lonely desolation of forty-two years of desertion in this forsaken spot, were complex.

The construction of this house, and the life which its occupants led for nearly two years within its four walls, have been graphically described by Nordenskjöld, and it is particularly well shown in the various excellent photographs illustrating his book, which is one of the great classics of polar exploration. Facing page 108, in my edition, there is a photograph taken by Skottsberg, showing it partly built, with the lower part, of stout vertical beams, still not planked in; two unidentified members of the party are seated on the ground runners at its base, evidently in animated conversation. Another photograph, by Bodman, facing page 150, shows us the house in its pristine and newly completed state. It was constructed, so Nordenskjöld tells us, from plans which had been drawn up for Amdrup's[4] first wintering expedition to East Greenland, and was erected in the early months of the year 1902 on its present site: 'to our inexperienced eyes it seemed as though the place enjoyed complete shelter from the cold south-winds'. The box-like structure, sustained originally at each corner by stout rope cables, only two of which still remained in position, seemed surprisingly small to us, being slightly over twenty feet long by fourteen feet wide. The outside had originally been covered with tarred paper, which now flapped in tatters in the gusty wind. The windows were gone, leaving blank holes through which, in the gloom of the interior, we could dimly see a table and chairs, covered with all kinds of debris, and embedded in mounds of ice. The door was inextricably jammed, and it was through one of the window openings that we finally made our entry into the house. Awestruck, we tiptoed reverently from room to room, conversing in whispers, like pilgrims going through the echoing galleries of a national shrine or the flagstoned alcoves of a great cathedral.

In addition to the loft under the roof, there were five rooms, the largest of which had served as the general living quarters; of the others, three were sleeping cabins, one the kitchen, and the remaining one had obviously served as the lavatory. The main entrance door led into a little porch or alcove giving access to the living room. It was into one of the cabins that we had first penetrated by entering through the window, and here there were two bunkbeds, the lowermost almost buried in ice, with the names of the occupants – Gösta Bodman and Erik Ekelöf – carved on their sides with creditable skill, and still containing the sodden and decayed remnants of striped flock-filled mattresses.

Snow and ice lay in drifts and mounds everywhere in the interior, and we had to use a shovel and a hammer to pry loose the articles scattered around and partly embedded by the alternate thawing and freezing of the accumulated snow. The party had, of course, left the house with great precipitation when unexpectedly relieved on November 8th, 1903, by the Argentine naval vessel *Uruguay*, and so it was very natural that the articles left behind had been strewn in confusion and disorder. The photographs of the interior taken during the sojourn of the party show us that they had normally maintained everything in a state of characteristically Scandinavian tidiness. Now, empty bottles, rusty tins, kitchen utensils, parts of meteorological instruments, a few candles and remains of oil lamps, and other odds and ends littered the exposed parts of tables, chairs and bunk beds, and sheets of peeling cardboard had collapsed off the inner walls and now lay randomly draped over these miscellaneous objects. In the loft, which was greatly weighed down by the accumulation of snow, we found some more unused candles, which we took, a camera tripod, a case half full of packets of baking powder, and a tin containing some mouldy tea. Two sealskins, hard as boards, were hanging from the crossbeam of the roof.

Having made our reconnaissance, and taken a number of photographs of the house from various viewpoints, Taylor and I returned to our sledge on the sea ice a short distance offshore and unloaded it to make camp. A bitter south-west wind was blowing, and Taylor pointed out to me the remarkable steepness and depth of the *sastrugi*, or wind-blown snow ridges, around us; this seemed indeed to be a particularly windy spot, probably on account of the col on the island, to the south of the Swedish base, acting as a funnel to intensify the force of the prevailing south-westerly gales. Nordenskjöld's party soon found that they had picked a bad place for wind, and during their stay there they experienced some exceptionally severe hurricanes, up to seventy miles per hour in velocity, with the temperature going down to as low as −22 °F, a lethal conjunction of wind and cold, such as we ourselves had happily as yet only once experienced, on the occasion of that night in the tin galley shortly after our landing at Hope Bay. Nordenskjöld writes that the first omen of such a blizzard would be a warm wind from the south, followed later by a few strong blasts, after which the storm would be unleashed in its full violence, and continue for forty-eight hours or longer. On such occasions, he says, inside the house 'everything reminds one vividly of the sleeping-car of an express-train rushing along a line which is not too solidly constructed'. In our modern days, on a similar occasion, I had in the same way compared the experience with a flight in a not too solidly constructed aeroplane.

Just as we had finished pitching camp, James and Russell arrived with the news that they had found the depot at Cape Hamilton* and, having joined us inside our tent, they displayed some of the foodstuffs which they had found there: dried apple rings and prunes, tea, and some cans of preserves, mostly in a remarkably good state of preservation and perfectly edible.[5] We gratefully supplemented our evening meal with the Swedish supplies which had lain in their

---

* Now Hamilton Point.

hiding place for over forty years, and topped off the repast with an excellent dish of tea of rare old vintage, matured in ice.

Two days later[6] we left Snow Hill on the first stage of our homeward run, and set a course somewhat to the right of the isolated, cone-topped mass of Cockburn Island, in Erebus and Terror Gulf which extends from the north-east coast of Ross Island to Vega Island and the mainland of the Palmer Peninsula. We made our first night's camp on the shores of Seymour Island, which lies about fifteen miles north of Snow Hill. On raising our tent, Taylor and I made the annoying discovery that a fairly large hole had been worn in the outer fabric by friction against a carelessly loaded ration box, and I spent a very unpleasant quarter of an hour sewing up the rent with needle and thread in a blustery wind with a temperature of −18 °F. The following day was devoted to the exploration of Seymour Island, where the Swedish expedition had made some of the most important geological discoveries in the annals of polar science, finding there fossilized remains of almost the earliest representatives of our present-day temperate flora.

Seymour Island consists of soft friable sandstone of a terracotta colour, worn into deep ravines and gorges, and affording a landscape of a soft, polychromatic quality which contrasts utterly with the hard, sombre, black-and-white scenery of Hope Bay and the rest of the mainland. It had in it something of the colourful luminescence of Claude Monet or Sisley[7] in comparison with, shall we say, the work of Vlaminck,[8] and I found it hard to believe that this friendly looking, though arid landscape was situated in one of the most severely exposed climatic regions of this sector of the Antarctic.

We left the camp standing, and crossed the island on foot by way of a low valley which extended right across it. On the way I found the ground literally strewn with fossils in many places; bivalve molluscs, the teeth of *Zeuglodon* (an extinct giant shark), belemnites (the spear-like 'bone' of a bygone race of cuttlefish), coiled ammonites with intricate patterns of convoluted sutures, and whole trunks of fossil wood. At the eastern side of the island we parted company, going in different directions, Taylor following the shoreline to the north, James and Russell to the south, and myself returning to the valleys of the interior to make as complete a collection as possible of fossils and lichens.

From these several excursions, each of us returned with great profit late that afternoon, and with exciting tidings to relate inside the tent in the relaxing warmth of the singing pressure stove. Taylor had walked right around the northern end of the island, a distance of twelve miles, and had found a cairn marked with a pole, at the base of which was deposited a capsule containing a letter, written in French, left by the Argentine relief expedition under Commodore Julián Irízar, and dated November 7th, 1903, that is to say the day before they landed at Snow Hill and took off Nordenskjöld and his party; its text I am not free to divulge.[9] Meanwhile, James and Russell had succeeded in finding the Argentine depot[10] in the southern part of the island, and returned bearing a large quantity of white sugar, agglomerated into large lumps like blocks of marble, large cans of corned beef (partly rusted through), dried beans, rice, and – marvellous to relate – a case of a dozen brown barrel-shaped bottles of a liquor identified by the highly ornate label as 'Hesperidina de Bagley', with instructions in Spanish to accept no substitutes, which in the circumstances we considered entirely reasonable. Some years later I was to become considerably familiar with this harmless and pleasant beverage, a refreshing and rather weak orange bitters, but on this occasion the watery contents of the bottles were frozen solid, and the supernatant sixth part, which we decanted off and drank, consisted of approximately absolute alcohol, and elevated our spirits very considerably. Together with the foodstuffs, they found a small tin canister sealed with adhesive tape, obviously containing a message; we deferred opening this until our return to the base.

Finally, I made my contribution to the display of wonders by exhibiting my collection of fossils and lichens, expounding enthusiastically on the superiority of that class of plants and of those who study them, and quoting portentously from Thoreau's *Journal*[11] in support of my views: 'The lichenist extracts nutriment from the very crust of the earth. A taste for this study is an evidence of titanic health, a sane earthiness ...' ('Earthiness is right,' interrupted James.) 'It fits a man to deal with the barrenest and rockiest experience. A lichenist fattens where others starve ...' ('You bet he does, but not on lichens,' said Taylor).

The essential part of our mission had now been accomplished, and it remained only for us to make a quick dash across Erebus and Terror Gulf, through Sidney Herbert Sound which runs between Ross and Vega Islands, and pick up our depot on Vortex Island. This would replenish our now very depleted supplies of fuel and dog food and allow us to accomplish the last stage of our journey across the peninsula back to the base in leisure and comparative luxury. The distance of about fifty miles separating us from Vortex Island should, we calculated, by the light of a candle stuck in one of the Bagley bottles, be covered easily in five days, or even three if the surfaces were very good, and it so happened that our supplies in hand, with the exercise of economy, would last out just exactly that time. In addition to which, we thought (being optimistically affected by our potations), we had every chance of meeting up with seals along the Ross and Vega coastlines, and more or less living off the land during the course of our return journey, with seal steaks and fried liver every night.

Yes, sir, altogether a wonderful trip, from start to finish – wonderful, wonderful ...

Pounded in the Mortar of Affliction[1]

AT THE OUTSET of our journey next day, as I was driving our team across the low snowfield between rocky mounds and hillocks, on the northern end of Seymour Island, to reach the sea ice of Erebus and Terror Gulf, I met with a strange experience, which now, on looking back at it in memory, appears insignificant and even ludicrous. Nevertheless, in the circumstances at the time, it impressed itself upon me rather strongly, leaving me with a vague feeling of uneasiness which wore off only slowly as the day progressed.

Taylor had gone ahead on snowshoes to assist James and Russell with the running survey, leaving me to bring up our sledge team half a mile behind. The sky was covered with continuous grey cloud which seemed to press down on us like a low ceiling. While keeping the foremost party in sight most of the time, I made several detours inland to examine the more conspicuous rock outcrops for their vegetation of lichens and mosses, and was able to add a number of these to my collection of the previous day.

Returning from one of these detours, I took the team down a lightly snow-covered slope towards a notch between two large rocks, from which there would be a straight run onto the sea ice to join up with the tracks of the preceding party. At a distance of about ten yards from this notch, the dogs suddenly stopped simultaneously, and the sledge ran into them from behind before I could bring it to a halt with the ski-crampon brake. They stood there motionless, all facing in the same direction, with the hair on their necks rising up into bristly fringes, and paid no attention to me and my angry swearing, even when I grabbed the dog whip off the handlebars of the sledge and commenced to lay it about them in exasperation. This was something which I had never experienced before, and I looked more closely at the notch between the rocks to find out what was scaring them. Then I too was seized with irrational fright when I saw, supported against the face of the rock on the left hand side of the notch, what appeared to be a human corpse in an advanced state of disintegration.

Taking my nerves in hand, I left the dogs and walked closer to investigate. Even after I got right up to it, it took me a few seconds to realize that it was just the half-decomposed carcass of a large seal which by some strange chance had come to lie in an upright position, supported by the almost vertical rock face. Its resemblance to a human corpse was most disconcerting; the skull was still covered by a tuft of hairy skin, and the teeth projected in the sardonic grin of the human death's-head, below the eyeless sockets. The rib casing was exposed down one side, and the rest of the body, in its glutinous investment of decaying skin and blubber, was amorphous like a corpse that has rotted down in the charnel house to a shocking armless and legless mass. It was the upright position of the carcass that caused the feeling of dismay, and made me unwilling to touch it. Probably it had died on top of the rock – for seals often crawl inland when they feel death approaching – and then by the melting of the snow been gradually lowered down the side into an upright position, where it remained, frozen into this strange quasi-human stance.[2]

Although it was in an advanced stage of decay, there was still enough organic matter left on it to give the dogs a much needed meal, and I tried to lead them up to it. But not one step would they advance; bristling and whining, they kept their eyes fixed on the object in obvious terror. I retraced my steps, and gave the rotting thing a rude push with my ski pole; it collapsed with a thump prone

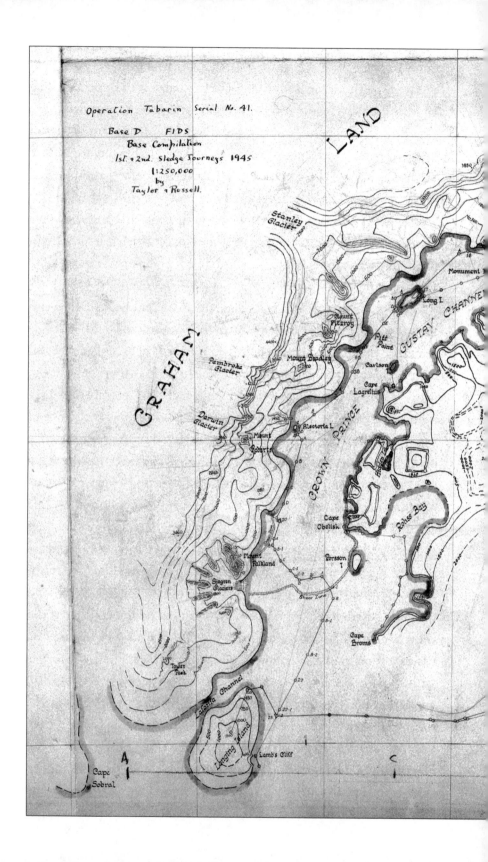

Operation Tabarin   Serial No. 41.

Base D   FIDS
Base Compilation
1st & 2nd. Sledge Journeys 1945
1:250,000
by
Taylor & Russell.

LAND

GRAHAM

PRINCE GUSTAV CHANNEL

Stanley Glacier

Monument

Long I.

Mount Fitzroy

Pitt Point

Pembroke Glacier

Mount Bradley

Carlson

Cape Lagrelius

Darwin Glacier

Mount Robert

Victoria I.

Rosa Bay

Cape Obelisk

Mount Falkland

Persson I.

Sjogren Glaciers

Cape Broms

Shear Zone

Taylor Peak

Lafond Channel

Longing Island

Lamb's Cliff

Cape Sobral

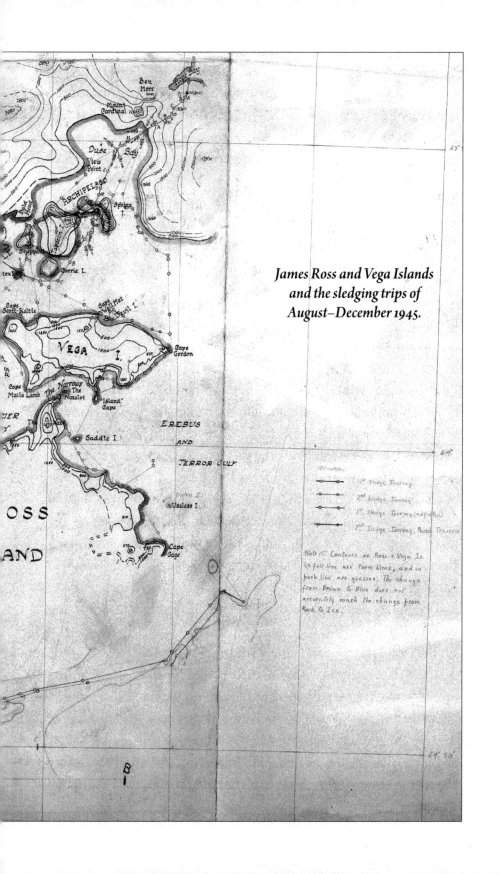

James Ross and Vega Islands
and the sledging trips of
August–December 1945.

onto the snow, and in the same instant the dogs found their voices and leaped forward with a headlong rush, and almost before I had time to step back out of the way they were tearing the skin and rotten blubber to bits and crunching the bones to splinters between their powerful teeth.

Out on the sea ice again, catching up with the other team, I thought: the respect which these animals have for Man, their master, is absolute, even in death – *but only so long as he retains the distinguishing mark of his species, the upright position . . .*[3]

*

From here, our route homewards lay across Erebus and Terror Gulf, that westernmost embayment of the Weddell Sea which is delimited by the coastlines of Seymour, Ross and Vega Islands, and which for its greater part lies in the sheltered lee of the vast domed snowfield of Ross Island. Directly across our course lay Cockburn Island, a small island of pepperbox-like form which for me, at least, possessed considerable interest, as being the first locality in the Antarctic to be systematically investigated from the botanical point of view. I refer, of course, to the visit made to it by Joseph Dalton Hooker[4] on the British *Erebus* and *Terror* Antarctic expedition of 1839–1843. For many years, up to the beginning of the twentieth century in fact, the sum total of our knowledge concerning the Antarctic flora was based on the few plants – algae, lichens and mosses – which Hooker had hurriedly collected on this little island during a brief landing from the ship.

The clouds lay low, and after a while descended to the level of the sea ice to the north and west of us to form a fog bank which swallowed up the landmark for which we were heading. Before it disappeared altogether, we took a compass bearing on Cockburn Island by which to steer our course through the dense fog which soon enveloped us completely. A feeling of intensified isolation came over us as we thus made our way blindly through the grey and clammy murk, the virgin and unvarying white surface opening up endlessly a few yards ahead of us, and our parallel tracks sliding silently away out of sight behind.

Towards noon we reckoned that we must have traversed the four or five miles which had separated us that morning from Cockburn Island, and began to wonder whether we had not missed it altogether in the fog. The united shouts which we emitted at intervals brought back no echo to us, and yet we knew that the high cliffs and rocky talus slope could not be more than half a mile away, at most; but in which direction?

Suddenly Taylor, who was walking ahead on snowshoes, came to a halt, and shouted back to us something which I did not catch, at the same time pointing upwards with his ski stick. Gazing up into the grey limbo in the direction indicated, I was startled to see a great dark mass of jumbled rocks suspended, as it seemed, in the fog bank almost directly above our heads. The drifting wraiths of cloud above and below gave it the impression of movement, the illusion of thousands of tons of rock slowly dropping downwards on us from above. We were actually right at the base of the steep cliffs of Cockburn Island, and a few more yards brought us to the tide crack and the scree slope of loose basaltic blocks. The matrix of the island consists of a soft bedded sandstone, surmounted by almost vertical cliffs of dark conglomerate. In places along the talus slope were evidences of an Adélie penguin rookery, with numerous deserted nests and the mummified carcasses of chicks which had died there in various stages of their growth. Lichens were tolerably abundant on the rocks near sea level, and I made a collection of about a dozen species, the majority of which had already been found, perhaps in that self-same spot, and duly recorded, by Hooker a century before.[5]

After consuming our noonday rations we headed off once more into the fog, and traversed another four miles in a direction slightly west of north, which should lead us directly across Erebus and Terror Gulf for thirty miles or so of unhindered travel over the sea ice to strike eventually the channel running between Ross Island and the southern side of Vega Island. Through this channel, the Sidney Herbert Sound,* another ten or fifteen miles of sledging (assuming the existing chart to be approximately correct) should bring us out again into the northern end of Crown Prince Gustav Channel, not far from our outgoing depot on Vortex Island. Shortly after four in the afternoon we made camp for the night, being still surrounded by dense fog on all sides. The temperature had dropped somewhat, the mercury standing at 8 °F, and fine snow crystals were falling through the mist. We had covered this day a distance of eleven and a half miles.

Next morning, September 1st, dawned gloomily through persistent fog banks crowding round us on every hand. The barometer was falling rapidly, and we decided not to travel that day. Russell and James joined us in our tent to economize our low stock of fuel, and we spent an uneventful day plotting the survey results of the last few weeks, mending dog harnesses, and making an inventory of the rations still in hand.

Our supplies were indeed running very low, and it was obviously imperative that we should make good time across the gulf and through Sidney Herbert Sound to our depot before they became completely exhausted. Only half a can of kerosene remained, which meant that henceforth we could use it only for the preparation of our food, and not for warmth or for drying clothing and footgear. We restricted ourselves to one meal that day, and did not feed the dogs at all. Fortunately, we possessed the additional supplies from the Seymour Island depot, some of which we could use to supplement our rations, about two dozen large rusted cans of doubtful corned beef, forty-two years old, to eke out the dog's ration for a day or two, and we ourselves could chew up a limited quantity of the dried beans, which we were unable to soak or cook for lack of fuel. Apart

---

* Now Herbert Sound.

from that, all we could use from the depot was a rather large quantity of white sugar, consolidated into slabs and blocks of marble-like consistency.

The following day was just as foggy as the two preceding it, but we could not afford to lie up another day in camp, and accordingly loaded the sledges and set out on compass bearings as before. We felt ravenously hungry, and ate large lumps of sugar from the sledge bags; this would give us the needed calories, it was true, but what of our wasting bodily tissues? The dogs were also obviously half starved, and that morning I saw several of them fight for steaming human excreta. Before the day was over they would be eating their own...

Much soft snow had fallen during the night, and after a while the going began to get very heavy. At last, towards noon, the dogs, weakened by hunger, were barely able to keep the sledges moving. I put on our only pair of snowshoes and the man-harness, and struggled along pulling with the dogs, while Taylor pushed the sledge from behind by the handlebars. The other team with James and Russell, following in our beaten-down tracks, had less difficulty in making headway.

Two miles more and the snow was knee-deep. To make further progress, we were forced to dump half of our loads and relay in mile-long stretches. In this painful fashion we covered a further couple of miles in the fog, and were finally forced to pitch camp at two in the afternoon by the insurmountable exhaustion of man and beast. We fed the dogs each a can of corned beef in addition to their single pemmican block, and both disappeared down their gullets in a flash. I tried to supplement our own pemmican mush by adding a handful of the dried beans to it, but they were so hard that we could not masticate them.

Shortly before sundown Taylor left the tent and returned with the news that the fog was lifting at last. He had spent some time in conversation with James and Russell in the other tent, and for some time after his return lay quietly in his sleeping bag, gazing upwards at the peak of the tent. Finally he turned towards me and spoke his mind.[6]

'We're no further from the base than a good day's journey by road in an automobile. On a good surface we could make our depot at Vortex in two days with full rations. On a moderate surface, in four days on half rations. On a surface like this, in perhaps ten days, six of them without food or fuel. But the dogs can't pull the sledges more than a day, or two at the most, after their rations are finished; even now they're a lot weaker than they were yesterday. We're on the north-east side of Ross Island, and the prevailing wind is south-westerly. That means that the snow cover on Ross gets blown off and settles deep over the sea ice. We may have to go out of our direct course and head more eastwards to get out of the zone of deep drift. Question is, how far? Senseless to think of returning to Snow Hill and using the lumber there for fuel; we'd still be without food supplies, unless we met up with a seal, which seems unlikely from what we've seen so far around these parts. You know, Mack, our great mistake was to leave the skis and second pair of snowshoes at Vortex. On skis, with just a pressure stove in a rucksack for drinking water, one of us could get through to Vortex in a day, and right back to the base if need be by travelling twenty-four hours at a stretch. It could be done – if we had our skis.'

'What about our radio?' I asked. 'We contacted the base from the bottom of Crown Prince Gustav Channel, and it ought to be possible to get them from here too'.

'In the first place, the batteries are pretty well run down, and the set would have to be warmed up for about an hour, which we don't have the gas to do; in the second place, what would they do about it there, without any dog team, only a few untrained pups and nobody practised in sledge driving? No, we are the only ones who can help ourselves out of this jam, and we'll do it, don't worry. Men lost in the Northwest Territories of Canada have got back with much less in their favour than we have.'

And so, in the full knowledge of our somewhat absurd predicament, we pulled the flaps of our sleeping bags about our ears and lapsed without effort into a dreamless slumber to rest ourselves against the efforts which the morrow would bring.

> *Sept. 3.* Calm, fairly clear; −14 °F. Floundering NW through deep snow; 3 hours to go 1 mile! Halt exhausted every 50 yds. Last of dog pemmican used up this evening; feed dogs on last of depot corned beef. Snow up to dogs' bellies, Taylor ahead on snowshoes hauling in man-harness. Heading away from lee of Ross. Think three miles covered today, but sledge meter out of order. Awful cold this evening, −27 °F. Hungry.

Three miles in one day!

To add to our troubles, the temperature on the night of September 3rd/4th fell to an all-time low: −40 °F. I woke up in the hours of dawn, curled up in a ball down in the bottom of my sleeping bag, with my teeth chattering violently and an alarming cold gripping at my back and shoulders. The inside of the tent was glistening with a dense fur of projecting rime crystals, and our breath issued from our mouths and nostrils in vaporous puffs. I could feel the mucous membrane inside my nose crackling as I inhaled the lethally cold air. I fished out my damp socks and sealskin boots, which I had taken with me into the sleeping bag to keep them from freezing to board-like stiffness, as we no longer had the fuel to dry them out at the end of each day's journey. Painfully I worked them onto my swollen feet, which had lost all sensation and were of an unhealthy waxen colour, and stamped them on the floor of the tent in an effort to revive something of the circulation. We had to postpone our departure for about an hour, until the sun came up and raised the temperature to a more bearable −28 °F. Everything we had to handle – knots, buckles, guy ropes, sledge lines – was of steely hardness and stiffness, and cost us many minutes of painful fumbling with frozen and almost useless fingers. Finally we got going, in clear weather at last, across the trackless waste of knee-deep snow, heading in a north-north-easterly direction away from the drift-infested coasts of Ross Island on the horizon to our left.

By noon we had covered not more than two miles, and were exhausted and running with perspiration, in spite of the low temperature. The dogs were almost useless; stopping every few yards and lying inert on their bellies with glazed and hopeless eyes, their legs completely buried, until we urged them on with voice and whip to recommence their frenzied leaping and floundering. At this juncture we decided to offload the sledges and leave behind everything which was not absolutely essential to us in gaining the safety of our depot.

An hour later we started off again, leaving behind us a mound of boxes, instruments, cameras, radio, specimens and equipment, surmounted by a theodolite tripod to which we had tied a small flag of red bunting. A round of compass bearings taken from the spot was recorded in Taylor's notebook to enable us to locate the dump again if and when it should ever prove possible to return and pick up the goods on some subsequent occasion. Taylor and Russell, the former on snowshoes, went ahead hauling on a line with the 'Big Boys' team, while James walked, or I should say struggled, behind the sledge, and by their united efforts they succeeded in keeping it in constant motion at a speed of about half a mile per hour. The dogs were by this time a negligible factor, merely keeping pace with the sledge and at times straggling beside and behind it, with slack traces trailing over the snow. I followed about half a mile behind with the 'Odds and Sods', propelling the more lightly loaded second sledge forward in the tracks of the first, between waist-high walls of soft snow, by a continued series of convulsive heavings on the handlebars, with but little help from the poor exhausted animals. I had left my dog whip behind in the cache, not so much to lighten the load, but because I no longer had the heart to use it on them. By an irony of nature, the day had become calm and fine with excellent visibility, wonderful travelling weather were it not for the deep snow which engulfed us like a quicksand and kept us rooted in this spot with little prospect of getting much farther by nightfall, in spite of the most strenuous exertions which we could possibly muster.

I doubt if there can be any more exhausting mode of progression, even those inflicted upon themselves by Asiatic pilgrims, than that of plunging each leg alternately in snow up to the thigh and then raising it out of the hole by an acrobatic contortion which involves bringing the knee up to the level of the chin. I found it much more restful to shuffle along behind the sledge on my knees, using the backwardly extended shin as a snowshoe, but unfortunately this method did not give sufficient purchase to heave the sledge bodily forwards when it came to a standstill every few feet. It was progressing inch by inch like a snow plough, pushing up a large pile of snow in front, and from my sunken position down behind the rear end I was unable to see the dogs at all, except when one of them lay down and allowed the sledge to pass him by until he was again pulled forward by the tightening of his trace line.

After a while my feet began to come up covered with saltwater slush, and the following interesting fact dawned on me: we were travelling, not over sea ice at all, but over open sea covered with a thick bed of soft drift snow! The enormous quantities of drift, blown into the gulf off Ross Island by the prevailing south-westerly winds, obviously lay upon the waters in a thick insulating mantle which prevented them from freezing over, and so the surface was literally bottomless, a mere raft of soft snow floating directly upon the surface of the sea. And it was into the midst of this, right out in Erebus and Terror Gulf, ten miles or more from the nearest land, that we had unwittingly wandered, and our feet were now plunging straight through the floating snow into the sea itself. One way of walking on the waves, I thought.[7]

The acrid perspiration got into my eyes and blinded me as it ran down my face, and every few seconds in passing I rubbed my features in the wall of snow on each side. My breathing seemed to have synchronized itself with the rhythm of my heartbeats, and when I halted to allow it to slow down a little, I was oppressed by a feeling of asphyxiation, no matter how much air I tried to gulp down into my convulsively labouring lungs; the only way I could get my breath was to keep moving as before, so that heart and lungs pulsated in unison. Some of my senses began to play little tricks on me, auditory and olfactory hallucinations; I heard distinctly the pattering rush of a heavy rainstorm among foliage, replete with the tinkling murmur of the run-off rivulets, and for one instant my nose seemed to be assailed with the warm, mawkish, dusty smell of privet flowers, such as I remembered from my earliest infancy along the hedge in front of our house in Scotland on the hottest summer days.

Finally my legs crumpled sideways beneath me and I found myself leaning backwards, like a half closed jack-knife, but not uncomfortably, against the handlebars of the sledge, viewing the expanse of snowy landscape at eye level with minute but completely disinterested attention. My breathing seemed to have stopped altogether, but I could not be sure of this. I was very drowsy, and perfect peace lay all around . . .[8]

*

I found myself blinking in a flood of brilliant, cold, clear and splendid sunlight. I was sitting upright in the snow, beside the sledge. Crouched in a semi-circle around me, at the ends of their traces, were the seven dogs of my team, backing slowly away from me on humbly bent legs, with their tails pulled tight in below their hindquarters; they were uttering little moans of terror and submission, and never before had I seen them so completely abject. I lurched suddenly to my feet and flapped my arms vigorously about me, and the dogs recoiled onto their haunches with little yelps of dismay, as if they had been flicked expertly with the dog whip. Something had put the fear of their God into them. Becoming aware of a stinging, burning sensation in my right forearm, I took off my gloves, rolled up my anorak and sweater sleeve, and looked: there on the skin were two opposite V-shaped rows of red impressions, from some of which a trickle of blood was slowly oozing . . .[9]

My eyes travelled along the furrowed trail ahead, and at the end of it, about half a mile away, I saw the other sledge stationary, with two figures standing beside it, while a third, which I correctly took to be Taylor, had left their side and was coming in my direction on snowshoes. I waved to him, called up the dogs, which responded with unusual alacrity as if eager to please, hauled back the main trace, and braced my shoulder against the front of the sledge, with a firm grip on the nearside runner. 'Huit!'

With a wrench on the sledge, and the impact on the main trace as the dogs leaped forward simultaneously in their harnesses, we were in motion, and shortly met Taylor on the trail. He looked at me and the dogs with an expression of obvious relief at seeing that we were still in the sledging business, having no doubt started back with some anxiety on observing my sledge stalled in the distance and myself lying prone behind it in the snow. His first words struck a welcome note:

'I've got good news for you, Mack. I think we're out of it at last. I walked on for about a mile on snowshoes, and came to the end of the drift, onto a good hard surface with bare sea ice in places, and it seemed to go on like that as far as I could see towards Sidney Herbert Sound. If that keeps up all the way along, we ought to be at our Vortex depot tomorrow afternoon.'

I said nothing, but took his gloved hand in both of mine. Something warm was running down my cheeks and freezing into little beads on my three weeks' growth of beard.

*

It proved, however, that our troubles were by no means over. Our release from the prisoning grip of soft deep snow gave us in one respect the means of attaining the safety and comfort of our depot on Vortex Island, but left us still comparatively helpless due to lack of traction. For both the dogs and ourselves were debilitated by the effects of slow attrition, especially the former. For some days past we had been living almost exclusively on a diet of pure cane sugar, the congealed and marble-like lumps excavated from the Argentine depot on Seymour Island. This chemically pure carbohydrate, taken at frequent intervals from the sledge-bags as we travelled, stilled the pangs of hunger to a large extent and promoted short bursts of energy, but did nothing to replace the rapid loss of fatty and protein reserves from our bodily tissues; we noted in each other, and then in ourselves, an increasingly lean and finally a cadaverous and almost skeletonic aspect. The extreme disrepair of our worn out clothing, now hanging loosely on our bony frameworks, heightened our resemblance to poorly constructed scarecrows.

With the dogs, matters were worse, for they would not eat the sugar which we offered to share with them. Perhaps they thought that we were serving them with lumps of snow, and may even have imputed sadistic tendencies to us in doing so; although I doubt this, taking into consideration the essentially trusting quality of canine nature. Their only source of nourishment now was excrement, theirs and ours, and even this commodity was latterly in sadly short supply. Not only could the dogs no longer draw the sledges, but they could only with the greatest difficulty totter on slack traces alongside, and two of them, Mutt and Jimmy, finally collapsed altogether, and were placed on the sledges, which we continued to drag painfully forward ourselves.

The surface here was comparatively good, windblown and tolerably smooth, as we worked slowly in a north-westerly direction towards The Naze, that stony finger of land that projects northwards from Ross Island and lies across the entrance to Sidney Herbert Sound, the gateway to our destination. Our forward rate, taking into account the frequent pauses of exhaustion, was something in the order of one and a half miles per hour.

Light variable airs now began to fan our cheeks from different quarters, and these, together with the gloomy mantle spreading rapidly across the sky, told us what to expect next. The accustomed routine of light airs, stiff breeze, south-west wind, falling temperature, horizontally flying sheets of granular snow, and finally the howling blizzard in its full development, was unfolded about us. A following blizzard may be borne, but this one, deflected by the icy heights of the two islands between which we sought to penetrate, blew directly in our faces. Our beards and eyes were clogged with the congealing crust, and we sought for a while to travel on with heads withdrawn into our cowls and averted downwards. Fingers and cheeks soon took on the numbness and waxy pallor of frostbite, and no choice remained to us but to halt and camp until the thing blew over. It was about four o'clock in the afternoon, and we had covered a distance of nearly nine miles, which was rather a remarkable achievement in the circumstances.[10]

By our stratagem of hauling up the peaks of the tents with a line, while simultaneously spreading them at the base and dumping large quantities of snow onto the flaps, we succeeded in getting them pitched as well as was possible, that is to say with just enough space inside for two men to rest, half crouching and half lying, inside their sleeping bags. The force of the snow-laden gale, like a sand-blast, filled our sleeping bags with snow even as we transferred them off the sledges into the tents, and I spent half an hour inside scooping the white powder out of them with a spoon before we could insert ourselves. We had no kerosene at all now left, and so did not bother to unpack the stoves off the sledge. We were not conscious of hunger to any great extent, but were considerably inconvenienced by thirst, which we could allay only by sucking the juice out of our sealskin boots and outer clothing as they thawed to softness with our bodies inside the bags. The dogs outside were not chained, but left where they flopped down in inanimate heaps, incapable of moving even a short distance from the camp.

The following day was mercifully fine and clear, with a temperature of −22 °F, and we loaded up the sledges and commenced to drag them forward once more, round the tip of The Naze and into Sidney Herbert Sound. The dogs now tottered far astern, dragged forward on their traces, most of the time on their feet, but sometimes on their bellies or their backs; Mutt and Jimmy as before comatose, and carried curled up on top of the sledges.

A halloo from Russell broke the air, and we halted to discern, our eyes screwed up and focused to infinity, what he was pointing out to us with the tip of his extended ski pole. There, in the farther entrance to the sound, bathed in the blue effulgence of the sunlit icy wastes, lay the rusty columnar spiral of Vortex Island, our haven of salvation in Crown Prince Gustav Channel, at a distance of approximately twenty miles. Spurred onwards and heartened by the sight, we pulled desperately for six hours more until our legs refused to have any more to do with it, and we finally made camp in the middle of the sound, beneath the sheer black basalt heights of Cape Scott Keltie, dominant sentinel of these immutable wastes.*

---

* Now Keltie Head, on NW Vega Island.

Final Footprints
on the White Expanse

'WELL, I'M AFRAID there's only one thing to do now,' sighed James, as he flipped open the breech of our service revolver and reached into the cardboard ammunition box for four bullets. They rattled dryly under his fingers like the disjointed members of a skeleton hand. It was shortly after sunrise, and we crouched together, all four of us, in one of the two tents. The last half hour had been spent in serious discussion, and we had now arrived at an agreement. There was no more to be said, and James, carrying the revolver, slipped outside through the tent flap, and waited for us. We left the tent silently in turn and joined him standing there. Rosy shafts of light diffused the eastern sky behind the bluffs of Vega Island, and the gradations of nacreous colour in the sky, and over the wrinkled icefields below, were unbelievably subtle and tender in their unconscious artistry. Antarctic nature was at its purest and most sublime that morning, and spoke to us of life, not death. But our minds were made up, and the question settled once and for all.

Slowly James made his way behind the tents, to the spot where our fourteen poor comrades lay in the snow, stupefied tumuli of brute exhaustion. We remained standing where we were, silent, our eyes cast down on the ground, embarrassment and shame written all too clearly on our faces. We heard the voice of James speaking warmly and comfortingly to one of his favourite animals behind the tent, and then the air was shattered by the whanging report of a shot, followed two seconds later by another. The cliffs of Cape Scott Keltie repeated them to us alternately, and once again all was still. From a corner of my shamefully averted eye I caught a glimpse of James re-entering the tent, something white, shaggy and inert clasped to his bosom. A minute later the groundsheet of the tent was extruded through the opening. We remained motionless outside, silent as before.

Five minutes elapsed. Then we heard James call to us from inside the tent, in a steady, uninflected voice.

'It's all ready. I can cut it into thirteen pieces, or seventeen. Taylor?'

'Thirteen.'

'Mack?'

'Thirteen.'

'Vic?'

'Thirteen.'

Another five minutes, and a ration box emerged from the tent, pushed out from within. James followed, and carried it over to where the dogs were lying. Their seventh sense seemed to tell them what was in it, and they snapped out of their lethargy, regained their wasted legs, and crowded up to him drooling and whining. He served each one in turn, and a dismal sound of sucking and crunching filled the air. James re-joined us, and I saw that the front of his anorak was crimson and moist.

'Better give them an hour to digest it before we start.'

'Poor old Mutt, squint-eyed, bad tempered old bugger. It won't seem the same without him.'

'Well, better get the tents down and the sledges loaded.'

An hour later, when the time came to harness up the remaining thirteen, two things surprised me. First, the restored vigour of the animals, who ran forward to the full extent of their traces at the front of the sledges and even jumped and whined a little in a pale parody of their former riotous eagerness; and, second, that nothing, nothing at all, remained on the snow, not even a spot of blood, except a large patch in the place where one of tents had stood. They all pulled, feebly to be sure, but with some accession of their former spirit, and with our help carried the journey forward another nine miles, almost to the western opening of Sidney Herbert Sound, where we encamped within a few miles of its debouchment into Crown Prince Gustav Channel, with the chocolate tower of Vortex Island in full view before us, twelve or thirteen miles distant.

'Listen,' I said to Taylor, as we stood outside our tent preparing to push the bedrolls into it. 'The air's so still that I almost think I can hear the penguins over there on Vortex.' We stood motionless, unbreathing, straining our ears. The air was indeed exceptionally calm that evening, and to both of us was unmistakeably wafted, flooding and ebbing in faint waves, a confused murmur of some indeterminate activity from the wide and isolated stretches of the channel to the westward.

Perhaps we were mistaken; at a distance of twelve miles, even given the remarkable stillness of the atmosphere, such a thing does not seem possible; and yet, may not our ears, after our long sojourn in the wintry wastes of Death, have become preternaturally attuned to the first faint murmurings of returning life?

'Penguins. Penguin liver with oatmeal. Penguin breast *à la suprème*. Maybe penguins' eggs. And a seal. No, two seals, three seals, a dozen fat seals basking on the ice there at the foot of Vortex. Tomorrow evening at this time, Taylor, we'll all be full and burping and warm, and our boots will be drying up in the peak of the tent over a roaring stove, and I'll melt about ten gallons of snow to drink as we never drank before.' Now for the first time, with abundance almost palpable before us, did I realize how hungry and thirsty we were, and had been for longer than I could now remember.

Next day we covered the remaining thirteen miles with a will, and arrived below the cliffs of Vortex at four o'clock in the afternoon. Hours previously, at a distance of five miles, the clamour of the penguins had become manifest, and on rounding the point near which our little depot lay, we came into full sight of their several scattered colonies. No change in their circumstances appeared to have occurred since our last visit, and still they wandered aimlessly to and fro, on and off the land and out onto the sea ice, which lay, as previously, thick and unbroken out in all directions, with not even a crack through which they could dive to get their sustenance.[1]

And now intense activity consumed us all. There were the tents to be erected, the cache to be dug out, the stoves to be filled up, the dogs to be attached along their wire – for now, in view of their returning vigour and what we had to give them, the chances of a free-for-all at feeding time were once more possible – and a raid to be made on the unsuspecting penguins around the corner. As I came to the fourteenth chain on the line, I involuntarily looked about me for Mutt before I remembered . . .

Those penguins – hunger artists indeed, beyond the imaginings of a Kafka or the holy playboys of the eastern world. With nothing but a little greenish mucus in their bowels, how could they remain erect and stroll about so unconcerned, day after day, week after week, finding strength even for nest-making and nuptial rites of which the outcome would be more than questionable? It seemed as if the injunction, 'Take therefore no thought for the morrow,'[2] perhaps together with others from the same authority, had penetrated pole-wards and at last encountered devotees who took it seriously.

Double ration of pemmican for each dog, and a penguin as dessert; for us, fried penguin livers and oatmeal coming up, faithfully fulfilling my prediction in all details, even unto the burping. The Primus stoves, filled to overflowing, and pumped to dangerous pressure, roared out a circle of blue flame and raised the temperature inside the tent to such a degree that Taylor and I, stripped to our soiled singlets, had to stick our heads out of the tent opening and gulp in lungsful of the cold refreshing air. I motioned towards our skis, now exhumed from the cache and stuck upright in the snow beside the tent; we both laughed, as we could now afford to do, at Taylor's jest that we should never in future go anywhere without them, even in the streets of Montevideo.

On the morning that followed, our high living of the previous evening had taken effect, not altogether favourably to efficiency. A relaxed and holiday spirit filled the air, and we moved leisurely, pipe in mouth, among our recovered chattels, humming brief snatches as we lifted and transported bedrolls and ration boxes to the sledges. The day was well advanced before we got under way, headed this time due north into the 'Bay of a Thousand Icebergs'.

The events of the day continued to enhance our festive attitude, for shortly before noon, when we were about halfway across the bay, we surprised a group of three seals basking at the foot of an embedded tabular iceberg, and massacred them. After the choicest morsels and a goodly supply of blubber had been boxed for our own use, the two teams, which had been meantime detained in the offing, were taken singly, still attached to the sledges, to the carcasses, and there allowed to despoil them *in situ*, wallowing and gorging themselves to repletion in the steaming gory masses. It was indeed a savoury sight to see the gallant creatures choking down great gobs of juicy nourishment and swelling by the minute; but I wished that fourteen, not just thirteen, could have been called to table.[3]

We were now only two days' easy journey from our base, and having supplies in hand and not feeling unduly energetic, we resolved to make camp early in the afternoon, having covered about three-quarters of the distance separating us from the point on the mainland where we would commence our ascent over the top of the peninsula and down the other side to Hope Bay. The free time in the tents that afternoon gave me the opportunity of trying out a little experiment, along lines which I had long been privately contemplating off and on, namely the utilization of seal blubber for fuel. At one time, with supplies of kerosene exhausted, recourse to blubber for warmth and cooking was necessary and obvious, but then we had none; now we had both kerosene and blubber in abundance, and so had no need to occupy ourselves any further with the subject. But I was reluctant to return from what was probably our last sledging trip without having had experience of the use of this classical polar fuel, and so, that afternoon, talked Taylor, against his sounder judgement, into acquiescence, and set to work to make a blubber stove exactly according to the details remembered from the passages in Nordenskjöld's book describing the construction of what Duse and Anderson called a 'smoker'. How appropriate that designation was, we were shortly to find out for ourselves. You proceed as follows:

First, take a good-sized tin container of about a half-gallon in capacity – we used an empty pemmican can, but if you are working in your own home anything similar from the kitchen will do – and fill it three-quarters full with chunks of blubber cut to about the size of an ox's eyeball (uniform symmetry is not essential except for aesthetic reasons). The cut-around lid of the can, not completely severed, is lifted up at an angle of forty-five degrees and then bent level at its free side so as to form a shelf upon which a block of blubber may conveniently rest. A short piece of lamp wick, such as you might snip off an old dog harness, is then squeezed down among the blubber in the can until it becomes saturated with the exuded oil, this also serving the purpose of cleaning the fingers and allowing you to see their natural colour. Applying a match to the wick, you are agreeably surprised to see it burst readily into a steady yellow flame, not unaccompanied by smoke. The basic philosophy underlying the entire operation, fascinating in its simplicity, is that blubber, although in the raw state not readily flammable, parts company with its oily fraction when heated, and the function of the burning wick is to bring about this exudation from the lump superimposed upon the lid above it. The fragrant oil drips down therefore onto the flame of the wick, thereby augmenting it and from thence onwards the process is one of increasing returns; the more the flame is fed from above, the stronger it burns, this in turn releasing an increased supply of fuel from above, until at last not only the wick, but also the entire contents of the can, are mantled in a sheet of leaping yellow flame, and the wick, having fulfilled its fertilizing function, collapses after the manner of its kind. No further attention is needed but to throw a fresh block of blubber from time to time into the spattering conflagration, and the amount of heat given out is all that could be desired.

But where there is fire, also there is smoke, and a blubber stove confirms the soundness of this dictum beyond all possibility of doubt or contradiction. Furthermore, the smoke in this instance is of a peculiar solid constitution, not merely ethereally gaseous. It was Taylor who drew my attention, with some signs of mild irritation, to the slow descent upon us, from the smoke-filled upper reaches of the tent, of myriads of beautifully formed flakelets of utter blackness, little stygian gondolas of exquisite feathery lightness, which ebbed downwards with a wavering motion and finally settled on our hair, hands and faces, as well as on every other solid which they might encounter.

The efficiency and workability of the blubber burner had now been amply demonstrated, and demands for its removal became peremptory. Accordingly it was deposited outside in the snow to burn itself out without causing further annoyance. But it had done its work. When I crept back into the tent and lit a candle to replace the light of the smoker, Taylor looked at me wide-eyed for an instant and then broke into loud guffaws of laughter, which coming from him must have been caused by something really very funny; and as I turned to meet his gaze, I too was seized with uncontrollable mirth.

'You going in for the blackface minstrel business, Mack?' he chuckled, and then, surveying his own hands and rubbing his face and head with them, 'Christ Almighty!'

It was then that we both simultaneously noticed the inside walls of the tent, now that the smoke had subsided. 'CHRIST ALMIGHTY!

Don't you ever bring another bit of that stuff inside this tent! Look at those walls! His slight annoyance, I felt bound to confess, was not unjustified; for not only the walls and our persons, but also the bedding, clothing, exposed food and utensils were richly encrusted with a lustrous patina compounded of lampblack dissolved in double-distilled seal oil.

Thenceforth we had to accustom ourselves to grey sugar and dusky porridge, and a faint but omnipresent taste and odour in everything we ate and drank, and to resign ourselves to total bodily nigrefaction until our return to the base, provided we could get enough hot water even there. And so was fulfilled the saying of the prophet Nahum: 'All faces shall gather blackness.'[4]

That night, we revolved listlessly on our sooty pallets, and sleep would not come to our eyes. We felt hot and oppressed. Giving up all thoughts of sleep, we fell to discussing what might be the cause of our discomfort. The seal liver, the penguin breast *à la suprème*, and of course the fumes from the blubber smoker, were all taken into consideration. Finally, I suggested that the influence might well be meteorological, and crawled outside the tent to verify my hypothesis by observation. And for once I was correct.

The warmth of the north-westerly wind almost took my breath away, like the first suffocating rush of steamy vapour from a Turkish bath. Heavy banks of cloud were racing away from us in the south-east and shooting almost perpendicularly up the sides of the massive dome of Ross Island, there to dissolve in a clear-cut line against a violet-coloured sky. Not being enough of a meteorologist to understand or explain this remarkable weather phenomenon, I could only bring to mind what I had read about the North African sirocco, that hot wind which blows intermittently from across countless miles of the superheated Saharan wastes. But one thing I understood perfectly: that our present position, out here on the sea ice in the middle of the 'Bay of a Thousand Icebergs', would shortly become untenable. I looked down, and my feet were in two inches of water; only a few emaciated cakes of snow, rapidly melting, remained on the tent flaps. I heard tricklings and gurglings on all sides. In a matter of a few hours, at this rate, the sea ice would break up, and commence to disperse out of the bay in great floes, hastened forward by the inexorable onthrust of the many huge tabular bergs which, becoming loosed from their imprisonment, would bear out before the wind like so many ships under full press of canvas. Our lease had expired, and we ran the risk of summary eviction onto an ice floe somewhere out in the Weddell Sea.

It took us exactly three-quarters of an hour to dismantle and pack our tents and gear in the lurid half-light of a livid sky, and start our precipitous rush towards the mainland, some ten miles away. We pulled with the dogs, attired only in boots, woollen drawers and sweatshirts (ourselves, I mean, not the dogs), and thanks to the good condition of all of us after two days of rest and feeding, managed to strike up and maintain a spanking five miles per hour over the slushy surface.

For two hours we raced forward thus, in a lather of sweat. Our course took us past several rocky islands, large and small, upon which we could have taken refuge; but to what purpose? As well to be marooned upon an ice floe as upon a small island in the open 'Bay of a Thousand Icebergs'. And the increasing roar of cascading waters down the slopes of those islands had a sinister sound to our ears.

At last we came within hailing distance of the mainland, close to the place where we made our initial descent on the outward journey. I might almost say within wading distance, for by now the dogs were scampering through six inches of water on top of smooth ice, and the sledges pushing up quite a bow wave before them. This was fresh water, flooding outwards over the sea ice from innumerable waterfalls and rivulets cascading over the face of the land in front of us. To get the sledges safely up onto wet land was going to be quite a tricky undertaking. Taylor went on ahead to prospect a possible route, and following him came James and Russell, with the 'Big Boys' team – minus one. Some distance behind I came in their tracks with the 'Odds and Sods' drawing the heavier sledge.

At a hail from Taylor, now standing on top of the cascading ice foot, the first team made a rush for the bank, and the sledge, carried on by its momentum, lodged halfway up it, in the midst of a waterfall; a few hearty heaves, and it was resting securely among the rocks. I urged my dogs on to join them, and we splashed and scudded through the slippery pools, with me pushing on the handlebars from behind. And then it happened.

It took me a few seconds to realize that the ice had broken beneath the sledge, and that we were sinking, within twenty yards of land. It did not make much noise in doing so, only a faint *crump*, followed by various hissing and seeping sounds as the water welled up between the fragments. The sledge and part of its load disappeared from view, and I, instinctively clinging to the handlebars, watched the water come up to my knees, then higher, and shivered. The dogs I did not have time to observe, but they must have been thrashing the water into a turmoil at the ends of their traces, to keep their heads above the surface. In a split second of time, with curious detachment, I made a calculation of the probable depth of water at that spot, taking into account the distance from the land and the slope of the latter; and the answer, dancing in figures of uncompromising black before my eyes, was five fathoms, or thirty feet. Before the water came to my waist, I had propounded and resolved yet another interesting problem: would it be possible for me to swim the remaining twenty yards or so to land, breaking up the rotten ice before me as I swam? Again the answer: *No, it's not possible, but I've got to do it.* But I found that I could not let go of the sledge; my hands, beyond my own volition, grasped the handlebars in a paroxysm which I was powerless to unlock. It was as if I were part of the sledge, sinking into ... Would it be black down there?[5]

Since I am not writing these lines at a desk in limbo, you are assured that it did not happen thus. I never now treat tales of miracles with scorn, since experiencing this near approach to one. A simple explanation, on the surface of it. True, I broke the ice. So far, so good. But it was ice formed on the surface of four feet or so of fresh water which had cascaded during some previous warm spell over the surface of the real sea ice below. And it was on this real sea ice, of satisfying thickness, that the sledge and I now came to rest, leaving me standing half out of the water at one end of the sledge, like the misplaced figurehead of a scuttled sailing ship. Really nothing to it, thankfully.

I can take no credit whatever for the subsequent proceedings. The others waded out to me, breaking the thin ice before them, and first liberated the dogs from their traces, letting them flounder ashore themselves. The sledge was pushed forward out of its watery resting place onto the land, and quickly offloaded; surprisingly little water had penetrated the enveloping tarpaulin. Lastly, they led me ashore, dazed, by the hand, and the dogs kindly revived me with an icy shower. Soon I found myself in the tent, in a fairly dry sleeping bag, with the pressure stove beside me going full blast, and Taylor carefully decanting for me into an enamel mug the absolute cream of a carefully hoarded bottle of half-frozen Hesperidina Bagley from the Argentine depot.

A thought occurred to me. 'Taylor,' I said, 'what's the date today?'

'The date? It's six o'clock in the morning of September 10th, 1945. Why?'

I closed my eyes blissfully as I sipped the fiery nectar. 'My birthday,' I replied.

*

A delicious feeling, to lie in one's sleeping bag on the last morning of an easy day's journey home, and to let flit before the mind's eye delightful images of hours of torpidity in a real bed, broken only by regular visits to the mess table and elsewhere; a real bath with steaming hot water in the big kerosene drum next to the galley;

being woken in the mornings by Tom Berry plucking at the coverlet and handing up a cup of strong, sweet, fragrant tea; plates of fresh white bread and delicious sliced Spam thrown prodigally on the table, with its dazzling off-white napery and all but glittering cutlery; a good book between times beside the roaring stove, and cigarettes and chocolate bars thrown at you at the drop of a hat; and last but not least, the husky mellifluous song of Bing Blyth to soothe one's soul and attune it to higher things, as he cheerfully completes his chores about mess room and galley.

In spite of these heartening prospects, I lingered with faint tinges of regret over my task of preparing breakfast, dismantling the tent and loading up the ration boxes that last morning of our trip; conscious that in all foreseeable probability I was doing these things for the last time. Never again would I spill kerosene into the oatmeal, or watch the eyes of my companion light up at the sight and aroma of my *plats du jour*, seal liver *bonne femme* and penguin breasts *à la suprème*. And in future retrospect these regrets would be intensified, only the fine days, the laughs, the gladsome sights, the good companionship remembered, and the frostbite, hunger and exhaustion quite forgotten . . .

*

'Penguins that might have been men,' I chuckled, paraphrasing Gorky's title.[6] As if to compensate for the error made by Andersson, Duse and Grunden on October 12th, 1903, when they mistook the members of Nordenskjöld's sledging party for penguins in the distance, we, on September 11th, 1945, not far from the same spot, mistook three penguins for human beings.

They were first spotted high up on the snow slope above our camp near the ice foot, three small black specks apparently coming down to meet us. We had everything packed on the sledges, and were just about ready to start, when Russell's keen eyes discerned them. It was impossible to judge their relative magnitude on the featureless snow slope, but they certainly looked like three members of the base party walking down towards us at a distance of about a mile. We indulged in some speculations as to their identity. 'That fat one in the middle, I bet that's old Tom,' I surmised. 'That's almost certainly Doc there on the left,' said Taylor; 'I'd know the way he walks anywhere.' 'Wonder what brought them up over here today of all days; they couldn't possibly have known that we were coming back today.' The only way to make sure was to get out the binoculars, and then we remembered that we had left them in the cache out in Erebus and Terror Gulf. So we started off up the slope to meet them, waving gaily and shouting to them; but they failed to return our salutations. Worse than that, they suddenly, when we were still about half a mile distant, turned their backs on us, and started to climb back up the slope away from us. 'The *bursted rockers!*' we stormed, and urged the dogs forward to overtake them, stringing together in our minds a selection of choice epithets with which to greet them. Not until we were a few hundred yards away from the fleeing figures did we establish the fact that they were pygoscelean, all too pygoscelean.[7] But our indignation against Tom Berry, Doc Back and a further unidentified member of our base party was slow to evaporate entirely. Great stuff for cobs to work on.[*]

Up on the summit plateau, the tilted Pyramid hove now in sight, and on the rapidly steepening downward slope it seemed only minutes until we passed 'Knob Nunatak' and suddenly, over the brow of the slope, caught sight of the settlement below, a couple of matchboxes with two upright toothpicks off to one side. Drawing nearer, we made out the veritable Tom Berry standing on a heap of ashes, monarch of all he surveyed, a garbage can under one arm. All at once he dropped it, and his arms flew up in expressive gesticulations. In a few seconds other figures poured out of doors and windows, one of them hurriedly adjusting his clothing, and ran hither and thither like ants in their excitement and confusion. We

---

[*] This term, meaning disgruntlement, is explained on p. 145.

bore down the slope triumphantly towards them, our voices and the dogs' raised in a paean of salutation. The scene below us had all the activity, homeliness and squalor of one of Breughel's winter landscapes. Instants later we ran the sledges up onto the cinder pile outside the back door and were surrounded on all sides, having our backs thumped and our arms joyfully wrung out of their sockets. It was impossible even to attempt to give answer to all the questions being simultaneously shot at us. Willing hands unharnessed the dogs and took them round the back for a good feed; while we, preceded by Tom Berry, were pushed indoors in the midst of a vociferous group, and found ourselves with the unaccustomed feeling of walls around us and floorboards underneath our feet, the heat of the roaring stove enveloping us in breathtaking luxury. A jar of rum and a bottle of gin made their appearance on the mess room table, and we put down a half-tumblerful of each before divesting ourselves of the sooty remnants of our outer clothing.

'How clean you buggers look!' was our first remark. Times of ease and fullness, after exactly five weeks spent outside in the White Expanse, were upon us at last.

The Hunter

DURING THE FIRST week in October that year we were besieged
by an unusual quantity of pack ice in Hope Bay. For day after day
the wind blew steadily from the north-east, rafting immense masses
of ice floes through both sides of Joinville Sound, so that one could
have walked dry-shod across to all the islands which cluster round
the tip of the Palmer Peninsula. From the high outlook point of
'Knob Nunatak' above our base, an even whiteness embalmed the
face of the waters as far as the eye could see, and way out in the
distance towards the north, concentric zones of flat-topped tabular
icebergs rose up perpendicularly out of the barren ice pastures like
vast impregnable fortresses guarding the gateways between us and
the human habitable world beyond.

And with the pack ice came the snow petrels. As I afterwards
learned, these birds are the faithful companions of the pack, and
their presence an unfailing signal of its proximity. They are said at
times to mark the open leads to icebound vessels, and show the way
through danger into havens of safety; but this, I must confess, I have
never seen myself. Certain it was that the now close-knit pack around
us had brought them to us in large flocks, winging their way high
up over our heads so swiftly that one could not make out whence
they came nor whither they went; they seemed eternally suspended
errantly in the sky, and never on any occasion were they seen to
alight on land or ice. Their scientific name is *Pagodroma nivea*; a bird
about the size of a dove, and somewhat similar in form also, but pure
white, except for its black eyes, bill and feet. So much for the gross
ornithological details; but their weird, faint, unearthly cry, uttered

whilst they cleft the heavens high above us in their concerted darting flight, and accompanying their continual passage back and forth in droves, seemed to hint at some mysterious mission which we could not even dimly comprehend. As they flashed, wheeled and plunged in the blue sky above, their snowy white, fleecy plumage reflecting satiny glints in the rays of the sun, they made one think of nothing so much as a choir of angels on the wing.

Seeing them thus abundant at this time, I was reminded of the fact that in the collection of bird skins which we had prepared at various times during this and the previous season as part of our scientific collections, we still lacked one of the snow petrel. Not only had they been but very rarely seen hitherto, but always they had flown at such heights above our heads that even with a shotgun we could not easily have brought them down. And our single shotgun had been left behind at Port Lockroy. At first I entertained the thought of trying to get one with a service rifle, but on riper reflection hit on a different plan to capture one of them for the sake of its skin. For I had noticed that on their flights over the col at the side of Mount Flora, they winged their way quite low over the rocky pile of 'Knob Nunatak' at the summit of the ice slope, so low in fact that often a cast stone might easily attain them from the ground.

I made my way into Chippy Ashton's workshop beside the galley, where he was fabricating a new cowl for the fluepipe to replace one carried away in a recent storm. The inevitable cigarette, with an ash two inches long, lay as usual burning itself out athwart a matchbox beside him on the bench.

'Go away,' said Chippy, 'Whatever it is, I haven't got any.'

Unabashed by this prickly reception, which I knew concealed a heart of pure gold, I snooped around his worktable and shelves, poking my fingers into this box and that until I finally found what I wanted.

'Hey, you can't take those bolts; they're the only ones that size I've got, and I want them for the new cleats on the radio poles. Just walk in here, some people do, and clean you out of all your gear right under your flaming nose.'

I counted seven into my hand, and weighed them thoughtfully. 'Yes, they'll do. Thanks, Chippy.' He watched me go with an air of long-suffering tolerance, sighed, lit another cigarette, and returned to his task.

I've seen mousetraps and mantraps in my time, but this would be something new in traps, set in the sky instead of cheese or a mess of mouldy porridge. You have to be a cunning hunter to get the snowy Pagodrome, and this is the way I did it. I tied the seven bolts to the ends of seven two-foot lengths of twine, and fastened the other ends all together to a central brass ring. Then I cut about thirty feet of the twine, and knotted one end of it firmly also to the ring. And that was all there was to it: a very fine and highly original line, for fishing in the clear sky instead of deep down in troubled waters. It worked on the principle of the gaucho's *bolas*, and would get me a *Pagodroma* skin in a nice clean way, without any bloody mess over the glinting feathers.[1]

Arriving at the summit of the snow slope, I took my stand on top of the rocky mound of 'Knob Nunatak', the highest point nearby to which, as a wingless creature, I could ascend. Several droves of the petrels flashed across the sky not far away, and I crouched down among the rocks and waited quietly, my snare beside me ready to my hand concealed, for I remembered a proverb to the effect that the net is surely spread in vain in the sight of any bird.[2]

Half an hour passed away without any coming near, but at last I descried in the south, over the snowfield, a dense flock of them winging their way with the swiftness of arrows northwards directly towards the place where I lay in wait. I draped the line in loose coils on the rock, and swung the seven bolted ends free for an upward throw. Seconds later they were right over my head in their silent ghostly onrush, barely fifteen feet above the ground, and with a vigorous swing I launched my weighted snare straight upwards in their midst. It spread out and revolved like Ixion's wheel[3] in its swift ascent, intercepted the flock in its densest part, and wrapped itself around one of their number. The bird, inextricably trapped in full flight in the intertwining weighted coils, plummeted down to earth in a slanting trajectory, and landed in the mud beside a little trickling creek of snowmelt water issuing from the rocks. I rushed to the spot and eagerly grasped my treasured prize, trellised and helpless in my snare, and with its virgin plumage sadly sullied by the mire into which I had brought it down. I placed it on the rock before me, fished my clasp knife from my pocket, opened it with my teeth, and prepared to plunge it in the snowy neck.

But then I saw its jet black eyes, which surely seemed to my imagination to be welling with unshed tears, looking up mutely into mine and filled, not with fear, but with an inscrutable sadness. For a minute or more we two things, children of the same Creator, one temporarily, the other permanently earthbound, eyed each other silently, and unspoken question and answer passed in our reciprocal glance. Then, as gently as possible, I disentangled the weighted cords, and freed its fluttering body; I tried to wipe away the earthy stain with which I had besmirched this heavenly creature; and raising it aloft in my hands, I let it go and commended it freely back to its exalted home.

Fly up again, my beautiful white brother, and join the rest of your snowy blessed throng. Never forget that I, unaided, once brought you down to earth, and that then I freely let you go again. Tell them up there that, even without a blessing, we down here are human, knowing compassion, and not ashamed of it. Perhaps we both shall finally reach the same chosen destination, you in your way, I in mine. But even if not, I let you go all the same.

*

'What d'you want this time?' asked Chippy; 'Whatever it is, I haven't got any.'

'I don't want anything more, Chippy,' I replied. 'I've shot my bolts, and it worked the way I wanted.' And with my clasp knife I cut them off the snare and dropped them back in the box on the shelf above the bench.

Falklands Bound

IT HAD ALL HAPPENED so quickly. Although we knew that our final departure had been slated for some time in January 1946, and that a new party was on its way out from England to relieve us, we somehow could not reconcile ourselves to the fact that we were now, as of January 18th, on board the SS *Fitzroy* and bound northwards towards civilization. Our departure from the shores of two years' habitation had been brusque and prosaic, lacking in the lingering quality of romantic leave-taking which would have been appropriate to the majesty of the place and the depth of our spiritual connections with it. True, we had received instructions from Port Stanley to have all our gear packed and ready for immediate departure; we knew that we were going away any time from New Year onwards, and that our embarkation would have to be carried out smartly, the Bransfield Strait being notorious for its rapidly fluctuating ice conditions; and yet when it did happen, it wasn't at all the way in which we had envisaged it.

The *Scoresby* steamed into Hope Bay at 3.30 in the morning, shortly after sunrise, on January 14th, and sent a boat ashore. We were awakened from the sound slumbers of the righteous by the clumping of sea boots through the mess room and a hearty voice shouting 'Well, don't you *freezers* want to be relieved?' After that, there was such a concentrated rush of activity that we had no time to pause and reflect on what was happening until we found ourselves, some hours later, leaning against the rail of the *Scoresby* and watching the ice-capped peaks of Antarctica dwindling on the horizon, by most of us never to be seen again.

My first concern, as one dedicated to science, had been to get the boxes of botanical and geological specimens safely on board. There were two dinghy-loads of them, representing the fruits of over a year's painstaking collecting and research activity on the part of Flett and myself, all carefully packed and labelled and nailed up in wooden boxes. Each box had painted on it a number and superscription describing its contents. It was no easy matter to get them up from the dinghy and over the *Scoresby*'s rail, for the swell was rising and falling about five feet, and accurate coordination between the giver and the receiver therefore difficult. One box, containing botanical specimens, missed the connection and fell into the drink, but fortunately did not sink immediately, and was rescued; how much sea water got into the specimens I would not know until we arrived at Port Stanley. I stacked the first load along the sides of the covered gangway outside the radio operator's cabin, and then had to wait until the dinghy came back from shore, where it was being loaded up with surveying equipment and personal baggage. A keen cold wind was blowing across the bay, and made my eyes water. The sound, as far as I could see, was remarkably free of drift ice, only a few brashy patches running before the wind here and there. On shore, a continual procession of tiny figures going to and fro between the house and the ice foot, laden down with heavy burdens.

I made for the warmth of the galley, and there found Fleck, the first mate, making his breakfast from sliced mutton sizzling in a pan on the stove, and helped him to dispose of it. He gave me all the local news from the Falkland Islands, much of which was to me singularly uninteresting, as it dealt with the social exploits of prominent residents most of whom I did not know even by name. The town hall of Port Stanley had burned down a short time previously,[1] he told me, and this was an inconvenience insofar as the Saturday night dances now had to be held in the less sumptuous quarters of the Customs shed. The *Fitzroy* and another vessel, the *Trepassey*, were lying at anchor at Deception, which would be our first port of call. Commander Bingham,[2] who had taken part in the British Graham Land Expedition of 1934–37, was there with the new base parties, and was the new leader of the whole outfit, which was being continued under the title of the Falkland Islands Dependencies Survey. All this and more Fleck told me. Our day was over, and our connection with the continent in which we had come to take an almost proprietary interest was being severed once and for all.

When all of us and our gear had been brought aboard, and the relieving party left to take over our habitation, the *Scoresby* weighed anchor and stood out into Bransfield Strait without delay. I had been so occupied with the transfer of the scientific collections that I had had the opportunity of meeting only one member of the new party, the doctor, to whom I was introduced by Lieutenant Marchesi. His name was Andrew,[3] and he seemed to be genuinely interested in continuing the biological research which we had initiated. While getting the remainder of the boxes out of the back passageway of the house, I had caught a glimpse of Tom Berry instructing the new cook in the complex functioning of the Esse stove; Tom's heart must have been sorely cleft at having to leave his anthracite-burning prodigy, which had been unto him as a cloud and a smoke by day, and the shining of a flaming fire by night.[4]

We lingered a while at the rail, observing the peninsula from angles hitherto unknown to us, until at last it sank below the eastern horizon. The wind blew doubly keen here out on the open sea, and we made our way to the *Scoresby*'s saloon, where we partook of tea and slices of an uncommonly fine caraway seed cake baked especially for us by the wife of one of the Colonial Secretary's staff; bless her kindly motherly soul.

That evening we reached Deception, and as we steamed through Neptunes Bellows into the black and cindery domain of a bygone whaling civilization, three other vessels at anchor loomed before us: the *Fitzroy*, an oil barge, and a new ship to these parts, the *Trepassey*, a diesel powered job from Newfoundland under the command of our old friend Captain Sheppard. Without delay, we transferred our stores to the *Fitzroy*, which was to take us back to Port Stanley. Captain Pitt[5] greeted us and gave the steward instructions to feed us and allot us our berths. The steward was of Chilean origin, and his charming urbanity would not have been out of place on board the *Queen Mary*; we were greatly intrigued by the sight of his spotlessly laundered white mess jacket.

An hour later, Commander Bingham came aboard from the settlement with some members of the new party, and invited us all to join in a cocktail before dinner in the *Fitzroy*'s saloon. He greeted us individually and collectively, expressing his cordial appreciation of the work we had done, in some respects putting it on a par with that accomplished by the British Graham Land Expedition in which he had taken part ten years previously; to me, who had read Rymill's *Southern Lights*,[6] the official account of that expedition, and had had the opportunity of working on some of its outstanding biological collections, this was high praise indeed.

Night fell, and after an excellent dinner we sat in the saloon in comfort and warmth, and had time at last to reflect on our sudden translation to civilization and the circumstances accompanying it. Here we were, hirsute, dishevelled and grimy, about to be precipitated abruptly into the midst of the polite society of Port Stanley; would we all be able to acquit ourselves with the necessary distinction and avoid in our conversation in social gatherings the usage of certain expressions which to us, in our two years of isolated comradeship, had lost all intrinsic meaning and served only to lend a certain expressiveness and colour to our everyday speech? We were not too optimistic about it.

Doctor Back and I settled back in the comfortable swivel chairs and started one of those desultory conversations of ours which nearly always hinged on profound problems but seldom led to clear-cut or tangible solutions; we could tear down, but had some difficulty in building up. In some circles this type of discussion is simply called beefing, or belly-aching.

'It's just incredible, the way the Governor and his clique in Port Stanley ignored us and our work,' fulminated Doc. 'Almost the whole time we were down there, hardly a word of friendly greeting or appreciation. Stony silence, even our requests for vital information often ignored. And when you and Taylor and Vic and James came back from your trip with all that area properly surveyed for the first time, all those data on the Snow Hill base and the Nordenskjöld and Argentine depots, and all that scientific material, and Taylor sent a long signal to the Governor describing it all, what did we get back? A measly half-dozen words or so, little more than a bare acknowledgement, no encouragement whatsoever. Couldn't they understand that we were cut off altogether from things down there, and some sign of life and appreciation from them once a month or so would have made all the difference in the world to us and our morale? Complete psychological ineptitude. And when we did succeed sometimes in wringing a signal out of them, why did it have to be so brief and cryptic? After all, we were their trusted emissaries doing a job of work, often unpleasant and dangerous, for them, at their command; they sent us down there for their own reasons, and the least they could do was to give us a sign of life and contact with the originators of the whole scheme now and then. As it was, we began to wonder sometimes whether they hadn't forgotten our existence altogether. One can easily lose one's entire faith in the whole business when that sort of thing happens.'[7]

'Doc', I replied, 'I felt it as much as you did, but maybe the old Governor and his staff weren't so much to blame as you think.' (I was feeling in a charitable and expansive mood after the good dinner which they had served us on the *Fitzroy*.) 'You see, in the first place, we were called upon to go down there and live there for a while as you say, but we were not chosen to be the recipients of all the information available to the high command. That would have been impossible. Even if all the information about the whole scheme of things and its management had been supplied to us, do you really think for a moment that we would have been able to understand it? All the intricacies of protocol and international political science or international law, how could we ever hope to understand such matters of higher policy? The cryptic stony silences of which you complain were entirely justified, in my opinion; indeed, it couldn't well have been otherwise. If the Governor in his wisdom chose to conceal certain things from us, I am sure he had a perfectly good reason for doing so. Who are we to demand explanations of general policy from higher sources? All we know for certain is that we were sent down here to do as good a job as we could, in the light of our own instinctive limited judgement, which we can only hope conforms to the ultimate aims of the authorities that sent us. They realized that in London and Port Stanley, and left us to our own devices, confident that we would do our best not to let them down, as far as lay in our limited powers and understanding. Their very silence showed that they reposed trust in us, and we should have equal faith in them, even though they remain aloof and silent, and don't answer our signals. All we need is to be able to feel, somehow, significant in the scheme of things generally, and that we know we are, otherwise we wouldn't have been sent here.'

Doc snorted; perhaps the fourth helping of curried mutton had not soothed his digestive tract as effectively as it had mine. In addition to that, he was a non-smoker, and so deprived himself of the grateful mild opiate of the cigars which Captain Pitt had kindly handed round, and on one of which I was now puffing contentedly.

'Bullshit,' was his verdict.[8]

*

On January 18th we passed to the west of the bleak, ice-crested peaks of Elephant Island, between the South Shetlands and South Orkneys, scene of Shackleton's remarkable exploit in 1916 when, marooned there with his party after the shipwreck of the *Endurance* in the Weddell Sea, he made his way in an open boat for seventeen days across 800 miles of freezing tempestuous ocean to South Georgia, there to hike on foot over the glaciers and mountain peaks to a whaling station on the other side to get help for the remainder of the party left bivouacked on Elephant Island. I would rank this as perhaps the greatest single feat in the annals of polar history, because it was crowned with success in the face of almost impossible odds, and represents one of the most mysterious achievements of human willpower and endurance.

Three days later we reached our destination. Cruising up the sound towards Port Stanley, we were wildly excited by the vivid greenness of the tussock-covered islets which we passed, and by the nostalgic aroma of peat smoke in the air; Jock Matheson of Skye was particularly affected, and I doubt if he could have replied if spoken to just then. And five minutes later, rounding the point, the sudden vista of the bare brown heathy hillside with the brightly coloured little houses spilling down to the water's edge: Port Stanley, the metropolis of the Falklands.

As the *Fitzroy* slowly nosed up to the jetty, and the mooring ropes were thrown over the bollards among the assembled crowd, we lined the bulwarks of the main deck and felt ourselves under the scrutiny of half a hundred pairs of eyes. We felt somehow embarrassed and out of place, as not of this world. And there was one in particular at the edge of the throng on whom the gaze of all of us was fixed, in awestruck fascination.

'Hullo, John!' rang out her silvery voice, as she waved to somebody behind us.

The *Fitzroy*'s second mate pushed his way through between us, leaped over onto the jetty, and the two figures were silently locked in a loving embrace.

We looked elsewhere, sudden sadness stealing into our hearts . . .

Epilogue

THE INTERNATIONAL GEOPHYSICAL YEAR of 1957–58 is almost
upon us, and the eyes of the whole world are turned again towards
the seventh continent.[1] Parties from many nations already are abroad
in the White Expanse, erecting bases from which they may explore
and further probe into its secrets. Dwellings of men spring up overnight along its icebound margins, and from them mechanized armies
under many flags will invade the frozen realm. Will they eventually
bring back from thence the knowledge which up till now we fruitlessly have sought? We cannot tell as yet. All we can hope for is that
the united efforts of the nations of the earth, bent towards this single
end, may give us some kind of answer to many matters which now are
shrouded in uncertainty. Let us wish all possible success to this great
joint venture, joyfully greeting any new discoveries, under whatever
nation's banner they are made, for the extension of nationalistic aims
and rivalries into this snowy treasury of God is futile and out of keeping
with its mystery, its glory, and its elemental undiscriminating force.

Let us not persist in the vain and impious attempt to divide this
great white realm into conflicting sectors, for it is universal, holy,
one and indivisible, and in its barren glory belongs equally to us all!
It contains in its midst the invisible centre on which our whole world
pivots and revolves; and that, being but an imaginary geometrical
point, can never be partitioned. And from whatever side we approach
it, and in whatever attitude – submissive, or weeping, or laughing, or
fearlessly erect – it will receive us all, whatever our nation, race, or
creed, impartially into its blank and pure depths.

Notes

Abbreviations used in the notes include:
BAS: British Antarctic Survey
IML: Ivan Mackenzie Lamb
RILS: Ronald Lewis-Smith (editor)
SPH: Stephen Haddelsey (editor)
TNA: The National Archives, Kew

Editors' Introduction

1. Neptunes Bellows (without an apostrophe) is the formally adopted name for the narrow passage that gives access to the interior of Deception Island. See G. Hattersley-Smith, 'The History of Place-Names in the British Antarctic Territory', *British Antarctic Survey Scientific Reports*, No. 113 (Part II) (Cambridge: British Antarctic Survey, 1991).

2. Gordon Howkins, meteorologist on Operation Tabarin, to SPH (personal communication) 4 July 2012.

3. Alister Hardy, *Great Waters: A Voyage of Natural History* (London: Collins, 1967), p. 161.

4. For comprehensive accounts of Argentinian claims and British policy, the reader is referred to John Dudeney & David Walton, 'From *Scotia* to "Operation Tabarin": developing British policy for Antarctica', *Polar Record*, Vol. 48, 4, October 2012, pp. 342–60, and Stephen Haddelsey & Alan Carroll, *Operation Tabarin: Britain's Secret Wartime Mission to Antarctica, 1944–46* (Stroud: History Press, 2014).

5. See José Manuel Moneta (trans. Kathleen Skilton & Kenn Back; ed. Robert Keith Headland), *Four Years in the South Orkney Islands* (London: Bernard Quaritch, 2017). An annotated translation of *Cuatro Años en las Orcadas del Sur* (Buenos Aires: Ediciones Peusar, 1939).

6. TNA, PREM 3/141, Most Secret Cipher Telegram from Air Ministry to Mideast, 2 February 1943.

7. Vivian Fuchs, *Of Ice and Men* (Oswestry: Anthony Nelson, 1982), p. 23.

8. BAS, AD6/1/ADM (Item 22), Operation Tabarin Political Instructions, November 1943.

9. Ibid.

10. Ivan Mackenzie Lamb, 'How I came to the Antarctic', *Hope Bay Howler*, Vol. 1, No. 5, 21 October 1945.

11. J. W. S. ('Scout') Marr, *Into the Frozen South* (London: Cassell, 1923).

12. J. W. S. Marr, 'The South Orkney Islands', *Discovery Reports*, Vol. X (Cambridge: Cambridge University Press, 1935).

13. Andrew Taylor, *Two Years Below the Horn: A Personal Memoir of Operation Tabarin* (Norwich: Erskine Press, 2017), p. 205.

14. Lamb, 'How I came to the Antarctic'.

15. See Chapter 1.

16. See Chapter 1.

17. BAS, AD6/16/1986/4.1, transcript of an interview with Eric Back, 8 October 1986.

18. David James, *That Frozen Land* (London: Falcon Press, 1949), p. 156.

19. See Haddelsey & Carroll, *Operation Tabarin*, p. 122. Also M. W. Holdgate, 'An experimental introduction of plants into the Antarctic', *British Antarctic Survey Bulletin*, 3, 1964, pp. 313–16.

20. Interview with Eric Back, 1986. Sir Joseph Dalton Hooker (1817–1911) served as botanist during James Clark Ross's Antarctic expedition of 1839–43.

21. BAS, AD6/1A/1944/A, J. W. S. Marr, 'First Report on the Work of Operation Tabarin, Part I: The Work at Base A, 1943–44', p. 5.

22. I. M. Lamb, 'Further observations on *Verrucaria serpuloides*, the only known permanently submerged marine lichen', *Occasional Papers of the Farlow Herbarium of Cryptogamic Botany*, No. 6, 1–5 (1973).

23. Interview with Eric Back, 1986.

24. Taylor, *Two Years Below the Horn*, p. 205.

25. James, *That Frozen Land*, p. 160.

26. George A. Llano, 'I. Mackenzie Lamb' (obituary), *The Bryologist*, 94 (3), 1991, pp. 315–20. The editors would like to acknowledge their debt of gratitude to George A. Llano's obituary of Lamb for much of the detail relating to Lamb's biography.

27. University of Manitoba, MSS 108, box 8, folder 22, Andrew Taylor, 'Private Report on Personnel', 21 May 1945.
28. Taylor, *Two Years Below the Horn*, p. 40.
29. Taylor, *Two Years Below the Horn*, pp. 341–2.
30. J. M. Wordie, 'The Falkland Islands Dependencies Survey, 1943–46', *Polar Record*, Vol. 4, 32, July 1946, pp. 372–84.
31. Gwion Davies to Alan Carroll (personal communication) 4 September 2002.
32. Cryptogams are plants that have no true flowers or seeds, i.e. they have hidden or inconspicuous reproductive structures, and reproduce by spores. They include ferns, mosses, liverworts, algae, lichens and fungi. IML was a cryptogamic botanist.
33. Dr Irwin Brodo to SPH (personal communication), 9 August 2017.
34. Carroll W. Dodge, *Lichen Flora of the Antarctic Continent and Adjacent Islands* (Canaan: Phoenix Publishing, 1973).
35. Lamb's notes and descriptions, bound in three volumes containing 470 pages, are housed in the British Antarctic Survey Archives. See R. I. Lewis-Smith, 'I. M. Lamb's unpublished contribution to Antarctic lichenology', *Nova Hedwigia*, 70 (2000), pp. 491–504. RILS and D. O. Øvstedal came close to fulfilling IML's goals with their publication, *Lichens of Antarctica and South Georgia: A Guide to their Identification and Ecology* (Cambridge: Cambridge University Press, 2001); it should be noted, however, that this publication was based largely on the collections made by RILS, rather than those made by IML. In *Lichens of Antarctica and South Georgia* the authors state '. . . it was the ambition of one of us (RILS) to see that the pioneering efforts of Ivan Mackenzie Lamb (the late Elke Mackenzie) . . . who revised many lichen genera and large collections of specimens between 1938 and the late 1970s, were brought to fruition'.
36. Telephone conversation between SPH and Nina Lamb, 6 October 2017.
37. Ibid.
38. Interview with Eric Back, 1986.
39. See Chapter 1.
40. See pp. 84–6 and accompanying explanatory notes.

Author's Introduction

1. Walter E. Traprock [George Shepard Chappell], *My Northern Exposure: The* Kawa *at the Pole* (New York: G. P. Putnam's Sons, 1922).

Chapter 1: A Polar Portrait Gallery

1. Under the terms of the 1964 agreement between the US Advisory Committee on Antarctic Names and the UK's Antarctic Place-Names Committee, the name Palmer Land should be applied only to the area of the Antarctic Peninsula that lies south of a line joining Cape Jeremy on the west coast and Cape Agassiz on the east. Prior to 1964, the USA called the entire peninsula Palmer Peninsula, while the UK described it as Graham Land. IML's use of the American nomenclature is probably a result of his longstanding residence in the USA, though he seems also to have accepted American claims to precedence in the discovery of the peninsula region.

2. Originally launched as a Research Steam Ship (RSS) in 1925 (later Royal Research Ship), the 370-ton *William Scoresby* had been built for whale-marking activities in the Southern Ocean. At the beginning of the war, it was commissioned as a Royal Navy minesweeper and its designation changed to His Majesty's Ship (HMS) *William Scoresby*. At the same time, its 12-bore whale-marking gun was replaced with a Boer War-vintage 12-pounder.

3. The Shackleton–Rowett, or *Quest*, Expedition of 1921–2. Marr served as a deckhand.

4. James William Slessor Marr was born in Cushnie, Aberdeenshire, on 9 December 1902. As a volunteer Boy Scout, he accompanied Shackleton's *Quest* Expedition of 1921–2 and published his account of the expedition under the title *Into the Frozen South* (London: Cassell, 1923). Having completed his BSc in zoology and an MA in classics, during the summer of 1925 Marr served as zoologist on the British Arctic Expedition organized and led by Grettir Algarsson and Frank Worsley. In 1927 he joined the staff of the *Discovery* Investigations under Dr Stanley Kemp and took part in three voyages into Antarctic waters: on board RRS *William Scoresby* in 1928–9; and on *Discovery II*, 1931–3 and 1935–7. In addition, between his voyage on the *Scoresby* and his first on *Discovery II*, he served with Sir Douglas Mawson's British Australian New Zealand Antarctic Research Expedition (BANZARE). Finally, in

1939 and 1940, he made a further southern voyage in the whale factory ship *Tede Viken* to investigate the possible use of canned or frozen whale meat to augment depleted British wartime stocks of food.

5. Born in Edinburgh in 1907, Andrew Taylor emigrated to Canada with his family in 1911. He trained as an engineer at the University of Manitoba in Winnipeg and, as a provincial surveyor, gained much experience in travelling in Arctic conditions. Recruited as Operation Tabarin's senior surveyor, in February 1945 he succeeded Marr as commander-in-the-field. Taylor's *Two Years Below the Horn* is the most important and comprehensive eyewitness account of the expedition.

6. John Blyth joined the expedition in March 1945 following Marr's decision to repatriate Kenneth Blair on the grounds of his apparent unsuitability for polar work.

Chapter 2: Gaining a Foothold on the Seventh Continent

1. This landing was made on 7 February 1944.

2. Although IML makes light of the decision not to establish Base 'A' at Hope Bay, in his report to the governor of the Falkland Islands Marr admitted to being 'bitterly disappointed' and he clearly recognized that the reluctance of the Falkland Islands Company officers to risk the *Fitzroy* becoming iced-in could have dire consequences for the expedition's ambitious programme of survey and scientific investigation (BAS, AD6/1/ADM 4.2, Marr to Sir Allan Cardinall, 13 February 1944).

3. Fitzroy Island was not accepted as an official place name. Another island, in Marguerite Bay at *c.* 68° S, was given this name in 1947.

4. Dr Jean-Baptiste Charcot (1867–1936) led French expeditions to the Antarctic in 1903–5 and 1908–10. It was during the former that he first visited Port Lockroy and named the tiny island on which Operation Tabarin's Base 'A' would subsequently be established, Îlot Goudier. The island was renamed Goudier Island in 1929 following the National Oceanographic Expedition's survey of 1927.

5. Mount Français was not climbed until December 1955, when three members of the Falkland Islands Dependencies Survey (FIDS) Base 'N' on Anvers Island completed the ascent.

6. The huts, of a 'Spitzbergen type', were manufactured by Boulton & Paul, a company which, during the war years, was also responsible for supplying the armed forces with aircraft gun-turrets and packing-crates

for Spitfires. So late had the order for the expedition huts been placed that Boulton & Paul's managing director pointedly demanded to know which of the government's many orders should be given priority.

7. Sir Allan Wolsey Cardinall, KBE, CMG (1887–1956), was Governor of the Falkland Islands and Dependencies from 1941 to 1946. Cardinall advocated clear and unambiguous action in response to Argentinian incursions into British Antarctic and sub-Antarctic territories during the war and initially suggested that members of his staff should visit the Dependencies on board Royal Navy vessels.

8. This first message from Port Lockroy was transmitted by Farrington on 15 February 1944.

Chapter 3: **A Visit to Cape Renard**

1. This is IML's first, albeit oblique, reference to the primary purpose of Operation Tabarin: to respond to Argentina's incursions into the Falkland Islands Dependencies and to reassert British hegemony in the region.

2. *The Antarctic Pilot: Comprising the Coasts of Antarctica and All Islands Southward of the Usual Route of Vessels* (London: Hydrographic Department, Admiralty, 1930).

3. Sub-Lieutenant Fleck, RNVR, first lieutenant of the *Scoresby*.

4. Robert Edward Dudley Ryder (1908–86) served as master of the *Penola* during John Rymill's British Graham Land Expedition of 1934–7. He was later awarded the Victoria Cross for his role in the St Nazaire raid in 1942.

5. The *Scoresby*'s captain was Lieutenant Victor Aloysius John Baptist Marchesi (1914–2006) who had previously served as fourth officer on the RRS *Discovery II*.

6. According to Marchesi's account, the submerged rock was spotted too late to avoid it; however, the engines were put into reverse early enough to reduce the *Scoresby*'s speed and no serious damage was done to its hull. Victor Marchesi to Alan Carroll (personal communication, 1999), see Haddelsey & Carroll, *Operation Tabarin*, pp. 81–2.

Chapter 4: **The Onrush of Winter**

1. On 2 March 1944 Lamb left the building for a few minutes, noting in his diary that 'there was a vague glare of moonlight behind the ruffled

clouds, the wind was whining desperately, and the landscape looked so savage and inhospitable that I was seized for a moment with a sort of fear, and I was glad to get back to my bunk again, thinking that even this, so warm and comfortable, was separated from [the elements] only by four inches of wood and paper'. See BAS, AD6/1A/1944/B, Lamb, Operation Tabarin (Base A) Official Diary.

2. The editors have been unable to find any reference to Francisco Goya's inverted warning angel, or an explanation of its significance. However, close examination of Goya's 1772 oil fresco of 'Adoración de Nombre de Dios' ('Adoration of the Name of God'), also known as 'La Gloria' ('The Glory'), on the ceiling of the cupola over the Small Choir of the Virgin in the Basilica de Nuestra Señora del Pilar in Zaragoza reveals that one of the cherub-like angels is, in fact, upside down!

3. Although Operation Tabarin's geopolitical objectives were clear – to reassert British sovereignty in the face of opportunistic Argentinian incursions – its primary movers, James Wordie, Neil Mackintosh and Brian Roberts, always intended that the field personnel should undertake an ambitious programme of survey and scientific investigation. During the expedition's first year this programme was severely curtailed by the inability to establish Base 'A' at Hope Bay, as had been intended. The existence of strong currents, and the resulting failure of the Gerlache Strait to freeze over, make Port Lockroy a very poor base for sledging operations. Anxiety over this failure almost certainly contributed to Marr's depression and his decision to resign his command. See Haddelsey & Carroll, *Operation Tabarin*, pp. 66–7.

4. On 12 August 1944, IML records in his diary that he spent the night in his igloo, rather than in a tent. Given that his record of the experience is in all other respects almost identical (even down to the recorded temperature), it appears that he has substituted one form of accommodation for another in this account. See Lamb, Operation Tabarin (Base A) Official Diary.

Chapter 5: **Preparations and Small Excursions**

1. Writing of similar preparations for the 1945 sledging season, an amused David James wrote: 'Looking at the various lists of ration scales, used by various expeditions, giving daily quantities to 0.1 of an ounce, we had always imagined nutrition experts poring over test tubes and

saying, "Let's cut down 0.2 ounces on the pemmican and give a bit more biscuit and pea-flour, it will give a better balance between fats and carbohydrates." On closer inspection, however, it seems that if you multiply the daily quantity by twenty (ration boxes for two men, ten days) the answer is the amount that the manufacturers sell in their tins!' See James, *That Frozen Land*, pp. 119–20.

2. The Seamless Robe of Jesus (or Holy Robe or Holy Tunic) allegedly worn by Jesus at the time of his crucifixion. 'Now the coat was without seam, woven from the top throughout' (John 19: 23). The robe is housed in the Cathedral of Trier (Trèves) in Germany, near the eastern border of Luxemburg.

3. Lamb is probably referring to Andrew Croft and Brian Roberts, 'Notes on the Selection and Care of Polar Footwear', *Polar Record*, Vol. 3, 19, January 1940, pp. 235–67, which states in relation to the manufacture of *kamiks*, or knee-length boots: 'The skin is scraped and then soaked in urine for two or three days to extract the fat. The thicker sole-skin is finally softened by chewing.'

4. This event occurred on 7 September 1944.

5. Probably Graham Rowley, 'Snow-house Building', *Polar Record*, Vol. 2, 16, July 1938, pp. 109–16.

6. These events took place between 18 and 20 November 1944; however, IML makes no mention of his fall in his diary.

Chapter 6: Snow-Blindness

1. William Campbell Posey, *Hygiene of the Eye* (Philadelphia: J. B. Lippincott, 1918).

2. The editors have been unable to identify either the work or its author. Given IML's enjoyment of literary jokes at his reader's expense, it is entirely possible – if not probable – that this book is a figment of his imagination.

Chapter 7: Fifteen-Mile Odyssey

1. According to Andrew Taylor, 'The pelt of the Weddell seal . . . is composed of a coarse hair, greenish-yellow in colour, though parts are almost black, and these hairs have a definite grain, lying towards the tail. We used strips of these pelts to cover the underside of our skis, firmly laced in place, and they prevented any backward slip of the skis

in pulling heavy loads, or in climbing a slope. Care had to be exercised in cutting the strips so that the grain was parallel to the ski, as otherwise some difficulty was experienced in steering': Taylor, *Two Years Below the Horn*, p. 64.

2. The sledges were actually brought up on 18 September 1944; a series of delays caused by poor weather then prevented the team from continuing their journey until the 22nd. The intervening period was spent at the base.

3. 1 Kings 19: 12.

4. According to other accounts, the sledgers were unable to undo their harness straps in time. 'We couldn't get out of them,' Taff Davies recalled, 'Our fingers were too frozen to let go so, instinctively, I think, we just lay down on the snow, "head to sea", as it were, as you might in a small boat.' See BAS, AD6/16/1986/2.1, transcript of an interview with Gwion Davies, 13 September 1986.

5. IML refers to the two statuesque figures on either side of the title plaque on the frontispiece of *The Holy Bible, Conteyning the Old Testament, and the New.* They were engraved by Cornelis Boel (*c.* 1576– *c.* 1621), a Flemish draughtsman and engraver, for the first edition of the King James or Authorized Version of the Bible, published by royal authority in 1611.

6. IML's experiment actually occurred on 20 November 1944, during another short sledge trip to Wiencke Island in company with Blyth and Ashton.

7. Presumably in order to maintain the narrative pace, IML has compressed the events of the Wiencke Island survey, which actually lasted from 22 September to 18 October 1944. See Haddelsey & Carroll, *Operation Tabarin*, pp. 97–115.

Chapter 8: **Rustle of Spring**

1. In fact, Blyth and Davies both fell into small crevasses – not when digging the shelter, but while running around afterwards in an attempt to dry out! See Haddelsey & Carroll, *Operation Tabarin*, p. 113.

2. From Edward Fitzgerald's translation of *The Rubáiyát of Omar Khayyam* (London: Quaritch, 1859):

> The Moving Finger writes; and, having writ,
> Moves on: nor all thy Piety nor Wit

Shall lure it back to cancel half a Line,
Nor all thy Tears wash out a Word of it.

3. H. G. Ponting, *The Great White South: Or with Scott in the Antarctic, being an account of experiences with Captain Scott's South Pole Expedition and of the nature life of the Antarctic* (London: Duckworth, 1921). IML might also have mentioned George Murray Levick's Heroic Age classic devoted entirely to the subject: *Antarctic Penguins: A Study of Their Social Habits* (London: Heinemann, 1914).

4. Charles Baudelaire (1821–67), 'L'Albatros':

> Scarcely have they placed them on the deck
> Than these kings of the sky, clumsy, ashamed,
> Pathetically let their great white wings
> Drag beside them like oars.

5. IML's somewhat verbose disquisition on natural selection and its philosophical interpretation has been reduced in length by the editors.

6. *Belgica antarctica* was discovered by Adrien de Gerlache's Belgian Antarctic Expedition (1897–9) and named after his ship *Belgica*. This wingless midge is endemic to the west coast of the Antarctic Peninsula. The loss of wings (brachyptery) is an adaptation to existing in habitats exposed to strong winds. It is the largest terrestrial invertebrate in the Antarctic, about 3–4 mm in length. The larvae reach about 6 mm in length and live amongst moss and algae on which they feed over a period of two years, surviving temperatures between −15 °C and 10 °C. In order to do this they produce 'antifreeze' compounds in their body. The adults appear on warm sunny days in summer but live for only a few days, the females mating within hours of emerging and laying eggs a few days later. There is another (winged) midge (*Parochlus steinenii*) known from a few locations in the South Shetland Islands, and also in South Georgia and Tierra del Fuego.

7. The *Scoresby* was forced to return to Port Stanley, arriving there on or about 12 November 1944. It again headed south on 2 December.

8. In order to consult more fully with the governor regarding the plans for the expedition's second season, on 9 December Marr returned to Port Stanley on board the *Scoresby*. He was accompanied by Gordon Howkins, Deception Island meteorologist, who was invalided home due to appendicitis, and by John Blyth, whose hand required an x-ray

234 *Notes to pages 82–86*

following a minor skiing accident. Bill Flett, base leader at Deception, remained at Bransfield House to undertake geological investigations of the area.

Chapter 9: **Deception**

1. The *Scoresby* reached Port Lockroy early on the morning of 3 February 1945. It had made a fleeting visit to Base 'A' on 1 February, which IML does not mention (see note 6 to this chapter, below).

2. Lieutenant (later Doctor) David L. Niddrie (1917–97) served with the South African Naval Force, and was later Professor of Geography at the University of Florida. The author of many books on geography, his post-war master's dissertation (1946) was entitled 'A contribution to the study of the climate and weather of the Falkland Islands'.

3. Captain David William Roberts, OBE (1886–1970); as Marine Superintendent of the Falkland Islands Company, he commanded the FIC schooner, *Gwendolin*, followed by RMS *Falkland* and *Lafonia* (later renamed *Fitzroy*). From 1939 to 1949 he was Colonial Manager of the FIC. Roberts had accompanied the expedition at the beginning of 1944, and had been one of the most influential voices in the decision not to establish Base 'A' at Hope Bay.

4. Operation Tabarin's Base 'B' was first established on 3 February 1944. The five-man team for the first year was comprised of William 'Bill' Flett (leader and geologist), Norman Layther (radio operator), Gordon Howkins (meteorologist), John Matheson (handyman), and Charlie Smith (cook).

5. IML appears to be enjoying an elaborate (and obscure) literary joke at the reader's expense, mixing his own well-documented experiences on Deception Island with elements lifted from the novel *Le Plan de l'Aiguille* (Paris: Au Sans Pareil, 1927) by the Franco-Swiss novelist Frédéric-Louis Sauser (1887–1961), writing under the nom de plume Blaise Cendrars. 'Community-City' is the name of the settlement established on the fictional Sturge Island by Sauser's eccentric English hero, Dan Yack William, and the seal-liver pills stamped with a picture of a baby and the mechanical juke box all feature in the novel. The whaling station's population of 711 has its origins in the same source; in fact, the population of the whaling station on Deception Island was usually around 100 during the summer months, reducing significantly

during the winter. See José Valencia and Roderick Downie (eds), *Workshop on a Management Plan for Deception Island* (Instituto Antártico Chileno, 2002), Appendix II, 'Deception Island and Antarctic fiction', and Blaise Cendrars (trans. Nina Rootes), *Dan Yack* (London: Peter Owen, 1987).

6. Back had sailed from Port Lockroy on 1 February 1945, on board the *Scoresby*. The ship made only the briefest of stays at Base 'A' as the purpose of the voyage was to collect the doctor and take him to Deception Island in order to tend to Captain Sheppard of the *Eagle*, who had broken a number of ribs in a fall, as IML recounts.

7. In his confidential report on Marr's state of health, Eric Back wrote that 'Lt-Cdr Marr is suffering from mental and physical exhaustion associated with depression. He requires very careful observation and treatment since suicide is not unknown in such cases' (BAS, G2/1/3/4, Back, 'Recommended treatment for Lt-Cdr JWS Marr, RNVR', 8 February 1945).

8. Captain Robert Carl Sheppard, MBE (1897–1954), served with the 1st Newfoundland Regiment during the First World War, being severely wounded at Beaumont Hamel on 1 July 1916. He subsequently worked as lighthouse keeper at Fort Amherst, St John's, and as a master of square-riggers. Early in the Second World War, he brought a convoy of confiscated French vessels across the Atlantic and then served as harbour master of St John's. He was awarded the MBE for his work on Operation Tabarin and with the Falkland Islands Dependencies Survey (gazetted 13 June 1946).

9. *Recuerdos de Provincia* [*Recollections of a Provincial Past*] (Santiago: Belín, 1850).

10. Domingo Faustino Sarmiento (1811–88) was an Argentinian activist, intellectual, writer, statesman and the seventh President of Argentina (1868–74).

11. Crabgrass is a genus of warm temperate and sub-tropical grass (*Digitaria*). It was later identified as the common temperate grass *Poa pratensis* (Common meadow grass or Kentucky bluegrass).

12. During their year on Deception Island, the five-man party led by Flett completed a fairly extensive programme, including survey, meteorology, and zoology. See Haddelsey & Carroll, *Operation Tabarin*, pp. 133–6. Given Smith's desire to join the expedition, his apparent unwillingness

to leave the base seems odd. Unfortunately, sources covering the year spent at Deception Island are scarce and the editors have been unable either to prove, or disprove, IML's claims.

13. NOIC: Naval Officer in Charge; NAAFI: Navy, Army and Air Force Institutes; WAAF: Women's Auxiliary Air Force. According to the most recent issue of 'MoD Acronyms and Abbreviations' (published by the Ministry of Defence, 15 August 2014), PUS is an acronym for Permanent Under Secretary; the letters OIC usually indicate 'Officer in Charge', though OICR is an acronym for 'Operational Intelligence Collection Requirements'. However, it may be that PUS, OICS and CUSCI were all wartime creations, now obsolete – or IML's own creations.

14. Twillingate is a small town located on the Twillingate Islands in Notre Dame Bay, off the north-eastern shore of the island of Newfoundland in the province of Newfoundland and Labrador, Canada.

15. IML's manuscript account of his conversation with the young man from Newfoundland has been substantially reduced by the editors.

16. In his diary entry for Tuesday 6 February, IML states that he dined on board the *Fitzroy* and that, afterwards, Marr asked him to help loading coal with James, Marshall and Russell. He makes no reference to a party, but Eric Back, in his diary, mentions that on the evening of 9 February (the day of Marr's departure on the *Scoresby*) 'a boozy party developed which was much enjoyed by all'. The following day, Back states: 'Most people feeling rather the worse for last night's party.' IML refers to meeting the Colonial Secretary, Kenneth Bradley (1904–77), on the 3rd, and again on the 7th, and it is possible, though far from certain, that the CUSCI is actually Bradley.

In his own very brief account of this, his first and only visit to the Antarctic, Bradley described his period visiting the Tabarin bases as 'some of the most exciting weeks of my whole life'. He also refers to consuming 'an enormous meal and a hilarious amount of drink', but at Bransfield House, Port Lockroy, on the evening of 3 February 1945 rather than at Deception Island. Bradley described himself as an amateur horticulturist rather than an amateur botanist, but this description might support the identification of Bradley as the original of the CUSCI. See Bradley, *Once a District Officer* (London: Macmillan, 1966), pp. 137–40.

Chapter 10: **Hope Bay Revisited**

1. It had been intended that Farrington would be a permanent member of the Hope Bay contingent and that Donnachie would serve as radioman at Deception Island; however, after a small fire in the Deception Island wireless room on 21 February 1945, Farrington volunteered to take Donnachie's place as Base 'A' wireless officer. Donnachie arrived at Hope Bay on board the *Scoresby* on 6 March and served at Base 'D' throughout 1945. See Haddelsey & Carroll, *Operation Tabarin*, pp. 147–9.
2. This copy of Otto Nordenskjöld's classic work, inscribed by Marr, Lamb and Taylor, is now held in the library of the British Antarctic Survey in Cambridge.
3. In his unedited manuscript, IML mentions meeting Professor Carl Skottsberg, one of the men who overwintered on Paulet Island, at a meeting of the Linnaean Society in London before the outbreak of war.
4. Tom Carroll's demonstration was completed on board during the evening of 12 February.

Chapter 11: **The Birth of Base 'D'**

1. In fact, the landing at Hope Bay was made on 12 February. Adverse weather conditions and the decision to hunt for seals meant that the first supplies and equipment were not landed until the following day. The tin galley was completed on 14 February.
2. According to Lamb's diary, the launch of the sledge boat actually took place on 12 July 1945.

Chapter 12: **Phenomena**

1. This temporary expedient became a permanent fixture after the *Eagle* was driven from Hope Bay on 17 March, with the missing sections of the Nissen hut still in its hold.
2. This ice formation is commonly referred to as 'pancake ice'.
3. Near-contemporary *Polar Record* articles addressing the subject of dog-management include C. G. & E. G. Bird, 'The Management of Sledge Dogs', Vol. 3, 18, July 1939, pp. 180–8, and E. W. Bingham, 'Sledging and Sledge Dogs', Vol. 3, 21, January 1941, pp. 367–85.
4. Ixnay: Pig Latin, or jargon, for 'nix', meaning in this case 'cancel'.
5. The four dogs that made up one of the two stronger teams, 'The

Drinks', were actually lost later in the year, on 28 May 1945.

6. Having been donated to the UK Antarctic Heritage Trust by Eric Back's son, Robert, during the austral summer months this greatcoat once again hangs on a peg at Bransfield House, Port Lockroy.

7. When seeking equipment with which to fight the fire that destroyed Base 'D' in November 1948, Dr Bill Sladen was unable to enter the Nissen Hut because the door opened outwards and was obstructed by drift-snow. However, he was able to enter the tin galley as its door opened inwards – just as Lamb describes. Following this fire, in which two FIDS personnel died, recommendations were made that all doors at Antarctic bases should open inwards. See Haddelsey, *Icy Graves: Exploration & Death in the Antarctic* (Stroud: History Press, 2018).

8. The storm that IML describes in such detail occurred on the night of 3/4 March 1945, and his account is based very closely upon his own lengthy diary entry. It should be noted, however, that the baulks of timber and bags of coal were not placed in position until 4 March, as a safeguard against any further storms. In addition, the barometric reading of 914.6 mb (686 mm) that IML quotes would, if correct, remain one of the lowest ever recorded globally. It appears that IML has exaggerated for dramatic effect, as Back, the meteorologist, in his own diary entry for 3 March, cites a low of 960 mb.

Chapter 13: The Meteorology of the White Expanse

1. Douglas Mawson, *The Home of the Blizzard: Being the Story of the Australasian Antarctic Expedition, 1911–1914* (London: William Heinemann, 1915).
2. Wilhelm Meinardus, 'Klimakunde der Antarktis', in W. P. Köppen & R. Geiger, *Handbuch der Klimatologie*, Vol. 4 (Berlin: Bornträger, 1938).
3. Job 38: 30.
4. Jeremiah 23: 19.
5. Matthew 8: 24–6.
6. Louis Charles Bernacchi (1876–1942) served as physicist on Carsten Borchgrevink's *Southern Cross* Expedition (1898–1900) and on Scott's *Discovery* Expedition (1901–4).
7. M. W. Campbell Hepworth, *Reports of the National Antarctic Expedition 1901–04. Meteorology* (1908).
8. C. E. Palmer, *Synoptic analysis over the Southern Oceans*. Professional

Note No. 1, 38 pp. New Zealand Meteorological Service (1942).

9. The editors are most grateful to Dr Steve Colwell, Professor John Turner and Dr John King of the British Antarctic Survey for providing the following explanation of Antarctic wind generation: 'Since the earliest days of Antarctic exploration those visiting the continent have noted the strong and persistent downslope (katabatic) winds. We now know that these are a result of the drainage of cold, dense air from the high interior plateau to the coastal region, especially down glacial valleys. As the air approaches the coast it is deflected to the left by the Coriolis force, which arises because of the rotation of the Earth. The fact that there is a coastal easterly wind around much of the continent gave rise to the idea that there was an anticyclone above Antarctica. However, modern meteorological analyses have shown that the Antarctic atmosphere is dominated by a cyclonic circulation through most of its depth.' For more details see John King and John Turner, *Antarctic Meteorology and Climatology* (Cambridge: Cambridge University Press, 1997), p. 409.

10. The editors have been unable to identify any evidence that the members of Amundsen's polar party were physically scarred by the conditions they encountered during their journey to and from the South Pole. That some at least bore the psychological scars of their experiences is more plausible.

11. 2 Kings 23: 10; Jeremiah 19: 6.

12. Verkhoyansk (and Oimekon), near the Arctic Circle in the Sakha Republic of eastern Siberia, is noted for its exceptionally low winter temperatures. The average January temperature is −45 °C (−49 °F) with a record low of about −68 °C (−92 °F) in February 1892. The temperature never exceeds freezing point between 10 November and 14 March, making it the coldest permanently inhabited place on Earth. The even colder Russian Vostok Station in East Antarctica holds the record low as measured with a thermometer, −89.2 °C (−128 °F) on 21 July 1983, although −94.7 °C (−135.9 °F) was recorded electronically from a satellite in August 2010, also on the East Antarctic polar plateau.

13. Dr (later Sir) George Clarke Simpson (1878–1965), meteorologist on Scott's *Terra Nova* Expedition (1910–13).

14. G. C. Simpson, *Scott's Polar Journey and the Weather: Being the Halley Lecture, Delivered on 17 May 1923* (Oxford: Clarendon Press, 1926).

Chapter 14: **A House Built on Sand**

1. Matthew 7: 26–7.
2. This seems to have been a general feeling, perhaps due to the poor quality of Eagle House's finish when compared with that of the very comfortable Bransfield House.
3. One of the most curious, indeed inexplicable, omissions in IML's narrative is that of the story of the near-loss of the *Eagle* on 17 March 1945. During a gale, the *Eagle* lost its anchor and then collided with an iceberg. With his ship badly damaged, Captain Sheppard was forced to choose between beaching it and attempting to sail back to the Falklands. He eventually chose the latter course and, by a miracle, his luck held. Given that this episode constituted one of the most dramatic incidents of the whole expedition, why did Lamb choose not to recount it? His decision seems even odder when one considers that the story would have given him ample opportunity for the kind of spiritual musings to which he was so often prone.
4. The work of transferring stores, which Lamb here describes as beginning in March 1945, did not commence until 7 May and ended on 21 June.
5. In conversation with SPH on 18 August 2017, Ken Blaiklock, one of FIDS' most experienced dog drivers, remarked: 'We had to stop every hour to undo the knitting – I don't know anyone who managed to keep their dogs in one place!' The experiences of IML and his companions were, then, far from unique.
6. The 'Leader Principle' which prescribed the fundamental basis of political authority in the governmental structures of the Third Reich: the *Führer*'s word was above all written law.
7. Fyodor Mikhailovich Dostoyevsky (1821–81), Russian novelist, who wrote *Debased and Insulted* (usually translated as *The Insulted and Injured*) in 1861.
8. The three teams referred to by Lamb were 'The Big Boys', 'The Drinks' and 'The Odds and Sods' (also referred to by David James as 'The Odds and Ends'). The Drinks were lost when they floated out on an ice floe, as recounted by IML in Chapter 12. It is much to be regretted that these teams are not commemorated on the FIDS/BAS sledge-dog memorial which stands at the main entrance to the Scott Polar Research Institute in Cambridge.

9. Honoré Daumier (1808–79), French painter, caricaturist and sculptor.
10. None of the other published and unpublished expedition records consulted by the editors mention this accident. Eric Back refers to the fact that IML hit himself in the eye with his own dog whip (diary, 11 June 1945), and IML states in his own diary that other members of the expedition broke a sledge runner and that they included a newly designed brake in their repairs (diary, 14 June 1945). In another entry (8 June 1945), IML also alludes to having damaged his own sledge runners.
11. Back describes the manufacture of sledge brakes in his diary entries for 12 and 15 May 1945.
12. Eagle House was destroyed by fire on the night of 8/9 November 1948. If we are content to accept that this 'daydream' is not a fiction introduced by IML at a later date, then it must be considered an extraordinary premonition. On the other hand, it is curious that he makes no explicit reference to the fire that killed FIDS personnel Oliver Burd and Michael Green.

Chapter 15: **Some Southern Horizons**

1. The 'cyclometer' was damaged as described on 28 June 1945. In his own account, Taylor observed that, 'The sledge meters which had come out with our supplies were nothing more nor less than cyclometers, such as are used in the bicycles which wheel around the English country roads. The meters were very small things made of aluminium and brass, and after testing a number of them, it was found that their average life expectancy was about two hours', Taylor, *Two Years Below the Horn*, p. 207.
2. Although Eric Back uses only the fisherman's initial 'M' in his diary, IML names him as Freddy Marshall (diary, 14 June 1945). Taylor also identifies the fisherman as Marshall, rather than Matheson.
3. Taylor states that the most successful bait was seal meat.
4. Alfred, Lord Tennyson (1809–92), *In Memoriam*, Canto 56.
5. Percy Bysshe Shelley, *Rosalind and Helen: A Modern Eclogue* (ll. 894–7).
6. This event does not feature in IML's diary for 16 July – the day on which the trip up Depot Glacier was made – or, indeed, on any other day.
7. IML describes the temperature as 'moderately cold' in his diary.

8. In fact, the four men were confined to their tents by a gale throughout 9 August 1945. The fine morning alluded to by IML dawned on 10 August.

Chapter 16: Smooth Running and Food for Thought

1. IML appears to be thinking of Vilhjalmur Stefansson's 1921 classic, *The Friendly Arctic: The Story of Five Years in the Polar Regions* (New York: Macmillan).
2. Actually the Antarctic Place-Names Committee of the Foreign & Commonwealth Office. According to IML's diary (14 August 1945), the island was named Vortex Island because of the 'whirlies' the field party encountered once they got there. For his part, in *BAS Scientific Report* No. 113 (Part II), *The History of Place-Names in the British Antarctic Territory*, Geoffrey Hattersley-Smith states that Vortex Island was 'so named because the survey party was forced to lie up there in a whirling snow-storm' (p. 591).
3. IML is conflating the two major sledge journeys conducted in 1945 (he took part in both). No mention is made of this penguin in the sledge diaries of IML, Taylor, Russell or James. However, Taylor describes the death of an Adélie penguin in similar circumstances on 24 December 1945 (Taylor, *Two Years Below the Horn*, p. 325)
4. Paul Siple (1908–68) was a distinguished American explorer and scientist who took part in Byrd's first and second Antarctic expeditions (1928–30 and 1933–5), the United States Antarctic Service Expedition (1939–41), Operation Highjump (1946–7) and Operation Deep Freeze I (1955–6). He made some important botanical discoveries in remote locations, but considered Pleistocene survival of any life-forms improbable. See Paul Siple, *A Boy Scout with Byrd* (New York: G. P. Putnam's Sons, 1931).
5. IML was very interested in the relationship between the distribution of Antarctic lichens and the movement of the Southern Hemisphere continents; this formed the basis of his Doctor of Science thesis in 1942 (Edinburgh University). Combined with his personal study of Antarctic lichens during Operation Tabarin, this convinced him that the large number of lichen species that are endemic to the Antarctic must have survived from the pre-Pleistocene epoch ($c.$ 2.5 million to 12,000 years ago), i.e. on nunataks and other ice-free refuges,

especially in coastal areas and possibly in 'dry' valleys farther inland. The evidence, he believed, lay in the fact that lichens, being complex organisms (a symbiosis between an alga and a fungus) had insufficient time to evolve new species (as endemics) during the Holocene epoch (i.e. since the glacial maximum, when ice sheets began receding globally 12,000 years ago). See IML, 'Antarctic terrestrial plants and their ecology', in M. W. Holdgate (ed.), *Antarctic Ecology*, Vol. 2, 733–51 (London: Academic Press, 1970). In this paper Lamb also refers to his earlier 1949 paper in which he 'expressed the opinion that from the genetic standpoint it is impossible to conceive that the present Antarctic endemic species could have evolved in such a relatively short space of time, especially in the case of such slow-breeding (bradytelic) organisms as the lichens'. He and other lichenologists considered, therefore, that most of the Antarctic lichen flora was established well before the Pleistocene, reaching what is now the Antarctic by a 'stepping-stone' type of long-distance dispersal via high mountain ranges from Arctic and tropical regions. Today many species, notably many mosses and non-endemic lichens, have a bipolar distribution.

6. The evolutionary history of penguins remains a somewhat controversial subject. Genetic analyses indicate that members of the Spheniscidae (penguin family) evolved from non-flying birds whose ancestors diverged from other groups of birds *c.* 71–68 (± 25) million years ago; however, another theory suggests that they evolved about 60–65 million years ago (Cretaceous) from flying birds related to the Alcidae (auk) family (e.g. cormorants, razorbills, puffins, auks), while a recent genetic study suggests that penguins are most closely related to the family Procellariiformes (albatrosses and petrels).

    From fossil evidence it appears that penguins probably evolved in that part of the Gondwanaland landmass that eventually became Australia, New Zealand, southern South America and Antarctica, which is where most modern penguins now occur. At that time much of Antarctica had a temperate or sub-tropical climate. Although the first collection of penguin fossils was made by Nordenskjöld's Swedish Expedition on Seymour Island, the oldest fossils, *c.* 60–62 million years old (*Waimanu manneringi*), were collected recently at a site at Waipara on the east coast of what is now South Island, New Zealand. It was a small flightless penguin. The most accepted hypothesis regarding their evolution into flightless birds is that such ancestors increasingly adapted to the marine environment where they obtained large amounts of food. This resulted in structural changes. By about 55 million years ago penguins were completely adapted to an aquatic life, but in a warmer environment than today. It appears that the evolution of modern penguins occurred over *c.* 3 million years, around 50 million years ago. The diversity of species was far greater than now, and several became extinct as they could not adapt to changing environmental conditions or competition for food from a rapidly diversifying marine fauna. In summary, IML's statement is broadly correct, with the one notable exception that we now know that penguins were not 'a purely Antarctic stock'. See www.penguins-world.com/penguin-evolution.

7. These remarks reveal IML's distinctly American-centric view of Antarctic history. The British are not alone in accepting that the Antarctic Peninsula was first sighted by Lieutenant Edward Bransfield, RN, on 30 January 1820 from the merchant brig, *Williams*. The other main contender is the Russian explorer Fabian Gottlieb von Bellingshausen, who may have spotted the shoreline of East Antarctica two days earlier. Palmer's sighting of the Peninsula did not occur until 17 November 1820.

8. The reference to a Japanese presence in the Antarctic may not have been made entirely in jest. In 1942 Churchill and others became concerned over the possible capture of the Falkland Islands by Japanese forces; this fear gave rise to Churchill's instruction that the amateur Falkland Islands Defence Force should be reinforced by a regular army battalion (see Dudeney, J. R. & Walton, D. W. H., 'From Scotia to "Operation Tabarin" – developing British policy for Antarctica', *Polar Record*, 2011). Furthermore, in 1940–1, six Japanese floating factories were operating in Antarctic waters (see J. N. Tønnessen & A. O. Johnsen, *The History of Modern Whaling* [London, C. Hurst, 1982], p. 481).

9. The term *Lebensraum* was used by the German geographer Friedrich Ratzel (1844–1904) to describe his theory that the development of all species, including humans, is primarily determined by their adaptation to geographic circumstances. Several decades later Adolf Hitler developed the belief that Germany required *Lebensraum* or 'living space' in order to survive. The conviction that this living space could be gained only in the east, and specifically from Russia, formed the core of

this geopolitical concept. It was elaborated in his book *Mein Kampf* and shaped his policy after he came to power in 1933.

10. Jean-Jacques Rousseau (1712–78) was a Swiss-born philosopher and writer whose political and educational theories strongly influenced the Enlightenment in Europe. His *Confessions* were first published in Geneva in 1782.

11. In his diary (14 August 1945), IML refers to finding penguin feathers and excrement, not a colony. Again, he has compressed events. A colony of Adélie penguins – not Gentoos – was discovered at Vortex Island on 20 November 1945, during the second sledging journey from Hope Bay. By suggesting that a penguin rookery was discovered so early in the year, IML creates a spurious conundrum – a curious, indeed inexplicable, act on the part of a man who dedicated his entire professional life to science. In his diary entry for 20 November, he remarks: 'Although there is no open water for many miles from here, the penguins were coming and going singly or in small groups across the sea ice; I wondered whether they might not be going down tide cracks to get food in the vicinity of the big icebergs nearby. Their excrement however was green from bile, containing no remains of ingested food.' The most southerly Gentoo penguin colony is on Petermann Island, at 65° 17'S on the western side of the Antarctic Peninsula. The most southerly Gentoo rookery on the east coast of the Peninsula is at Brown Bluff, a little to the north of Vortex Island.

Chapter 17: **Snow Hill**

1. This decision would imperil the lives of the entire party. Given that Andrew Taylor was recruited because of his experience in Arctic travel, his willingness to abandon the skis so early in the journey seems extraordinary.

2. IML is probably describing conditions encountered a little later in the journey, on 22 August 1945.

3. Taylor's judgement was probably correct, as Weddell and crabeater seals produce a weird high-pitched squeaking call interspersed with guttural gurglings: an ethereal sound not unlike whale 'song'.

4. Georg Carl Amdrup (1866–1947), a Danish naval officer and explorer who led two major expeditions to East Greenland (in 1898–1900, and 1900).

5. James and Russell did not reach Snow Hill Island until the following afternoon, 28 August.

6. The party left Snow Hill Island on 29 August 1945, two days after the arrival of Taylor and IML, but only a day after James and Russell joined them.

7. Alfred Sisley (1839–99), British Impressionist landscape painter.

8. Maurice de Vlaminck (1876–1958), French painter and one of the leading members of the Fauve movement, known for its use of bold colours.

9. Although the importance of secrecy was impressed upon the members of Operation Tabarin, it seems strange that, even as late as 1956, IML would not reveal the content of this letter, despite the fact that it had no relevance to the expedition's geopolitical objectives. James (*That Frozen Land*, p. 149), does refer to it, but it was Taylor who provided an accurate transcription (Taylor, 'Echoes of the Swedish South Polar Expedition of 1902–3', *Revue Canadienne de Géographie (Montréal)*, 4, 1950, pp. 47–62). For the full text of the letter see Appendix 1.

10. At the south end of Penguin Bay on the south side of Seymour Island, James and Russell found an Argentinian depot marked by a cairn and a wooden cross, to which was attached a canister containing a note. They brought it back to their camp, together with some of the food rations. This discovery, and that of Taylor (above), were made on 30 August 1945. The note was in English and is documented by James (1949, pp. 148 and 196), and Taylor (1950). For the full text see Appendix 1.

11. Henry D. Thoreau (1817–62), American natural philosopher, abolitionist, historian and poet. *Journal*, Vol. XI, 7 February 1859, p. 440. Republished as *The Journal of Henry D. Thoreau* (London: Constable, 1962).

Chapter 18: **Pounded in the Mortar of Affliction**

1. The phrase 'pounded in the mortar of affliction' has its prophetic origin in Ezekiel 34: 26: 'And I will make them and the places round about my hill a blessing; and I will cause the shower to come down in his season; there shall be showers of blessing.' However, the actual phrase was coined by Charles H. Spurgeon in his translation of sections of the Bible. In his sermon 'The Church of Christ', No. 28, *A sermon delivered*

on Sabbath Morning, June 3, 1855, by the Rev C. H. Spurgeon, at New Park Street Chapel, Southwark [London], he wrote: 'I truly believe there are some in my congregation to whom God has given power to preach his name; they do not know it, perhaps, but God will make it known by and by . . . I will make them a blessing. I will force them to do good. If I cannot make a sweet scent come from them in any other way, I will pound them in the mortar of affliction . . .' See *The Spurgeon Series, 1855 and 1856: Unabridged Sermons in Modern Language*, edited by Larry and Marion Pierce (Green Forest, Arkansas: Attic Books, 2012).

2. Carcasses of Weddell, crabeater and occasionally leopard seals are commonly found on James Ross Island, sometimes several kilometres inland and at considerable altitude (up to 250 m). Of the many encountered by RILS in 1989 some were of considerable antiquity, possibly several centuries old, while others had been dead only one or two years. See also A. E. Nelson, et al., 'Age, geographical distribution and taphonomy of an unusual occurrence of mummified crabeater seals on James Ross Island, Antarctic Peninsula', *Antarctic Science*, 20, 2008, pp. 485–93.

3. Major William Ellery Anderson, MBE, MC (1919–92), leader of the Hope Bay FIDS team of 1954–6, records a similar situation. While on a sledging trip across the Larsen Ice Shelf (about 110 miles/175 km south-west of James Ross Island), he was walking ahead of a sledge team to check the safety of the ice surface but broke through and, while in a prone position, was attacked by Murdo Tait's dog team. See William Ellery Anderson, *Expedition South* (London: Evans Brothers, 1957), pp. 166–7.

4. Sir Joseph Dalton Hooker (1817–1911) was the assistant surgeon and naturalist on James Clark Ross's expedition of 1839–43, in the ships *Erebus* and *Terror*. In the third year of the voyage the expedition entered the Weddell Sea and explored the north-western region of the Antarctic Peninsula, discovering James Ross, Snow, Seymour, Cockburn and many other islands. According to the descriptions given by both Hooker and Lamb, it appears that they collected plant specimens at exactly the same spot on Cockburn Island. Hooker became Director of Kew Gardens, London, in 1865.

5. In 1989 RILS visited Cockburn Island and collected at least 34 lichen species, 27 of which were from the site visited by Hooker and Lamb.

R. I. Lewis Smith, 'The vegetation of Cockburn Island, Antarctica', *Polar Biology*, 13, 1993, pp. 535–42.

6. The conversation to which IML fleetingly refers (and which receives no mention in his official diary) proved highly contentious and resulted in a breakdown in relations between Taylor and James. While Taylor advocated pressing on towards the Vortex Island depot, James believed that the party should retreat to Nordenskjöld's hut at Snow Hill Island, where they should wait – using the wood of the hut for fuel and the dogs for meat – until conditions improved and allowed them to return to Base 'D'. See Haddelsey & Carroll, *Operation Tabarin*, pp. 189–90.

7. It is highly unlikely that the survey party was traversing an area of floating snow. It is more probable that the seawater seeped through the underlying ice surface through fissures and tide cracks. Taylor states: 'There was by this time no doubt in our minds that the snow "bog" along this coast of James Ross Island was due to the drift snow from the southwest being sheltered from the wind by the bulk of the island itself; unless the snow is compacted by occasional winds, it has no strength. It became further obvious that the weight of the snow over the sea ice had caused the depression of the ice into the sea through which the consequent flooding produced the slush at the bottom.' See Taylor, *Two Years Below the Horn*, p. 258.

8. IML's account of this day's travelling is closely based on his diary entry for 4 September 1945. Although neither he nor any of the other members of the field team mention his collapse, at times the members of the party were separated and there is no definite evidence to suggest that the incident is fictional. At this point in his original manuscript, IML starts a new chapter entitled 'The Abyss', which begins with a 2,200-word description of a dream or hallucination experienced during his period of prostration. For the reasons outlined in the Editors' Note, the editors have chosen to delete this section. IML's stamina during the crossing of Erebus and Terror Gulf is commented upon with great admiration by both James and Taylor in their accounts of the expedition.

9. This incident would appear to be another example of sledge dogs' willingness to attack their drivers if – and only if – the driver is prone and thereby loses his distinctively human aspect. See note on William Ellery Anderson's experiences, above. As the attack is not mentioned in

IML's diary it is impossible to know whether the story is, at least in part, fictionalized.

10. 6 September 1945.

Chapter 19: **Final Footprints on the White Expanse**

1. Again, IML is describing the penguin colony as it appeared on 20 November 1945.

2. Matthew 6: 34.

3. The seals were found and slaughtered as described on 9 September 1945.

4. IML is slightly misquoting Nahum 2: 10, which states '... and the faces of them all gather blackness'. The phrase in the form used by IML is actually from Joel 2: 6.

5. Although this event, as described, is fictitious – in his diary entry for 10 September IML describes the surface as 'very good, hard and windswept' – it is based, at least in part, on the later experiences of IML and other members of the expedition. During the latter stages of the second major sledging journey from Hope Bay the temperature rose significantly. On 21 December, IML describes travelling 'over very wet snow and ice; at one place the dogs and sledge were moving through slush and water, and my skis disappeared completely under water'. Between 3 and 8 January, another team, consisting of Back, Marshall, Matheson and Davies, encountered even worse conditions and, on 7 January, Back wrote: 'We got off at 12 midnight and were very soon in the water again. We were bogged over and over again and eventually utterly stuck in two feet of water out of which neither we nor the dogs could move the sledge.'

6. Maxim Gorky, *Creatures That Once Were Men*, with an introduction by G. K. Chesterton (London: Alston Rivers, 1905).

7. None of the sledgers (including IML) make any reference to penguins in their diaries. This incident may well be a fictionalized recreation of the similar event that occurred during Nordenskjöld's Swedish Antarctic Expedition, as described in Chapter 10, and to which IML refers earlier in this passage. The term 'pygoscelean' refers to all penguins of the genus *Pygoscelis*, i.e. Adélie (*P. adeliae*), chinstrap (*P. antarctica*) and gentoo (*P. papua*).

Chapter 20: **The Hunter**

1. IML's description of his trap's design was originally incorporated in his conversational exchange with Ashton. As the resulting dialogue was extremely stilted, the editors have chosen to include the description in the first-person narrative, making only a very small number of essential changes to the author's language.

2. Proverbs 1: 17.

3. In Greek mythology Ixion was a king of Thessaly who committed parricide and attempted to rape Hera. As his punishment, Zeus decreed that he be bound to a perpetually revolving wheel in Hades. Hera happened to be Zeus's wife – and sister!

Chapter 21: **Falklands Bound**

1. In fact the fire to which IML refers occurred on 16 April 1944, destroying much of the mail so laboriously prepared by the personnel of the expedition.

2. Surgeon Commander (later Surgeon Captain) Edward William Bingham, OBE (1901–93): served as medical officer on Gino Watkins's British Arctic Air Route Expedition (1930–1) and John Rymill's British Graham Land Expedition (1934–7). He assisted in the selection of the dogs for Operation Tabarin and acted as overall Field Commander for FIDS in 1946–7.

3. Dr James Darby Andrew (1919–2006) served as Medical Officer at Hope Bay and Deception Island, 1946–7.

4. Isaiah 4: 5.

5. Keith Alan John Pitt joined the Falkland Islands Company as chief officer of the *Fitzroy* in October 1934 and served as master from March 1940 to early 1946.

6. John Rymill, *Southern Lights: The Official Account of the British Graham Land Expedition 1934–1937* (London: Chatto & Windus, 1938).

7. Though no doubt paraphrased, IML has accurately summarized Back's opinions regarding the authorities' perceived attitude to the expedition and its personnel. On 14 December 1945, for instance, Back wrote: 'The attitude of the authorities seems hard to justify; from here it looks like psychological persecution' (BAS, G12/2/3, Back, diary). In a later journal article, he would state that, 'In order to keep up the morale of isolated parties they should be kept informed of the work in hand . . .

The sense of frustration experienced by men completely isolated in the cold and given no information about future plans can be extremely galling and is often not appreciated by those at home' (E. H. Back, 'Cold Weather Hazards', *The Medical Press*, 9 November 1955).

8. At this point in the original narrative IML launches into a lengthy dissertation on the history of the Falkland Islands, and the counter-claims of the United Kingdom and Argentina. Because of its stilted conversational form, and as better sources are readily available, the editors have chosen to delete this passage.

Epilogue

1. The International Geophysical Year (IGY) was a global science programme involving 64 nationalities, 12 of which also undertook research in Antarctica at 55 stations. These were Argentina, Australia, Belgium, Chile, France, Japan, New Zealand, Norway, South Africa, United Kingdom, the United States of America and the USSR. It was during the IGY that Sir Vivian Fuchs made the first trans-continental crossing of Antarctica via the South Pole, a goal that Sir Ernest Shackleton had failed to achieve during his Imperial Trans-Antarctic (*Endurance*) Expedition of 1914–17. The IGY led directly to the formulation of the Antarctic Treaty in 1961. See G. E. Fogg, *A History of Antarctic Science* (Cambridge: Cambridge University Press, 1992).

Appendix 1

Messages Recovered
on Seymour Island

Recovered by Andrew Taylor , 30 August 1945

Les sousignés, de l'Expédition Argentine de Secours, commandant Capt. Julián Irízar, ont reconnu cette station le 7 novembre, 1903, en trouvent seulement une pointe indiquée avec des pierres et au milieu une canne en bois avec la signature de Andersson et Sobral: faite une enquête complète et minitieux dessous et autour de pierre ont y trouvé aucun, écrit.

[*Signed*]   José Garrachategui (Doctor)   Felipe Fleiss (Lieutenant)

On the back of the lined page of paper was also written:

Ont prie de les laisser dans le point pour le cas que les Expéditions Françaises ou Suède arrive. 'Avis Important'.

Rough translation:

The undersigned, of the Argentinian Relief Expedition, commander Capt. Julián Irízar, located this station on 7 November 1903, found only a feature indicated with stones [*a cairn*] and in the midst a wooden cane with the signature Andersson and Sobral: a full and thorough investigation made under and around the stones found nothing written.

Jose Garrachategui   Felipe Fleiss

Doctor   Lieutenant

Please leave this item in case the French or Swedish expeditions arrive. Important Notice.

Recovered by David James and Victor Russell, 30 August 1945

Republica Argentina,
Armada Nacional.
On board the *Uruguay* Argentine Navy
the 10th day of November of the year
one thousand nine hundreds and three.

The subscriber the Commander of the *Uruguay* in his voyage to the Antarctic regions to relieve the Swedish commission directed by Doctor Nordenskjöld, having arrived to Cape Seymour depot, and being so lucky as to find Doctor Nordenskjöld, and all the rest of the commission as well as Capt. Larsen Commander of the Antarctic, has decided to sail back with all thise [*sic*] gentlemen on board going to Paulet Island to pick up the Antarctic's crew.

In Cape Seymour Depot we leave the provisions as described in the adjoining list for the use of those persons reaching this point in need; in other depot which we shall leave also at Paulet Island, we shall leave also the same kind of provisions but in greater quantity as well as a report of the probable route which the ship will follow.

[*Signed*]   Julián Irízar
                 Commander
                 10th November 1903

[*Rubber stamped*]   Armada Nacional
                     Canonera *Uruguay*

*

There followed a list of eighteen food items and their quantities.

Appendix 2
Personnel of Operation Tabarin, 1943–1946

Base 'A' – Port Lockroy, 1944–45

Name	Born	Died	Position
Ashton, Lewis 'Chippy'	c. 1898	1956	Carpenter
Back, Eric Hatfield 'Doc'	30 Jan. 1920	21 Dec. 1992	Medical officer
Berry, Alfred Thomas 'Tom'	2 Feb. 1896	1978	Steward/cook/purser
Blair, Kenneth Cyril Gleeson	c. 1924	after 2005	Handyman (11 Feb.–24 Mar. 1944 only)
Blyth, John 'Johnny'	31 Oct. 1923	1 May 1995	Handyman/assistant cook (replaced Blair)
Davies, Gwion 'Taff'	3 Dec. 1917	22 June 2005	Handyman
Farrington, James Edward Butler Futtit 'Fram'	6 Apr. 1908	4 Oct. 2002	Wireless officer
Lamb, Ivan Mackenzie 'Mack'	11 Sept. 1911	28 Jan. 1990	Botanist
Marr, James William Slessor	9 Dec. 1902	29 Apr. 1965	Zoologist & field commander (all bases), 1943–Feb. 1945
Taylor, Andrew	2 Nov. 1907	8 Oct. 1993	Surveyor and (from Dec. 1944) temporary base leader

Base 'B' – Deception Island, 1944–45

Name	Born	Died	Position
Flett, William 'Bill'	29 July 1900	22 Aug. 1979	Base leader & geologist
Howkins, Gordon	3 Oct. 1919	—	Meteorologist
Layther, Norman Frank	28 Feb. 1924	1983	Wireless officer
Matheson, John 'Jock'	23 Mar. 1893	3 May 1970	Bo'sun
Smith, Charles 'Smitty'	13 Oct. 1911	—	Cook

Base 'A' – Port Lockroy, 1945–46

Name	Born	Died	Position
Biggs, John K.	—	—	Handyman
Layther, Norman Frank	28 Feb. 1924	1983	Wireless officer
Lockley, Gordon 'Jock'	4 Oct. 1916	14 July 1990	Base leader
White, Frank	26 Aug. 1895	19 Aug. 1952	Cook

Base 'B' – Deception Island, 1945–46

Name	Born	Died	Position
Bonner, Samuel	4 Apr. 1888	7 Mar. 1946	Handyman
Farrington, J. E. B. F. 'Fram'	6 Apr. 1908	4 Oct. 2002	Wireless officer
Reece, Alan William	31 May 1921	28 May 1960	Base leader & meteorologist
Smith, Charles 'Smitty'	13 Oct. 1911	—	Cook

Base 'D' – Hope Bay, 1945–46

Name	Born	Died	Position
Ashton, Lewis 'Chippy'	c. 1898	1956	Carpenter
Back, Eric Hatfield 'Doc'	30 Jan. 1920	21 Dec. 1992	Medical officer
Berry, Alfred Thomas 'Tom'	2 Feb. 1896	1978	Steward/cook/purser
Blyth, John 'Johnny'	31 Oct. 1923	1 May 1995	Handyman/assistant cook
Davies, Gwion 'Taff'	3 Dec. 1917	22 June 2005	Handyman
Donnachie, Thomas 'Tommy'	1921	1983	Wireless officer
Flett, William 'Bill'	29 July 1900	22 Aug. 1979	Geologist and 2 i/c
James, David Pelham	25 Dec. 1919	15 Dec. 1986	Surveyor
Lamb, Ivan Mackenzie 'Mack'	11 Sept. 1911	28 Jan. 1990	Botanist
Marshall, Norman Bertram 'Freddy'	5 Feb. 1915	13 Feb. 1996	Zoologist
Matheson, John 'Jock'	23 Mar. 1893	3 May 1970	Bo'sun
Russell, Victor	10 Nov. 1918	30 Dec. 2000	Surveyor
Taylor, Andrew	2 Nov. 1907	8 Oct. 1993	Field commander & surveyor

Further Reading

Anderson, W. Ellery, *Expedition South* (London: Evans, 1957)

Bagshawe, Thomas W., *Two Men in the Antarctic* (Cambridge: Cambridge University Press, 1939)

Boothe, Joan, *The Storied Ice* (Berkeley: Regent Press, 2011)

Charcot, Jean Baptiste, *The Voyage of the 'Why Not?' in the Antarctic: The Journal of the Second French Polar Expedition, 1908–1910* (London: Hodder & Stoughton, 1911)

Christie, E. W. Hunter, *The Antarctic Problem* (London: George Allen & Unwin, 1951)

De Gerlache, Adrien, *Voyage of the 'Belgica': Fifteen Months in the Antarctic* (Norwich: Erskine Press/Bluntisham Books, 1998)

Dodds, Klaus, *Pink Ice* (London: I. B. Tauris, 2002)

Dudeney, J. R. & Walton, D. W. H., 'From Scotia to "Operation Tabarin" – developing British policy for Antarctica', *Polar Record*, Vol. 48, 4, October 2012

Fuchs, Vivian, *Of Ice and Men* (Oswestry: Anthony Nelson, 1982)

Haddelsey, Stephen (with Carroll, Alan), *Operation Tabarin: Britain's Secret Wartime Expedition to Antarctica, 1944–46* (Stroud: History Press, 2014)

Howkins, Adrian, *Frozen Empires: An Environmental History of the Antarctic Peninsula* (New York: Oxford University Press, 2017)

James, David, *That Frozen Land* (London: Falcon Press, 1949)

King, H. G. R. & Savours, Ann, *Polar Pundit: Reminiscences about Brian Burley Roberts* (Cambridge: Scott Polar Research Institute, 1995)

Nasht, Simon, *No More Beyond: The Life of Hubert Wilkins* (Edinburgh: Birlinn, 2006)

Nordenskjöld, Otto, *Antarctica, or Two Years Amongst the Ice of the South Pole* (London: Hurst & Blackett, 1905)

Ommanney, F. D., *South Latitude* (London: Longmans, 1938)

Pawson, Ken, *Antarctica: To a Lonely Land I Know* (Manitoba: Whippoorwill Press, 2001)

Robson, John, *One Man in his Time* (Staplehurst: Spellmount, 1998)

Rymill, John, *Southern Lights* (London: Chatto & Windus, 1938)

Smith, Michael, *Polar Crusader: A Life of Sir James Wordie* (Edinburgh: Birlinn, 2007)

Speak, Peter, *William Speirs Bruce, Polar Explorer and Scottish Nationalist* (Edinburgh: National Museums of Scotland, 2003)

Squires, Harold, *SS Eagle: The Secret Mission* (St John's: Jesperson Press, 1992)

Stewart, John, *Antarctica: An Encyclopædia* (Jefferson: McFarland & Co, 1990)

Tatham, David (ed.), *The Dictionary of Falklands Biography* (Ledbury: David Tatham, 2008)

Taylor, Andrew (ed. Haddelsey, Stephen), *Two Years Below the Horn: A Personal Memoir of Operation Tabarin* (Norwich: Erskine Press, 2017)

Walton, E. W. Kevin, *Two Years in the Antarctic* (London: Lutterworth Press, 1955)

Index